FIFTY YEARS AFTER THE WAR

The People Who Were There
Recall the Major Events
of World War II

Tom Infield

CAMINO BOOKS, INC.
Philadelphia

Manufactured in the United States of America

The material appearing in this collection was originally published in
The Philadelphia Inquirer.

1   2   3   4   5   99   98   97   96

Library of Congress Cataloging-in-Publication Data

Infield, Tom
   Fifty years after the war: the people who were there recall the major events of World War II/by Tom Infield.
      p.   cm.
   ISBN 0-940159-34-1 (alk. paper)
   1. World War, 1939-1945—Personal Narratives, American.
   1. Title
   D811.A21535   1995
   940.53'73'000922-dc20
   [B]   95-33610
                                                                            CIP

This book is available at a special discount on bulk purchases for promotional, business, and educational use. For information write to:

Publisher
Camino Books, Inc.
P.O. Box 59026
Philadelphia, PA, 19102

CONTENTS

INTRODUCTION

When I was a kid in the '50's and '60's, it seemed that everybody's dad was a war veteran. Mine, too. But my parents broke up when I was only eight, and I never had much chance to know my father. By the time I was grown and wanted to hear about his experience as a ball-turret gunner on a B-17 bomber, it was too late. He had died, far too young.

Eventually, I decided to seek answers to my questions about my dad's life in the Eighth Air Force by tracking down 390th Bomb Group members he had flown with and asking them about their experiences. I ran into a remarkable cast of storytellers, then in their mid-60s: an ex-pilot from Bellingham, Washington; a former gunner from Long Island; a one-time navigator from a suburb of Chicago. All wanted me to understand that war, as they saw it, had little to do with heroics. For their generation, war was simply duty: *A man did what a man had to do.*

Though brought up during the Depression, they had never thought of themselves as deprived when they were kids. No one had had money. Straight from school, with no worldly experience, they had enlisted in the Army Air Force. The Army had shipped them across the Atlantic to airfields in England. Within days, they were fighting Germans in an alien, sub-zero world miles above the ground. It was bewildering, terrifying, and exhilarating all at once. "It was the kind of thing you'd never do again," James E. Keelan, the navigator, told me. "But I wouldn't take a million dollars for it now."

I had liked talking to these men. They embodied what we have come to think of as the American character. They were plain-spoken and unassuming, a little embarrassed at their own display of emotion in recalling men who were long dead. They were sentimental without being sappy, patriotic without being jingoistic.

Subsequently, when I heard that The Philadelphia Inquirer was planning a series of articles associated with the 50th anniversary of America's involvement in the Second World War, I rushed to enlist. That was almost four years ago. Since then, I have retraced the war, month by month, year by year, through the eyes of men and women who actually lived it, on both the battle front and the home front.

This volume contains most of their stories, from Dominic P. Gentile's recollection of the Japanese attack on Pearl Harbor—*I thought, is this how they do maneuvers on Sunday morning? Then we saw the red ball on one of the planes, and we knew this wasn't maneuvers*—to firsthand accounts of the atomic bomb strike on Hiroshima.

Fifty years after World War II may have turned out to be the best time to ask questions. For decades, many of these veterans had kept their feelings bottled up. Arthur C. Dietrich, a GI who late in the war was witness to the Nazi camp at Ohrdruf, put it this way: *You got home and thanked your lucky stars that you made it in one piece. And then you went on with your life. You thought about it a lot, but didn't talk about it much.*

But now in their 70s, most of them, they have realized they aren't going to live forever. Many want to share what the war was like in real life, not in Hollywood. I have never met so many people interested in keeping the peace as these folks.

World War II was the last time that Americans were yoked in a common cause. At home, citizens made sacrifices to help supply the troops abroad. Red meat, among other things, became scarce. But fish was always plentiful, and Ruth Wojtusik recalled her dad telling her, "If you *think* meat, it will *taste* like meat."

Even kids could help win the war. Ray Doyle, at age five, pitched in. *We collected tin cans and stamped them—crushed 'em, flattened 'em—and piled them up in the local air-raid warden's garage. We were told that we were helping to build weapons.*

The war brought out the best in Americans—and the worst. In Philadelphia, trash workers went out on a wildcat strike, a threat to war production, rather than work with newly hired black trolley operators. In Los Angeles, Mexican American "zoot-suiters" were attacked and beaten by a mob.

In researching the articles in this collection, I have been struck, time and again, by how much life in the United States has changed in the postwar period.

Most of the men and women I spoke with, having reached retirement age, seemed surprised and delighted at their prosperity. Those in good health—and that was the vast majority of them—had also found that age isn't what it used to be. Of the 16 million men and women in the armed services in World War II, more than 7 million are alive today.

Many remembered their parents seeming old at the time of the war. As I examined wartime photos, I was struck by this, too. The deprivations of the Depression must have had a lot to do with it. Mothers, especially, appeared to have settled into old-lady clothes and old-lady shoes. Yet their soldier and sailor sons were only 18 or 19 or 20. They couldn't have been more than 50, most of them.

After the articles here first appeared in print, I often heard from Inquirer readers offering still more memories. One of my favorites came from Maria C. Giampetro, of Voorhees, New Jersey. She was soon to turn 50 and was looking back.

My grandmother often told me that my birth . . . saved her from the despair which was to come when her son was killed at Anzio. She mourned him and spoke of him until she died. She lived on South Sixth Street in South Philadelphia, and she related how the neighborhood used to react whenever the Western Union delivery person would pedal his bicycle down the street and everyone holding their breath as he continued on. A memorial Mass was said for him each year on the Sunday closest to the date of his death at St. Mary Magdalene Italian American Church in South Philadelphia. She cried each year for the 30 years I could remember being there, as if it were just yesterday she learned of his death.

I wish to express deep thanks to many editors at The Inquirer for permitting me to undertake this series, a unique and wonderful experience. I start at the top with Editor Maxwell E.P. King, Deputy Editor Gene Foreman, former Metropolitan Editor Stephen Seplow, and Executive Editor James M. Naughton who conceived the project. Gene, who was a kid in Arkansas during the war, watched over the entire series with a protective eye. Ken Bookman, then the special-projects editor, got the project started. It was carried on by Nancy Szokan and Bob Filarsky. Tom Gralish was an especially imaginative and caring photo editor. Ed Voves, the news researcher, took a strong personal interest in the project, as did Mike Klein, the copy editor, and graphic artist Barbara Binik. My thanks, also, to Barbara Keeler, David Milne, Acel Moore, Claude Lewis, and David Taylor.

The research would have been difficult without the help of George Brightbill and his staff at Temple University Urban Archives. The same goes for John Slonaker, Louise Arnold Friend, and the other professionals of the reference branch at the Military History Institute of the Army War College, Carlisle, Pennsylvania. Many historians repeatedly lent their expertise to the series, among them Russell F. Weigley, Bruce Kuklick, Thomas P. Hughes, Philip Rosen, Carlo D'Este, Stephen E. Ambrose, Ronald Spector, Joseph H. Alexander, and Bernard C.

Nalty. I am thankful for the insights of Paul Fussell, Charles L. Blockson, Brooks E. Gray, Richard R. Lingeman, Charles Fuller, Ronald Klein, Susan Cooper, Edgar Williams, and others.

Finally, I owe a debt to every veteran and home-front survivor who talked to me, most especially the men of the 29th Infantry Division, with whom I revisited the beaches and bluffs of Normandy, and my friend Joseph P. Barrett.

—Tom Infield
Fall 1995

1 • Pearl Harbor Day
December 7, 1941

**The day that will "live in infamy"—and that brought
the United States into World War II.**

December 7, 1991

Domenic P. Gentile, a Marine from South Philadelphia, was padding
to the showers, naked except for a white towel.

Seaman Peter S. Ellmer of North Philadelphia was ironing his
dress uniform below deck on the light cruiser USS *Honolulu.*

Paul Brown, a sailor from Philadelphia's Crescentville section, was
asleep in his bunk on board the destroyer USS *Shaw.*

It was 7:54 a.m. Hawaii time, the last moment of peace for
America.

At 7:55, when the torpedo planes screeched overhead, "I thought,
is this how they do maneuvers on Sunday morning?" Gentile recalled.
"Then we saw the red ball on one of the planes, and we knew this was-
n't maneuvers. One of them turned around and came down and strafed
us."

In the next hour and 50 minutes, a force of 353 torpedo planes,
bombers, and fighters of the Empire of Japan sank or seriously damaged 19 fighting ships of the U.S. Pacific Fleet. The planes destroyed or
damaged 328 aircraft of the Army and Navy, killed 2,403 U.S. military
personnel and civilians, and wounded 1,178.

It was Sunday, December 7, 1941—50 years ago today.

America, finally, had been plunged into a war—a Second World
War—that had been burning and convulsing in Manchuria since 1931,
in Africa since 1935, in Europe since 1939. Only hours before, even as
the Japanese carriers were moving into attack position, American and
Japanese diplomats had been discussing peace.

At 2:22 p.m. on the East Coast, the Associated Press wired, "Flash: White House says Japs attack Pearl Harbor." In Philadelphia, it was 34 degrees. Many people got the news as they listened to Sammy Kaye and his orchestra on KYW or heard the Eagles game against the Washington Redskins on WFIL.

Stan Wojtusik, a 16-year-old from South Philadelphia, remembers coming home after playing football at Stinger Square at 33rd and Reed Streets in Grays Ferry. His dad, still in his church clothes, was bent over the Philco radio in the front room.

"He turned to me and he said the Japanese bombed Pearl Harbor. I vividly recall that. He said, 'How many ships do they have?' I said I had no idea. I knew Pearl Harbor was somewhere in the Pacific. But to associate it with Hawaii, I had no idea. None of us did."

■

When bullets and bombs started showering, the one thing Domenic Gentile wanted was his pants.

With the Marine Corps Fourth Defense Battalion, the 19-year-old son of a stonemason from 16th and Wolf Streets had landed in Pearl Harbor on December 2. The battalion's anti-aircraft batteries were still packed, and the men were in tents.

"I turned right around and went back to my tent, and I put on the nice, clean, starched khakis that I had laid out because I was going on liberty that morning. There was no time to dig into my laundry bag to get dungarees out. No socks. No underwear. No belt, neither. I picked up a belt later in the day from a dead Marine."

Their guns unavailable, the Marines were ordered to go down to the docks in trucks to pick up wounded on ships that had been hit. Gentile's truck was pulling up to a ship—he believes it was the destroyer *Shaw*—when it exploded.

"The whole ship went up. And all of a sudden, these big pieces of shrapnel were coming at you, and I mean they were big."

He paused.

"This is the part I never like to say. I pulled my friend off the truck because he didn't see the shrapnel coming at us. And as we landed on the ground, he said to me, 'Gentile, give me my arm back.' Here, a piece of shrapnel had cut his arm in half. He passed out, and I think I did, too."

Gentile spoke at his dining table in The Mansions apartments in Pine Hill, Camden County, New Jersey. He has seen much in 69 years. Born in the village of Casoli in the Italian province of Abruzzi, he passed through Ellis Island at age 9. After two years at South Philadelphia High School, he quit to enlist. After the war, he was a union painter.

Of Pearl Harbor, Gentile remembered: "It was hell that day. . . . We were on one ship where they opened up the doors and let some of the sailors that were down below come out. And they were shellshocked and burnt. One of the chief boatswain mates says, 'When we let these sailors out, don't let them jump over the side.' The whole harbor, the water was ablaze with the oil burning.

"I grabbed one of the sailors, not to let him jump overboard, and as he pulled—do you know what the hell I remained with? Just the skin. His skin came off."

The sailor disappeared over the side and, Gentile presumes, died.

"There was lots of heroes that day," he said. "Them sailors, they should of all got medals."

Later, Gentile said, "I was on the first convoy out of Pearl Harbor." He was at Midway Island on June 4 and 5, 1942, for the decisive Battle of Midway. He was on Tinian when the B-29 called Enola Gay took off to drop the world's first atomic bomb on Hiroshima.

He was there at the beginning, and he was there at the end. Most of all, he said, he'll remember Pearl Harbor.

Sailing from the harbor a few days after the attack, his troopship went slowly past the stricken giants of Battleship Row. The great warship *Oklahoma* had capsized—turned turtle, the sailors said—and men with cutting torches were ants all over the shell.

"All I could think about," Gentile said, "was them men in there, still inside."

■

In Philadelphia, the papers had been full of war scare for days.

The morning of the attack, the banner headline in The Inquirer said, "Roosevelt Sends Personal Note to Emperor in 'Final' Effort to Avert War With Japan."

At noon, WJZ broadcast a program called *Japan's Hour of Decision.* In those days, the East Coast was 5½ hours ahead of Hawaii time. By noon, Japan's decision already had been made: Its attack planes had been in the air for 10 minutes.

It's true, the cliché: People remember where they were when they heard of Pearl Harbor.

Charles Levy was at his parents' house on Spencer Street in Philadelphia's West Oak Lane section. He was a private first class in the Army, married three months, and was on weekend leave from Fort Meade, Maryland.

He recalls the football game on radio—"My father was a die-hard Eagles fan"—but not who won. (Washington did, 20-14, with Sammy

Baugh pulling it out in the fourth quarter for the 'Skins.)

"I knew, soon as I heard about Pearl Harbor, I was going overseas," said Levy, a former Philadelphia fire inspector, now retired in the Rhawnhurst section of the Northeast. He was right. In fact, 44 months after Pearl Harbor, on August 9, 1945, Levy was in a B-29 over Japan, accompanying the plane that dropped the second atomic bomb, on Nagasaki.

Others in Philadelphia got the news on December 7 as they emerged from movie matinées. *Sergeant York* with Gary Cooper was in its eighth week at Keith's theater, 11th and Chestnut Streets. Walter Brennan was playing in *Swamp Water* at the Stanton, 16th and Market, and Greta Garbo was in *Two-Faced Woman* at the Boyd, 10th and Chestnut.

Art Chaitt of the Strawberry Mansion section was at work in the old Broad Street Station, running the telegraph counter. "People would write messages on yellow pads; we would type it into the teletype." Each hour, on the hour, the Clocker pulled out for New York.

"I was by myself at the counter. I answered the phone—I don't remember who it was, probably a friend—and I got the news that Pearl Harbor had been attacked."

He had to work a double-trick that day, he remembers. Funny, but there was no rush of telegrams. "The day went on and on," and he had time to think.

"What it meant was, your whole life as an adult, which you had comfortably settled into, was about to be disrupted," he said.

Chaitt, who now lives in Glenside, Pennsylvania, waited to be drafted in June 1942. Later, as a member of the First Infantry Division, "the Big Red One," he saw action in the Rhineland and was "in at the end of the Battle of the Bulge."

■

Like lots of guys in the service from Philadelphia, Peter S. Ellmer was the son of immigrants.

His father was from Budapest; his mother from Wittenberg, Germany. They were Old World folks in every sense of the word. His mother, Ellmer said, hated the new music, swing. "She didn't like Benny Goodman. I thought it was the greatest stuff in the world."

The family lived on Delhi Street, near Tenth. After graduating in 1938 from Northeast High School, then at Eighth Street and Lehigh Avenue, Ellmer was an apprentice plumber and spent some time in the Civilian Conservation Corps, a make-work agency for the unemployed. Then he enlisted in the Navy.

That's how he found himself on the USS *Honolulu*, docked at

Pearl Harbor on December 7. For weeks, the ship had engaged in drills at sea, blasting away at towed targets with its 15 deck guns. Ellmer remembered thinking, "If we fight the Japs, two weeks it's gonna be over. The buggers can't see, they're blind as bats, they wear those Coke bottles for glasses, and all that other stuff. That's how we thought in those days. . . . We were invincible, so to speak. Then we found out during the Pearl Harbor attack that we weren't."

Ellmer, too, thought it was an air-raid drill when he looked up from his ironing and saw planes. Then the bombs began to fall, and at the same instant the ship's horns sounded. Ellmer skittered down a ladder and beat feet to his general-quarters station near the bow.

The USS *St. Louis*, moored next to the *Honolulu*, billowed backward from the dock. The *Honolulu* stayed put, but it got off 250 rounds of antiaircraft fire, 4,500 rounds of .50-caliber ammunition, and 2,800 rounds of .30-caliber shells, according to Capt. Harold Dodd's report.

Ellmer, now 71, a retired chief petty officer and Naval Shipyard worker, keeps a treasured copy of that report, stamped "DECLASSIFIED," at his home in the city's Feltonville section. At 9:20 a.m., Dodd told his superiors, a bomb slammed through the concrete dock at a 45-degree angle and exploded below the water, rupturing the hull of the *Honolulu.*

"When the thing hit, I was raised up off the deck," Ellmer said. "You don't know what the heck's going on."

Somehow, no one was badly hurt. Among the 800 crewmen was a young sailor, Jason Robards, who decades later would play the role of a general in the Pearl Harbor movie *Tora! Tora! Tora!*

The men of the *Honolulu* knew they were lucky.

"You could see all the battleships, the fires going," Ellmer said. "The one on the [battleship] *Arizona* must have burned for two or three days. There was black smoke coming out. There was a haze. You couldn't even see because there was so much smoke. Like a rain cloud. The whole damn Pearl Harbor area was smoking."

■

Rear Admiral A.E. Watson, commander of what was then known as the Philadelphia Navy Yard, got word to the radio stations immediately, ordering all sailors and Marines to their posts.

Police tapped the shoulder of every blue jacket and Marine uniform they saw on the streets. Police Red Cars, as they were called, cruised the neighborhoods. In theaters, ushers moved up and down the aisles, telling servicemen to meet officers in the lobby.

Ordinary citizens felt the rush of war excitement. By nightfall, a crowd of several thousand had gathered on the streets of Center City.

Cars ringed City Hall. But this being Philadelphia on a Sunday, bars were closed under the blue laws.

For the civil authorities, news of the attack seemed to pose a need to do something, anything. "The fateful hour is upon us," Mayor Bernard Samuel said in a radio address.

Authorities ordered the closing of the Delaware River Bridge (now the Benjamin Franklin) to protect against saboteurs. Police guards were posted at defense plants. At Midvale Steel, for one, the guards were issued shotguns and the whole vast property in the city's Nicetown section was set ablaze in lights.

No one knew what was happening in the Pacific. The next day's Evening Bulletin had the White House saying that one battleship had been capsized and "other vessels" damaged. German radio reported that the battleships *Oklahoma* and *Pennsylvania* had been lost. Although the *Pennsylvania* was not lost, the overall truth was far worse. By nightfall on the East Coast, word was out that the Japanese already had spread their attack to the U.S. possessions of the Philippines and Guam.

Spies were suddenly a worry. Twenty Japanese Americans, along with a crew of Finnish seamen, were taken to the U.S. immigration detention barracks at Gloucester City in New Jersey and held overnight. In Atlantic City, someone threw a brick through the window of a Japanese novelty shop.

Allen Okamoto of Abington, Pennsylvania, listening to the radio in the Cosmopolitan Club at Lehigh University, knew Pearl Harbor meant trouble for Japanese Americans. "Even before Pearl Harbor, we would always get some kind of prejudice," he recalled. For his safety, the university soon arranged for Okamoto to be escorted whenever he left campus to go into the town of Bethlehem. After graduation in 1942, he served in the famous "Go for Broke" outfit of Japanese Americans in the U.S. Army, fighting against the Germans. He won a Bronze Star and three Purple Hearts.

Now a retired engineer from Upper Dublin, Pennsylvania, Okamoto said, "I was surprised they attacked Pearl Harbor. . . . I didn't think they had a chance in the world, they're such a small nation."

■

"I heard all this scurrying topside," Paul Brown remembered. He was below deck on the *Shaw*. He could not hear the planes, only running feet. "I went up and looked out a passageway, and I saw two or three Japanese planes go by at very low altitude. You could see the pilot in the cockpit of the plane. You could see his helmet. Some guys swear you could see the gold fillings in their teeth. Some guys swear they looked down at you and smiled.

"I didn't realize these were Japanese planes. I said to another guy who was running by the passageway door—I says, 'What's going on?' He says, 'The Japs are attacking.' "

Brown was 21, a skinny kid from Reach Street near Rising Sun Avenue in Northeast Philadelphia. He had dropped out of Mastbaum High School to work and had joined the Navy a month before his 20th birthday. His mother was an Irish immigrant. His father was an engineer on the Reading Railroad.

His ship, commissioned at the Philadelphia Navy Yard in 1936, was now in floating dry dock at Pearl Harbor, undergoing repair after hitting a Navy tanker during a submarine patrol. The *Shaw*'s five-inch guns were not even armed. All the seamen had to fight with were rifles.

"They issued us .30-.30 Springfield rifles, bandoleers of .30-caliber ammunition, a gas mask, and a World War I helmet," Brown remembered. "They just put us up on the catwalk of this floating dry dock and told us to shoot."

At 9:12 a.m., in the second wave of Japanese attack planes, the *Shaw* took a hit.

"There was fire all around me," Brown said. "I was looking for an escape route. The flames and smoke and everything was so intense, I had to bail out over the side of this dry dock.

"I gently laid my rifle down on the catwalk. I kept the two bandoleers of ammunition around my waist, the gas mask, and the helmet. Climbed over the railing. I was ready to jump. And then the guy next to me jumped. I said, 'Oh, you son of a bitch.' I had to hang on there for 10 or 15 seconds to let him hit and clear. I didn't want to land on top of him."

He dropped about 50 feet to the water, he guessed. When he smacked the water in his blue dungarees and short-sleeved chambray shirt, his arms stung. The bomb hadn't even knocked him down. But the flash had burned his exposed skin. He swam, climbed out and was walking to the Naval Hospital, his back to the *Shaw*, when the destroyer blew up.

The instant is captured in a famous photograph. Flames had worked their way to the *Shaw*'s magazine, where 500 rounds of five-inch shells were stored. The explosion was "like the Fourth of July."

"Thank God I was a block away," Brown said. "If I was on the ship when that blew up, they'd still be scraping me off Cloud 15 with a razor blade out there."

He laughed, telling it. He is 71, retired from Bucks County Community College, where he was chief engineer. He spoke in the kitchen of his home on a quiet street in Southampton, Bucks County, Pennsylvania. His wife, Eleanor, was microwaving lunch.

He intends to record his memories for his 10 grandchildren, he said. Recently, he spoke to students at William Tennent Senior High School. For him, he said, the naval engagements off Guadalcanal were even more terrifying than December 7. "That's where we stood toe to toe and slugged it out."

But he'll never forget the Naval Hospital at Pearl Harbor.

"On one side of the walkway was a pile of arms, legs, parts of bodies. On the other was stacked-up dead bodies. They had no place to put them, so they just put them out on the front walk."

2 • The Day After
December 8, 1941

The day of shock was followed by a day of action, when Philadelphia's industrial power turned to the war effort.

December 8, 1991

It was the day that Roosevelt spoke of infamy and that Congress declared war. That young men rushed to enlist. That Philadelphia's unmatched industrial power was redirected in earnest to the production of tanks and bazookas and destroyers.

It was December 8, 1941. The day after. Fifty years ago today.

December 7, a Sunday, was a day of shock for most Americans after the Japanese attack at Pearl Harbor. But December 8, a Monday, was a day of action.

"I was anxious to get in in the morning to see what was going on, to see what was happening," recalled Tom Woods, a civilian workman at the Philadelphia Navy Yard. "I knew we were going to be very, very busy."

Not since 1776 had Philadelphia contributed as much to the nation as it would contribute during the 44 months of America's involvement in World War II. All those dead factories and warehouses dotting neighborhoods around the city today—they were alive then.

The city had 5,282 manufacturing plants, compared with 1,725 today. In them labored the largest body of skilled workers in the nation. Philadelphians could make anything.

Philadelphia made ships. So did Camden. So many shipyards built so many ships that the Delaware looked like a logging river, full of timbers from the launchings.

At the Frankford Arsenal, Philadelphia made bullets. At Midvale Steel, it made armor plate. At J.G. Brill Co., it made gun carriages. At

Philco Corp., it made fuses.

Budd Co., which in peacetime manufactured auto bodies, fenders, and doors, turned to war production eight days after Pearl Harbor. Before long, it was making bazooka rocket-bombs, ships' masts, aircraft manifolds. "Budd," recalls retired executive Norman Fesmire of Huntingdon Valley, Pennsylvania, "was 110 percent defense."

On December 8, at Eddystone in Delaware County, the Baldwin Locomotive Works rolled out the Army's first 60-ton tank. In Lester and Southwest Philadelphia, Westinghouse and General Electric were gearing up to turn out huge engines for ships.

"The war provided the moment when the full capacity of this city's and region's industrial capacity was released," said Philip Scranton, professor of history at Rutgers University's Camden campus. "It's just astonishing how much could be done."

Economically, the city was already on a war footing December 8, the day on which President Franklin D. Roosevelt declared, "No matter how long it may take . . . the American people, in their righteous might, will win through to absolute victory."

In Philadelphia, the Depression had ended in 1940. Employment had risen from 763,322 to 958,887 in 21 months. The city already was providing the materials of war to Britain, and the papers every day carried long columns of help-wanted ads. Already, there was a housing shortage.

But on December 8, said Woods, "we got really serious."

■

By 7:30 a.m., they were lined up outside the Navy recruiting office in the ornate hallways of the old U.S. Custom House at Second and Chestnut Streets. First in line was Charles Rogers, 30, of Melvale Street in Philadelphia's Port Richmond section.

"I got here at 12:30 a.m. and waited around like it was the World Series," reporter Ashley Halsey Jr. of The Philadelphia Record quoted Rogers as saying. "I made up my mind like that when I heard the news [of Pearl Harbor]. I told the wife and she said all right."

Boys of 14 jostled with scattered men who looked 40ish. "I'm fit, see?" said one.

The previous week, the Navy had had 79 applicants. This Monday, by noon, it got 250; by nightfall, 500. At the Army induction center, 33rd Street and Lancaster Avenue, it was a similar scene. By week's end, according to The Evening Bulletin's rough count, the Marines had accepted 400 to 500 men from the Philadelphia area. The Army had taken nearly 800 and the Navy 1,000.

Black applicants were few among those accepted. The

Philadelphia Tribune reported December 13 that blacks were getting "the brushoff." In an editorial, it said, "This is a war and all partisan and racial differences must be stifled."

Monday morning, at John Bartram High School in Southwest Philadelphia, Stan Wojtusik's social studies teacher tried to help his students understand the vastness of continents and the Pacific Ocean. World War II was nothing if not a geography lesson.

"Mr. Ott pulled a map down off the blackboard and was pointing to the area that was bombed by the Japanese—Pearl Harbor and [Wake Island]—and how far the Japanese traveled to get there," Wojtusik recalled. Mr. Ott had been to Hawaii, and he "could more or less describe the ships in the harbor as he remembered them."

City Hall teemed with activity. Mayor Bernard Samuel called an emergency meeting of the cabinet. All day long, people crowded into the offices of Deputy Air Raid Warden John Knecht, demanding to be enrolled as air-raid watchers. The city's 4,478 police officers were ordered not to leave town without permission; all leaves were cancelled. The Philadelphia Council of Defense met and designated firehouses as air-raid shelters.

The likelihood of aerial bombardment was remote, but the fear of it was close at hand. Samuel issued instructions on what citizens were to do in an air raid. He also said that police and fire sirens were banned for any purpose *but* air raids. Horns would have to do for other emergencies.

"People started building bomb shelters—clearing out spaces in their basements where they could claim a bit of security," recalled former police Captain James Reaves, who was a foot patrolman in South Philadelphia in 1941.

People were afraid of unseen planes in the sky. And they were afraid of unseen enemy agents, of spies.

The police and FBI continued their roundup of suspect foreigners. Amateur radio operators—hams, of whom there were 779 registered in Philadelphia—were ordered off the air by the Federal Communications Commission. Reaves recalls that police were ordered to scan rooftops for radio antennas.

Lewis F. Reynolds, a Budd Co. engineer, had to go to the Boeing plant in South Philadelphia that morning. "I remember all the agents of the government were there; I think it was the FBI. And they were taking out these fellows. . . . I saw them march them out." The atmosphere, he said, was "utter confusion."

At 12:30 p.m., as Roosevelt went before a joint session of Congress, Philadelphians were glued to radios: "Yesterday, December 7, 1941—a date which will live in infamy—the United States of America was suddenly and deliberately attacked . . ."

The speech was over in six minutes, and within an hour, the Congress had declared war on Japan.

"He was so emphatic using that word 'infamy,' " Wojtusik remembered. "My sister went to the dictionary and came back and told us what it meant. . . . There are times, still, I come across another word like 'information' in the dictionary and I think of that word 'infamy.' "

The patriotic fever burned. The longshoremen's union pledged not to strike for the duration of the war. The shipbuilders' union joined in. Society women did their bit, too, announcing cancellation of the city's major event, the Assembly, scheduled for January 2—just as they had done during the dark hour of World War I.

It was not a good day to go before a judge to be sentenced for failing to fill out one's draft questionnaire. But that was Richard Collins Baker's fate on December 8.

"This man has refused to obey the laws of his country and has attempted to set himself above the will of the majority. He therefore is not entitled to any leniency as far as I can see," said U.S. District Judge J. Cullen Ganey.

Ganey sentenced Baker, the son of a Haverford College professor, to spend a year and a day at the federal prison camp in Danbury, Connecticut.

Baker, now 72, of Boyertown, Pennsylvania, said he never regretted his action.

"Either we have a human species where each member cares about every other, or what's a species for?" he said. "There's enough famine and pestilence that can destroy the human species without humans turning against themselves."

Baker was a Quaker, a member of the Society of Friends, a firm believer in pacifism. But that didn't matter to the court. "There was a prosecutor that had such a high regard for human life," Baker said, "that he said I ought to be shot."

■

It was a different era, a much different city that December 8.

Coke—the fizzy kind—cost a nickel. Gimbel's advertised a 34-piece electric train set for $7.98 and a reversible raincoat in the thrift store for $12.95.

Philadelphia still had 239 farms, and almost every plot of land above Cottman Avenue had a cow on it. That year, 1941, the city had 112 homicides; in 1990, it had 500.

The city wage tax was 1.5 percent, for residents and non-residents. It had been imposed January 1, 1940. The Bulletin Almanac and Yearbook for 1942 said the tax "was to be only temporary."

Sports-wise, Philadelphia was the city of losers. Both baseball teams finished eighth—and last. The National League Phillies had a record of 43 wins and 111 losses. The American League Athletics were a little better, at 64-90. Hated New York teams, the Dodgers and Yankees, finished first in their leagues. In football, the Eagles' year-ending loss to the Redskins in Washington on Pearl Harbor Day left them at 2-8-1.

The skilled workers in the shops were mostly native-born men of Irish, German, Scottish, and English families, according to Professor Scranton, co-author of *Work Sights*, a book on Philadelphia manufacturing. Italians were "powerfully concentrated" in construction and material-handling trades, he said, and many Poles worked at Midvale Steel. Blacks mostly were consigned to dirty foundry work, though the war eventually made it necessary for companies to open the shop doors, a bit. At Sun Shipbuilding & Drydock Co. in Chester, Pennsylvania, the number of workers needed to build ships tripled. Eight hundred blacks were hired, but white steamfitters and riveters balked at training them. "Plant managers threatened to fire whites unless they trained these guys," Scranton said. "The response was, 'OK, we'll train them, but we're not going to work with them.' " After the war, the need for ships sank. Most of the workers in the so-called Negro Yard, Scranton said, ended up back in the low-paying jobs they had come from. The economic boom war was to continue for only a few years. Then began a slow decline. Today, two-thirds of the factories operating in 1941 are closed.

Around Philadelphia, there are only a few workers still on the job today who were on the job December 8, 1941. One is Charley Bradford, the senior employee at the Philadelphia Naval Shipyard. He's 80 and has been at the yard since 1939.

"Right away after Pearl Harbor, we went to seven days a week, 10-hour days," he recalled. "Sometimes, you worked 16 hours straight."

Bradford was—and is—a rigger. His job was to rig up heavy loads for lifting onto ships. On the wartime battleships *New Jersey* and *Wisconsin*, those loads included 16-inch guns. "Just the barrels weighed 109 ton," After Pearl Harbor, Bradford said, "I went to the shop and I told them I was going to re-enlist [in the Navy]. They said, 'Look, Brad, we think you're needed here more than you are in the service.' I went back and I said, all right. I worked hard. I felt that everything I did helped the poor guy out at sea. I didn't want to do a job that would fall apart at sea."

On February 12, 1942, at the Navy Yard, Philadelphia produced its first fighting ships of World War II—the destroyers *Butler* and *Gherardi*, launched 15 minutes apart.

It was the first drop of a torrent.

3 • The Atlantic War
January 14, 1942

The U.S. focused on fighting Japan in the Pacific, but the first attack by German U-boats showed serious weakness in the Atlantic.

January 14, 1992

A disaster worse than Pearl Harbor. That's how history has come to view a nearly forgotten battle of World War II that began off the East Coast 50 years ago today.

On January 14, 1942, a German U-boat surfaced 60 miles southeast of Montauk Point on Long Island and plowed three 3,500-pound torpedoes into the hull of a Norwegian tanker called *Norness*. Two seamen were killed; 38 were plucked from a lifeboat.

It was the beginning of a submarine assault against merchant shipping along the coast that threatened to take America out of the fight in Europe scarcely weeks after its entry into the war.

While the country's attention had been fixed on the Japanese menace in the Pacific Ocean after Pearl Harbor, an equally great German threat had popped up in the Atlantic, just miles off the beaches from New England to Florida and in the Gulf of Mexico.

The United States was totally unprepared. By the end of January, subs had sunk 40 tankers and freighters in Atlantic coastal waters. In February, they sank 65.

Naval defenses were nominal, and instead of sailing in convoys, as British ships had learned to do, vessels ventured out alone from U.S. ports. Resort towns such as Atlantic City blazed like strings of Christmas lights, making it easy for submarine captains to spot ships at night by their silhouettes.

"It was incredible to me," recalled Reinhard Hardegan, the last living captain of five *Unterseeboote* that arrived nearly simultaneously off the coast in January 1942 in an operation the Germans code-named *Paukenschlag*, or Drumbeat.

Hardegan, now 78, spoke from Bremen, Germany, where he is a retired marine businessman. "I thought that the United States Navy learned from the experience the British had for two years with submarine warfare," he said in his high voice. "And they did nothing. . . . The destroyers were in their harbors. There was no blackout on the coast and no blackout on the ships. They were all in full light."

The blow fell mainly on the civilian U.S. Merchant Marine, which in the first year of the war had a far higher casualty rate than any of the armed services. Nearly 6,000 mariners were to lose their lives in World War II.

One night, Bob Bright, owner of an appliance store in Wildwood, New Jersey, heard two thuds out at sea as he lay in bed. A day or two later, he recalled, a local funeral director, Benjamin Ingersoll, quietly asked him, "Can you get a couple of your men and come with me?"

In a flatbed truck, they rode down to the foot of Spicer Avenue. Splayed on the beach were the bodies of four seamen. The men labored to get the slippery corpses onto the truck and back to the funeral home, where they laid them parallel on the floor.

"I remember one man in particular," Bright said. "He was covered in fuel oil. A big, heavy, slimy mess. All of 'em were. But he was especially big. The thing I remember was looking at his wrist. He had this gold wristwatch on, and there wasn't a drop of oil on it. It just shined."

In March 1942, when 86 ships went down off the coast, the toll included the SS *Naeco*—"ocean," spelled backwards—captained by Emil H. Engelbrecht, a father of five from Williamstown, Camden County, in New Jersey.

The family had been to Grandmother's house for dinner the day word came. They had returned home to find the dog in the road, acting nervously. An agent of the Pennsylvania Shipping Co. was waiting at the door.

Gene Engelbrecht, the youngest son, recalled: "He said, 'Mrs. Engelbrecht, I have very bad news for you. Your husband's ship has been torpedoed. It broke in half and exploded. Only a few survivors have come off. No officers. There's very little hope for him.' "

The elder Engelbrecht was never found. His typewritten last letter, dated February 18 aboard the *Naeco*, arrived after the news of the sub attack. "Personally," he had written, "I do not desire to meet these underwater travelers of the sea, as I have neither the speed nor the guns to fight with, which makes this Battle of the Atlantic all one-sided."

His four sons took their revenge by joining the Merchant Marine and working the ships that carried arms and men to battle. The

Merchant Marine eventually put 250,000 men out to sea, up from 55,000 at the start of the war.

In April, U-boats sank 69 ships off the Atlantic shore. In May, it was 111. In June, the losses topped out at 121 ships. Then, oh so slowly, the havoc began to subside as the Navy made headway with improved defenses and, at last, blackouts and regular convoys.

Sinkings would persist, of course. By war's end, more than 700 American merchant ships would go to the bottom in all four oceans. But losses would never again approach the levels of what the elated Germans had dubbed "the American shooting season."

"The U-boat offensive . . . during the first six months of 1942 constituted a far greater disaster for the Allied war effort than did the Japanese attack on Pearl Harbor," said Michael Gannon, a University of Florida professor and author of the book *Operation Drumbeat*.

The assault took more lives than Pearl Harbor, and cost more in materiel. A wartime accounting said it was as if saboteurs had destroyed a half-dozen of America's biggest war plants.

■

Edwin Kremer was at sea when the Japanese hit Pearl Harbor, bound for a port in Gambia, on the west coast of Africa.

"We were never told that the war had broken out," he recalled. "When we sailed into the harbor, there were some British passenger ships that were carrying troops for the British desert campaign. And they were all blowing their whistles and ringing their bells, figuring the first American troops were arriving.

"We just had a few civilian aircraft technicians with us."

Kremer, a 1939 graduate of West Philadelphia High School, was off to see the world a month shy of his 20th birthday. His father was a doctor, a Jewish immigrant from Russia. The family recently had moved up to a townhouse at 19th and Pine Streets in Center City Philadelphia.

On June 15, 1942, Kremer was third mate on the SS *Cherokee*, a New York passenger liner pulled into war service. The *Cherokee* was on its way home from Iceland in a rare coastal convoy of six ships. It was 11:25 p.m., Eastern War Time, and Kremer was the officer on watch as the *Cherokee* headed toward the Cape Cod Canal.

Suddenly, an explosion. A British vessel, the *Port Nicholson*, had taken a torpedo in the side. Defensive measures called for the other ships to turn toward the noise, pointing nose or tail at the sub to show the smallest target.

"But before we even got turned around, the first torpedo hit the bow" of the *Cherokee*, Kremer said. "The explosion just picked up the ship and, bang, threw it down."

Kremer had barely grabbed his life jacket when a second torpedo slammed into the engine room, and almost before he knew it the *Cherokee* was listing hard to port. The black water had risen to his knees before he slid off the deck into the sea.

"I remember very clearly, something caught my collar and it was dragging me down. I fought and I fought. . . . They say that when you're drowning your whole life passes in front of your face. Believe me, it does. I remember how peaceful it was. And then my head popped above water. I figured, somebody is praying for me. . . . I looked around. The ship was sinking; it was going down fast."

Kremer spotted a raft and struggled aboard. "I heard voices of people struggling in the water. I managed to get hold of a couple of them and pull them on the boat. I went in after a couple of others. Hold onto the raft with one hand; grab the person in the water with the other. I remember starting to get cold even though it was June."

That night, they say, Edwin Kremer saved seven seamen.

Later, many of the 83 survivors and 87 dead were put ashore at Provincetown, Massachusetts, at the tip of Cape Cod, where the town hall was used as a morgue. At the dock, Kremer said, "there were doctors and nurses and Boy Scouts. I was helping this one guy who was bleeding, and they pushed him aside and grabbed me. My face was cut and I had oil all over me, and I didn't even realize it."

Kremer, who now lives in Bala Cynwyd, Pennsylvania, joined the Navy in late 1942 and ended up ducking bullets at Omaha Beach in Normandy on H-Hour of D-Day. After the war, he returned to the Merchant Marine, a civilian service that even in combat never got the recognition of the Army, Navy, or Marines. He felt he served his country just as much on the *Cherokee* as in France.

"There's nothing," he said, "quite like a sinking."

■

Oscar Blenman recalled that mariners didn't talk much about danger—that was an unstated taboo in the combat zone.

But after January 1942, Blenman said, he slept with his life jacket on. Sometimes he'd loosen his laces, but he would keep his shoes on, too. Sometimes he'd sleep on deck. Anything to gain an inch in a race to the lifeboats.

"You don't want to get caught in the room if you get hit," he said. "The ship could go down fast. The concussion will jam the door on you and you won't be able to open it."

Blenman spent five decades afloat. Born on the West Indies island of Barbados, he grew up in Harlem and went to sea soon after graduating in 1933 from Frederick Douglass High School. Now living in the

Mantua section of Philadelphia—in earshot of the rooster at the
Children's Zoo—he still has the green wallet card issued by the
National Maritime Union that identifies him as a "torpedoed seaman."

He, too, was in the Atlantic when the war broke out, headed for
Vera Cruz, Mexico. His freighter was on its return leg, he said, when the
U-boats all at once began their attacks.

A half-century later, it is hard to conjure a picture of the devasta-
tion the submarines caused. But Blenman paints one in vivid color.

"On the way back to New York," he said, "we saw furniture floating
in the shipping lanes. Drawers and boxes. Cans. Whatever was blown
overboard before a ship sunk, it floated. We saw lots of it."

The captain of his ship, the SS *Medina*, ordered lights out. No
smoking on deck. The captain even collected the crew's AM radios, lest
a sub zero in on the strains of Glenn Miller or Sammy Kaye.

Blenman was an able-bodied seaman, assigned to stand watch,
four hours on, four hours off. "We knew there were submarines out
there somewhere. We had men on lookout at all times. A man forward,
on both sides and, if there was a mast, a man up on the mast."

Mariners were in short supply in wartime. Though civilians, they
were required not to spend more than a month "on the beach" between
voyages. Blenman recalled a government agent stopping him as he win-
dow-shopped one time in New York. The agent demanded to see the
union-dues book that contained his record.

"See, a lot of guys were scared. They didn't want to go back out
there. It was dangerous out there. . . . They were drinking themselves to
death. Some were. Not to forget, maybe, but to ease their mind."

Blenman sailed regularly. The worst was over in March 1943, ironically, when he finally met his fate in the dark shape of an Italian submarine. On a ship called *Staghound*, he was torpedoed off the north
coast of Brazil. The crew spent 24 hours in lifeboats before an
Argentine ship picked them up.

These days, once a month, Blenman joins a group of black merchant mariners that meets at the Seamen's Church Institute at 249 Arch
Street in Philadelphia. In the military of their era, blacks were mostly
excluded from combat roles. So black seamen hold a special place in
history.

"Those were some days," Blenman said.

■

In six months, from January through July in 1942, the U-boats
sank nearly 400 ships in coastal waters. The late Samuel Eliot Morison,
the Navy's official historian, termed it a "massacre." Professor Gannon
called it the worst disaster at sea in American history.

Yet Adolf Hitler never freed more than a couple of dozen U-boats for the American campaign. Admiral Karl Doenitz wanted more, many more. Had he got them, Germany might have prolonged the European war almost indefinitely, if not won it.

"I guess, instead of 400 ships, perhaps we would have sunk 4,000 ships," said Hardegan, who as commander of Germany's U-123 fired the first shot by sinking the *Norness.* Since the war, Hardegan has been to the United States five times. He recalled that once, "I met the daughter of the captain of the *City of Atlanta.* Her father died when I sunk the ship, and she came to me and said to me, 'You didn't kill my father, you sunk his ship; that was a big difference.' It was impressive to me that she felt that way."

Time heals.

It has even softened the attitude of the U.S. government, which after World War II denied veterans' benefits to merchant seamen.

"There seemed to be a feeling they weren't military. They made more money than the guys in the Navy and could come and go as they pleased," said Shawn Aubitz, curator of a 1992 exhibit at the National Archives mid-Atlantic branch in Philadelphia, titled, "The Forgotten War: The United States Merchant Marine During World War II."

Merchant seamen often served on the same ships with men of the Naval Armed Guard. They helped load ammunition and in battle even fired guns that were put on the ships to protect them. But afterward, only the Navy men were considered veterans.

In 1988, a court ruled that the denial was "arbitrary and capricious." The Defense Department then granted war-veteran status for service from Pearl Harbor Day to August 15, 1945. A bill that has been hanging around in Congress for several years would extend that to December 31, 1946, the same as for members of the armed forces.

These days, 250 World War II-era seamen apply to the Coast Guard each month for a Merchant Marine discharge. Mostly, it's a matter of pride. Few have need of a college loan or low-interest mortgage. Kremer has applied for and received his; Blenman said he planned to apply.

"A military funeral," said Blenman. "That's about all I could get now."

4 • An Ethnic Roundup
February 19, 1942

In the panic after Pearl Harbor, Americans of Japanese descent were suspected of disloyalty, and many were detained in camps.

February 19, 1992

Like most Japanese Americans of her generation, Miiko Horikawa spent part of her childhood in concentration camps.

That's what she calls them: concentration camps. They weren't in Nazi-occupied Europe but in Arkansas and Arizona. The U.S. government officially called them relocation centers.

Fifty years ago today, February 19, 1942, President Franklin D. Roosevelt signed Executive Order 9066. In the name of military security, it permitted the Army to clear away everyone of Japanese birth or ancestry on the West Coast, where 80 percent of Japanese Americans lived.

In the panic after the Japanese attack on Pearl Harbor, America imagined that every ethnic Japanese was a potential spy, a saboteur. The government was at a loss to tell the loyal from the disloyal. "A Jap's a Jap," said Lieutenant General John L. DeWitt, who was in charge of the Western Defense Command.

And so 120,000 people—two-thirds of them native-born American citizens—were hustled from their houses and farms, packed onto trains, and deposited behind barbed wire in remote isolation camps. Without indictment. Without trial. Without appeal.

Horikawa, now of Bryn Mawr, Pennsylvania, was 8 years old when she interned amid the sticky heat of the Jerome Relocation Center near Dermott, Arkansas, along with her father, mother, sister, and three brothers. She was a year older—and had a fourth brother—when the family was moved to another camp in the baked desert at Gila, Arizona.

"They were concentration camps in that we were all herded away, put under guard, just because of who we were, not because of anything we did," Horikawa said. ". . . In Arkansas, I remember chiggers and mosquitoes because we were near a swamp. I remember my sister had sensitive skin. She was getting chigger bites that used to weep all the time. . . . It was just oozing everywhere on her body."

Yone Okamoto, now of Upper Dublin Township outside Philadelphia, was 23, still at home with her mother and siblings, when the order came to gather up whatever they could carry. The family was uprooted from Hollywood and put down on the Northern Plains at Heart Mountain, Wyoming. "It was desolate—and very cold," Okamoto said. "People from Southern California got their ears frostbitten, not knowing not to walk outside without covering their faces."

Charles Nagao, now of Vineland, New Jersey, was 25, married, with baby twin daughters, when his family was sent to Manzanar in the California desert. The barracks were built of tar paper over green boards. When the pine wood dried, the floorboards separated, and the dust blew into everything. Beyond the fence, he said, "there was nothing—just sagebrush." Yet the camp was ringed by guard towers, with searchlights and machine guns.

As the war dragged on—and no evidence was found to suggest Japanese American treachery—the nation began to get a moral itch about keeping tens of thousands of innocents in camps.

By 1944, though it still barred Japanese from the West Coast, the government was closing camps. It had opened War Relocation Authority offices in the East—including one at 21 South 12th Street in Philadelphia—and was seeking employers who would hire internees who swore loyalty to the United States. A few Japanese had been in Philadelphia before the war, but unlike those on the West Coast, Eastern Japanese had not been ordered evacuated.

Each internee who left camp got $25 and a railroad ticket.

As many as 2,000, including Miiko Horikawa and Charles Nagao, ended up in the crossroads village of Seabrook in Cumberland County, New Jersey, where the world's largest frozen-food plant needed labor.

An additional 1,000 or so, including Yone Okamoto, ended up in Philadelphia. Okamoto roomed at a Spruce Street boarding house and worked as a secretary at the old Women's Homeopathic Hospital.

A few hundred who came remain today.

It was not until decades later that America said it was sorry for the mass internments. On August 10, 1988, President Ronald Reagan signed legislation that granted an apology and awarded $20,000 in restitution to each of the estimated 60,000 camp survivors then living.

Today, the government's own Smithsonian Institution uses the term concentration camp to describe Jerome and Gila and other camps in an exhibit at the National Museum of American History in Washington.

"I need hardly tell you that there are lots of folks who think the government was perfectly justified in doing what it did, and I still get letters from folks—usually irate—who take that point of view," said Tom Crouch, curator of the exhibit, which opened in 1987.

"But most people, I think, understand it was wrong," he said. "Think what we did to Americans solely on the basis of their origin— lock them up behind barbed wire, threaten to shoot them if they got close to the fence. . . . When you add it up, you have something that fits the definition of concentration camp."

■

At 8, Miiko Horikawa was the oldest of six children in the family of Fuju Sasaki and his picture bride, Kikue.

Her father was born in Hiroshima in 1897, when thousands of Asians—mostly Chinese and Japanese—were migrating to the West Coast. By 1920, Japanese operated 4 percent of California's farmland and produced 10 percent of its crops. Ethnic prejudice was high. Immigrant Japanese were not permitted to own land or become citizens. In 1924, a new law basically banned all Asian immigration.

As a teenager, Fuju Sasaki left home for Hawaii. Unlike most immigrants, he got a college education, attending Park College in Kansas City, Missouri. He even did graduate work in Pittsburgh.

But by then it was the '30s—the Depression. The coming of the war found Sasaki driving a delivery van and making tofu from soybeans at a grocery near Sacramento.

A day or two after Pearl Harbor, agents came to the door and took him away. The family could only guess that it was because he had kept the records for a local Japanese association. Little Miiko's mother and uncle went to the Sacramento station three days later when they heard Sasaki was to be shipped out.

"They didn't see him because he was already in the train," Horikawa said. "The window shades were all drawn. They didn't know where he was going. They couldn't even see him. My mother got a letter saying he was in Bismarck, North Dakota. That's how we found out."

Bismarck was where the Army had opened a detention camp for suspected enemy agents. But all Japanese in this country, immigrant or not, were soon officially classified enemy alien.

Californians were near hysteria with fear of invasion, especially after a lone Japanese submarine fired a few shots on a coastal installation. There was much public support for the evacuation made possible by Roosevelt's Executive Order 9066.

The order said nothing about Japanese. It authorized the secretary of war to designate "military areas . . . from which any or all persons may be excluded." But everybody knew what it meant: The Japanese had to go.

And only the Japanese. Though individual Germans and Italians were picked up after Germany and Italy also became enemies, there was no wholesale roundup.

In May 1942, Kikue Sasaki reported with her children to be sent to an "assembly center" in Fresno, California. Though American-born, she grew up in Japan and returned for an arranged marriage. Fuju Sasaki had seen her only in a photograph.

She was lost without her more-Americanized husband, who was to remain in detention for six months before rejoining his family in Arkansas.

But in the eyes of a child, the uprooting was an adventure.

"As a kid, it meant lots of playtime," Horikawa said. "School wasn't so hard because the schools were sort of haphazardly put together. . . . There were all these other kids to play with. I didn't feel the resentment because I didn't know what was happening."

■

Charles Nagao was an adult. He knew.

"We had three meals a day, but they were always in the cafeteria. So they broke up the family style of living. . . . Children would leave in the morning and parents would never even realize where they were."

Nagao, who ran a bottled-water route before the war, found it astonishing that the Army recruited at the Manzanar camp for Nisei soldiers. The prefix "Ni" in Japanese means "two." The Nisei were the second generation, born in America.

"They said to me, 'We'd like you to volunteer.' I said, 'I respectfully decline that invitation. . . . I'm surrounded by barbed wire fence, machine-gun towers and all the privileges are gone. . . . I don't feel at this moment I'm up to volunteering.' "

But many did join. The Army's 100th Battalion, comprising Nisei from a National Guard unit from Hawaii, already was fighting in Italy when the all-Nisei 442nd Regimental Combat Team was being trained at Camp Selby, Mississippi. At war's end, the units had sustained awful casualties: 680 killed, 67 missing, 9,486 wounded.

Like other internees at Manzanar, Nagao was permitted to leave camp on work-release. Nagao was in Oregon doing farm work when representatives of Seabrook Farms traveled to Manzanar to recruit workers.

"They came with colorful brochures. My wife fell in love with it. She wrote to me and said, 'You better make arrangement to come home, because we're going to go out East. There's a frozen-food factory there.'"

Nagao wrote back saying he didn't want to go East. Too cold.

"She said, 'We are going to go, or else I'm going to go with my children.' . . . She just wanted to get out of the camp, I guess. You can't blame her."

Papers were issued, and the Nagaos set out in December 1944.

"They bused us up from Manzanar through the mountains to Reno, where we caught a train. I stood all the way to Chicago because the train was loaded with GIs. I thought, 'Oh, no.' But they were nice enough to let my wife and children sit. . . . I just stood there, hung onto a strap, and stared straight ahead."

The Nagaos arrived in late afternoon at the old B&O railroad depot in Philadelphia. They were greeted by volunteers from a hostel established at 3228 Chestnut Street by civic and church groups. In one busy month, the last April of the war, 120 Japanese spent at least a night at the hostel.

Setting out for the East had been a leap of faith. "We were facing the unknown," Nagao said.

A bus or truck from Seabrook met the train. By midnight, the Nagaos were ushered into the Seabrook Farms dining hall for lima bean soup and bologna sandwiches. Next morning, Charles Nagao got his first look at the utterly flat landscape. "I felt the cold, just as I imagined it would be."

A family business, Seabrook Farms had grown to encompass 23,000 acres of spinach, green beans, peas, asparagus, and other vegetables, with an additional 30,000 acres under contract.

The need for labor was enormous, but in war there was a labor shortage. Japanese started arriving in late 1944. They joined blacks from Jamaica and whites from Appalachia. German POWs, veterans of the Afrika Korps, worked the fields. After the Allied victory in Europe, displaced people from the Baltics came.

Japanese were housed in a government-built village of 54 barracks, each with six family units. The buildings, recently restored, are still in use. Only a few Japanese remain today in the village, but about 150 families are scattered across South Jersey, according to Ellen Nakamura, head of the Japanese American Citizens League chapter. The Seabrook Buddhist Temple has a mostly Japanese membership, and Japanese are prominent in a local Presbyterian congregation.

A Nisei group now intends to open a Seabrook Educational and Cultural Center in the local township building in 1994, the 50th anniversary of arrival. It will be dedicated to Charles F. Seabrook.

The Seabrooks were good folks, Nagao said. "They did well [financially], I'm sure," he said. "But they lived up to their commitments. If you went to Charles Seabrook for anything you wanted, he always did it for you."

■

In her best hat, Yone Okamoto arrived in Philadelphia at the Broad Street Station of the Pennsylvania Railroad. Her mother, who remained at the Heart Mountain camp, let her go because her best friend was going.

The date was September 12, 1943—the day an eight-alarm fire heavily damaged the station, warped all 16 tracks, destroyed six passenger cars, injured 350 people. The fire also burned 1,500 pieces of luggage, including one of Yone Okamoto's.

"I went back to the station. There were ropes and guards. And I could see my box. I just went under the rope. And a guard said, 'You're not allowed to be here.' I said, 'This is my crate.' He said, 'How can you prove it?' I said, 'It's got my typewriter.' "

The package was opened. Sure enough.

"The guard said, 'I'll tell you what. Why don't you take that typewriter home. And why don't you let me have those two golf balls you've got there for letting you have it.' "

That was Okamoto's welcome to Philadelphia—and to petty corruption.

She got along fine here. "I loved Philadelphia," she said. She typed for a while at the American Friends Service Committee, which then helped her get the hospital job.

The city's growing Japanese community attended charity dances at the International Institute, 645 North 15th Street, which became the center of Japanese social life. The arrivals attended a "splash party" at the Central YWCA. The Nisei founded a club and put out a newsletter, Penn Notes. They joined Red Cross blood drives.

Open hostility toward Japanese was rare. But there were instances—such as a highly publicized incident in Warren County, New Jersey, when locals ran off five Japanese men working on a farm.

After the Japanese surrender on September 2, 1945, some former internees returned to the West. Many had nothing to go back to. Homes had been lost, businesses destroyed.

Miiko Sasaki grew up and met Herbert J. Horikawa, a San Franciscan who had been interned at Poston, Arizona. They married, had two girls and a boy. Miiko is now library director at Springside School in Philadelphia's Chestnut Hill, and Herb is director of the counseling center at Temple University in North Philadelphia.

Nagao and his late wife, Mary, had a son after their twins. Nagao stayed with Seabrook Farms and became an executive. The company is gone, but two of Charles Seabrook's grandsons run an operation in South Jersey called Seabrook Bros. & Sons Inc., which produces 65 million pounds of vegetables most years.

Yone Okamoto, born Yone Watanabe, met a decorated veteran of the 442nd Nisei combat outfit, an engineering graduate of Lehigh University who grew up in Abington, Pennsylvania. She and Allen Okamoto have two sons and two daughters.

Many who were interned now fear a resurgence of ethnic hatred because of rising hostility between the United States and Japan. Said Miiko Horikawa: "I hear people on the radio saying, 'I don't trust those Japanese at all.' There's still so much racism."

But not long ago, Yone Okamoto had an experience that moved her. On a trip to Germany with a church group, she visited the Nazi concentration camp at Dachau.

"We saw the facilities. The barbed-wire fences. Where they were housed. Saw the horrible pictures of the starving Jewish people, enlarged and placed on exhibit in one of the buildings. . . . I just felt so awful that I [could not go] to the crematory, and I came back to the bus. All of us on the trip came back to the bus, and none of us spoke to each other. It was a complete silence for a good half-hour."

She became silent again, retelling it. And then she said:

"After thinking about that, I was so thankful that I was interned in an American concentration camp . . . that we were not treated as the Jewish people were in Germany."

5 • The Bataan Death March
April 9, 1942

The weak died along the way, some brutally, while the strong survived what may have been the low point of the entire war.

April 9, 1992

He still gets flashbacks, still has nightmares. In one dream, he is running, running, running . . .

"The Japs are chasing us, right? And they're cutting heads off. Then they're replacing the heads—your head—with a clay head. I'm running all through the night. Jumpin' all over. You believe that? You believe them kind of dreams?"

For Carmen J. Morelli, now 74, of Lafayette Hill, Pennsylvania, World War II has never really ended. "It'll never get out of my mind," he said. "You're never cured of it. Never."

Fifty years ago today, April 9, 1942, the Army corporal was among 78,000 American and Filipino troops who surrendered to the Japanese in the Philippines, most of whom embarked on what became known as the Bataan Death March. At the end, for Morelli and most others, lay three years of privation as a prisoner of war.

Together with the collapse of the last U.S. Army bastion at Corregidor on May 6, 1942, the Philippine surrender was the largest capitulation in American history. For the United States, it marked rock bottom in the Second World War.

Exhausted from three months of fighting in tropical heat, weakened from half rations and disease, the troops who surrendered on Bataan were in no condition to walk much of anywhere. But the Japanese needed to clear them out to continue their attack on Corregidor, a fortress island a few miles off the Bataan peninsula.

Prodded by bayonets and rifle butts, the strongest prisoners shuffled for five days over 55 miles of dirt to San Fernando. The weak fell out of line and died along the way. Some were stabbed, some were shot, some were clubbed. A few even were beheaded.

No one knows exactly how many were on the march or how many died. About 550 of at least 10,000 Americans died, according to historian Stanley L. Falk, an authority on the war in the Philippines. Between 5,000 and 10,000 Filipinos died.

The Japanese, expecting only half the prisoners they bagged, were unprepared to feed all of them. They had no means of transporting so many, either. The death of some weakened, sickened soldiers could not have been avoided, Falk said.

"It was an atrocity; it was a horrible atrocity. But it wasn't a deliberate atrocity" by Japanese leaders, Falk said.

But many guards were undeniably brutal—inflamed by a code that said surrender was dishonorable and by harsh discipline in their own ranks. "They mistreated their own soldiers," Falk said.

After the war, the two Japanese leaders in the Philippines, Lieutenant General Masaharu Homma and his superior, Lieutenant General Tomoyuki Yamashita, were tried as war criminals and executed.

"All I remember" of the death march, Morelli said, "is seeing guys lying on the roads, guys being kicked, hit with bayonets." Morelli, who grew up near Shibe Park in North Philadelphia, the son of Italian immigrants, is among a number of death march survivors living in the Philadelphia area.

Frank J. Basara of Aston, Pennsylvania, who lost a leg as a POW, recalled, "Guys would run off the road—they'd see a creek or something and want a drink—and the Japs would shoot 'em."

Dr. Luis R. Acosta of Philadelphia's Germantown section, who was a Filipino medical officer, recalled that at an aid station, "they just bayoneted those who were lying in bed. Helpless Americans. The poor people. Bedridden. With amputated arms, with amputated legs."

The outside world knew none of this. The Bataan troops slipped into a void after Major General Edward P. King Jr. dispatched a white flag at 6 a.m. on April 9—the 77th anniversary of Robert E. Lee's surrender at Appomattox in the Civil War.

The troops' fate did not become known until 1943, when three Americans escaped from a prison camp and made it to Australia, aided by Filipino guerrillas. On January 27, 1944, the Office of War Information finally issued a public report on what it dubbed "the march of death."

Readers of The Philadelphia Inquirer awoke the next day to a headline that said, "Japs torture, murder thousands of U.S. war captives from Bataan—Prisoners beaten and starved in wanton brutality."

By then, the war had dragged on long. In Europe, the Allies were bogged down at Anzio. In the Pacific, the Army was slogging through New Guinea, and the Marines were island-hopping in the Marianas. Iwo Jima and Okinawa still lay in the future.

Tales of Bataan atrocities fanned anti-Japanese hatred and helped stiffen Americans to the hard road of battle still ahead.

■

When Pearl Harbor was attacked at dawn on December 7, 1941, it was already December 8 in the Philippines, on the other side of the International Date Line. General Douglas MacArthur received word of the Hawaii attack. Yet he was taken by surprise hours later when bombers appeared out of the blue over his airfields.

Basara, then 20, a son of Polish immigrants in Chester, Pennsylvania, had been in the Army a year. He was a corporal in the 803rd Aviation Engineers, stationed at Clark Field.

"All of a sudden, all hell broke loose for us," Basara recalled. "Here we had I-don't-know-how-many B-17s, brand new ones that had just come over from the United States. They destroyed all our planes sitting on the ground. . . . They wiped us out."

From then on, the joint American and Filipino forces under MacArthur's command were on their heels. On December 20, a Japanese invasion force landed on the southern island of Mindanao. A larger force landed December 22 at Lingayen Gulf on Luzon, the same island where both Manila and Bataan are located.

MacArthur chose to abandon the capital of Manila and withdraw into the Bataan peninsula to wait for reinforcements from America— reinforcements that would never come. Slowly, the American-Filipino forces were pushed back. In February, a lull settled in and on March 11, under orders from President Franklin D. Roosevelt, MacArthur fled the Philippines in a torpedo boat. On reaching Australia, he pledged, "I shall return."

Feeling abandoned by their country, the American defenders took a cue from United Press correspondent Frank Hewlett and began calling themselves "the battling bastards of Bataan."

We're the battling bastards of Bataan,
No mama, no papa, no Uncle Sam,
No aunts, no uncles, no cousins, no nieces,
No pills, no planes, no artillery pieces.
And nobody gives a damn.

On the Japanese side, reinforcements poured in. The Japanese sprang forward with overwhelming force on April 3. The defenders fought, fell back, fought. But within days, their lines had disintegrated. Acosta, now an American citizen but then a 33-year-old captain in the Philippine Army, was assigned to a medical unit that had no weapons to fight with. And so the unit was ordered to withdraw.

"We were way up in the mountains of Bataan," he said. "At dawn, when we thought we were far away, we prepared for our breakfast. We used firewood to cook our breakfasts. The smoke attracted the enemy's artillery. They directed a barrage to us."

Shell fragments caught Acosta in the eye, arm, and back. It was his luck to be at Field Hospital No. 1 when it took a direct hit from a bomb dropped by an airplane.

"I was buried by other individuals who were on top of me. I lost my hat. All the buttons of my shirt were off. I cannot hear. . . . Everybody has to take care of himself. We were scattered. I did not know where I was walking to. I just have a towel to rub my head. I could feel the warm feeling of the flowing blood."

A short distance off, Acosta said, "I was intercepted by two Japanese with bayonets sticking in my side." He and other Filipino captives were ordered to go to an assembly point where, they were told, they would receive passes to go home. By the evening of April 9, word had reached Basara's unit that "we were to lay down our arms. We were to wait until the Japs come into our area and tell us what to do. And that's what we did."

Finally, the Imperial Japanese Army appeared—"two guys, two young guys on foot," Basara recalled. More soon followed. "We didn't eat for five days," Basara said, "and we marched almost 100 kilometers. . . . This guy, he was dragging another guy, and the guard made him let him go. He walked a few more steps and then he dropped. And after that, we heard a shot. We didn't look back or anything. We figured they finished him off. You can't walk, you're done."

For Filipinos, the promise of passes was a hoax. On the march, Acosta witnessed an American slip from line to grab a stalk of sugar cane on the roadside. "He was followed by the Japanese guard," he recalled. "He stabbed him in the body several times. He died crying."

After two days, Acosta himself slipped away and got into a house. "I was hearing my companions marching until dawn," he said. About daybreak, he said, he heard heavy feet on the stairs. He grabbed a stick and hid. "It was the old man who owned the building, and he was carrying a bowl of rice and fish. When he was inside the door, he called to me in our dialect, 'Son, I know you are there. Come out, I have brought you food.' . . .When I saw him, I cried."

The old man put Acosta in touch with the resistance. Though he had lost his right eye and much of his hearing, he spent the better part of the war hiding in Manila and elsewhere.

For Basara and Morelli, the death march was the beginning of suffering. Packed onto a train after his long march to San Fernando, Basara ended up at Camp O'Donnell, an American airfield the Japanese had taken over. During their first weeks at Camp O'Donnell, 1,600 Americans and 16,000 Filipinos died.

"O'Donnell had shelters, like shacks," Basara said. "Guys were lying on ground. We had all the running water you wanted there. The spigots were going continuously. But guys were so sickly, they were dying left and right. Dysentery and stuff."

Morelli remembers Cabanatuan—a camp 60 miles north of Manila. It was there that he witnessed the stuff of nightmares. Three POWs, he said, had a deal with a corrupt guard to let them slip under the wire at night to buy food—"canned fish, hard-boiled eggs, whatever"—from a Filipino. One night, the guard was switched, and the three got caught.

"They were tied to posts, hands behind their back, no food or water for three days," Morelli said. "And finally they beheaded them."

A guard did the job with a short sword called a bolo knife. The heads were stuck on posts.

"That's in my mind," Morelli said. "I can't forget."

Some prisoners, he said, lost the will to live.

"You know why I survived? A lot of guys wouldn't eat no more. They'd get a ration of rice and a cup of hot water. They'd be lying there and say, 'You got any [cigarette] butts for me today? You can have my rice if you give me a butt. I don't wanta eat. I'm gonna die anyway.'

"So when a Jap would drop a butt, I'd run over there, grab it, and put it out fast. Then I'd give it to one of these guys, and I'd get their rice. I'd eat double or whatever. Instead of eating one ration, I'd eat three or four. *That's* how I survived."

■

Basara remembers when he first knew—*really* knew—that he would be liberated. It was early 1945, when he was at Bilibid Prison in Manila. For some time, Navy bombers had been hitting Japanese garrisons in the city. Basara had taken to marking "X" on a calendar each day the planes came. "Man," he recalled, "that thing was loaded with Xs."

Then, one day, he saw P-38s—Army planes. Navy planes could have flown off carriers out at sea. Army fighters could only have come from airfields in the Philippines. MacArthur had returned.

"Everybody had their hopes up then, but everything just stayed the same for a long time," Basara said. "It was a couple more months before they come got us."

For Morelli, liberation came in far-off Japan. He had been moved to a labor camp there to keep him beyond reach of the American forces, which had been taking back the Philippines since October 1944. In one of the war's awful ironies, 5,000 American POWs—jammed into the holds of "hell ships"—had been killed when those ships were torpedoed by U.S. submarines or bombed by American planes. Morelli's ship had been one of three in a convoy to Japan. Only his got there.

"I always tell people—one out of three, and I was on the one. How come I made it?"

Morelli returned home with a chest full of medals, including four Bronze Stars and a Purple Heart. He had lost 60 pounds, and hard labor combined with malnutrition had given him curvature of the spine.

The war left Basara with hearing trouble. He almost died of a diseased liver, as did Morelli. Doctors say he still has anxiety neurosis. A good artificial leg now replaces the peg leg—"like John Silver"—that he wore after the war. He had lost his left leg below the knee while on a work detail out of a prison camp. A truck he was driving was attacked by Filipino guerrillas. The bullet burned. "It was like somebody took a whip and cracked it real hard."

Acosta, like Basara, has damaged hearing, and his ears still ring from the blast that took his eye. He has been in this country since 1985 and is one of a dozen Filipino survivors of the death march who belong to a VFW post in the Fishtown section of Philadelphia.

A half-century after the death march, all three survivors continue to suffer pains of Bataan. Along with other Philippine Army veterans, Acosta has a beef with the U.S. government. Even though he has a Purple Heart, awarded for action April 6, 1942, on Mount Samat in Bataan, the government does not consider him a U.S. veteran for benefits purposes.

He gets some benefits, but not what he would get as an American vet. A bill to redress the inequality has languished in Congress. Backers argue that because Roosevelt combined all forces in the Philippines before war broke out, there was no difference in service.

"The bullets of the Japanese did not select," Acosta said. "We were exposed to the same risks."

The American veterans, too, have a beef—but theirs is with the Japanese government. Their association, the American Defenders of Bataan and Corregidor Inc., is part of an international Allied veterans' effort to gain compensation for POW hardships. The ex-POWs want $20,000 each. They've tried—and failed—to get it through the United Nations.

Morelli said the money would be nice. But it wouldn't make up for what happened to him. Nothing could. Ever.

6 • The Battle of Midway
June 4, 1942

The historic six minutes of the historic American sea triumph, as told by the sole American witness.

June 4, 1992

From 14,000 feet above the Pacific, Lieutenant Dick Best could plainly make out the Japanese aircraft carrier. He opened the flaps on his dive bomber, nosed over, and plunged straight for the sea.

He remembers astonishment as the carrier *Akagi*, now seeming to rush up at him, grew bigger and bigger in his sights. "I thought, 'Look at these arrogant Japanese.'"

In contrast to decks of American carriers, stained ocean-blue to hide them from the air, the *Akagi*'s was a brilliant yellow, with "a tremendous rising sun on the bow."

He aimed right behind that sun. Below 1,500 feet, he let go of his 1,000-pound bomb. Behind him, other Dauntless dive bombers in his squadron dropped their bombs. Best flipped his airplane onto its side, looked over his shoulder, and counted one, two, three fiery eruptions on the deck.

"Funny thing, I don't remember any sound. Propeller noise, I guess. But I don't remember any sound of our bomb drops."

■

George Gay remembers noise aplenty. Explosion after explosion. If he'd had a .45-caliber pistol in each hand, he says, he couldn't have heard either go off.

Ensign Gay watched Best's attack while hiding under a floating piece of his torpedo plane. Moments earlier, he had been shot down.

His rear-seat gunner had been killed, and 29 of 30 men in his squadron had lost their lives.

He was the sole American witness to the entire historic Six Minutes of Midway, 50 years ago today. He saw not one but three Japanese aircraft carriers go up in flames. Later the same day, out of his sight, Navy fliers found and sank a fourth.

Although the Imperial Japanese Navy got in its licks, too, sinking the U.S. carrier *Yorktown*, the Battle of Midway was a lopsided U.S. victory—the most important naval battle of World War II.

"To me," said Midway historian Walter Lord, "it belongs with the crucial battles of all time. It belongs with Marathon. It belongs with the Marne. Until Midway, the Japanese had everything their own way. After Midway, they never pulled off another offensive move."

To Best, who dropped a second bomb later that day on the carrier *Hiryu*, it was "gorgeous. It was fulfillment. Happiness. Elation. And revenge—revenge for Pearl Harbor."

To Gay, it was a gut-wrenching experience, literally. He could feel the explosions throb as he bobbed in the sea. Picked up by a seaplane a day after the battle, the 25-year-old from Houston was taken to Pearl Harbor, where he was visited at his hospital bed by the commander in chief of the whole Pacific Theater.

"After asking how I was and if I had sent messages home to my family, he said, 'You know, I'm in charge of this thing, and I don't know what's going on out there. And I understand you've seen quite a bit of it. Do you feel like telling me about it?' "

Gay, now 75, of Marietta, Georgia, laughed at the recollection.

"He's Fleet Admiral Chester W. Nimitz, and I'm a little ensign. And he's asking me that. . . . He was impressed when I told him, 'Those carriers sank, Admiral. I didn't just throw a bomb at 'em and run. I sat there and watched the damn things.

'Not only that, Admiral, but when they went down—with the bulkheads and things compressing under the water pressure—I could feel it. It was shaking my guts. I *know* they sank. *Period.*' "

■

One big, decisive battle. That's what Admiral Isoroku Yamamoto had wanted. One big, decisive battle to destroy the American carrier fleet that had gotten away at Pearl Harbor.

His plan was this: He would invade Midway Island, a tiny atoll in the Pacific not quite halfway from Japan to Hawaii. The two coral fingers were an important outpost, manned by U.S. Marines. The American fleet would be forced to come out and fight. And then, with its overwhelming superiority in ships, planes, and men, the Imperial

Navy would smash the Americans. The United States would be forced to sue for peace.

So Yamamoto thought.

But his plans fell into enemy hands, as Lee's had fallen into McClellan's hands in the Civil War battle of Antietam. Unlike George McClellan, Chet Nimitz could fight.

McClellan found Robert E. Lee's orders wrapped around three cigars at a campsite. Nimitz came upon Yamamoto's plans by different means—a code break. A team led by Commander Joseph J. Rochefort Jr. was listening to everything the Japanese radioed among themselves—and making sense from a lot of it.

Rochefort had been right in predicting the Japanese venture into the Coral Sea, where on May 7 and 8, 1942, the world's first carrier battle had taken place—a rehearsal for Midway. The ships never saw each other; airplanes did all the damage.

Now Nimitz called his two carrier groups back to Pearl Harbor to prepare for the new threat. The *Yorktown*, badly damaged at the Battle of the Coral Sea, needed months of repair. "We thought we were going to have a little leave or something," said Raymond Kerr, now 70, of Clifton Heights, Pennsylvania, a Marine sergeant and gunner on the *Yorktown*.

But there would be no shore leave—captain's orders—and patchwork repairs would have to be done in 72 hours.

By May 29, four Japanese fleets were churning the ocean, all part of the Midway operation. By then, too, the Americans were headed for Midway in two task forces under overall command of Rear Admiral Frank Jack Fletcher, on board the *Yorktown*. Two carriers, the *Hornet* and *Enterprise*, sailed with Rear Admiral Raymond A. Spruance, standing in for Vice Admiral William F. Halsey, hospitalized with a skin rash.

"We were all apprehensive; we didn't know what to expect," said Meredith Johnston, now 71, a former gas-station owner from Feasterville, Pennsylvania, and a seaman on the *Yorktown*.

Johnston recalled, "If they would've told us before we left Pearl Harbor that we were going back to meet the Japs, everybody would have jumped over the side, probably. *I don't want to go out there again. I don't want to risk my neck again.*"

On the *Enterprise*, Best, as commander of a dive-bomber squadron, was summoned to a briefing in Admiral Spruance's cabin.

"Spruance laid out the entire Japanese battle plan," Best, now 82, of Santa Monica, California, recalled. "He said, 'On June 4, the carriers will come in from the northwest. The transport troops are coming up from the southwest, accompanied by the battle force. . . .' He went on and on. It was unbelievable."

Best remembered thinking, "We're lying behind the garden gate with an ax ready for the intruder."

■

A little after 7 a.m., June 4, 1942, Torpedo Eight squadron took off from the USS *Hornet*. Each of its 15 crews manned a flat-faced plane called the Douglas TBD-1, nicknamed Devastator.

"Devastated" would be more like it.

"I like to say it was a charming old collection of aluminum," Gay said at his Colonial-style home on the edge of the Kennesaw Mountain Civil War battlefield. "I thought it was a great airplane—for the covered-wagon days. It just wasn't World War II equipment."

Torpedo squadrons from three American carriers would set out that morning. Not one would score a hit, and only 14 of 82 crewmen would survive.

Gay, fated to be sole survivor of Torpedo Eight, was the greenest of ensigns. A graduate of Texas A&M, he had gone to Houston's San Jacinto High School, named for a great underdog victory of the Texas War of Independence.

He had never dropped a torpedo. "I'd never even seen one," he remembered. His rear-seat man, Robert K. Huntington of South Pasadena, California, was no more than an acquaintance.

Taking off, Gay's was last in the string of torpedo planes that head-ed out in search of the Japanese. By then, the Battle of Midway was already under way.

The emperor's own torpedo planes and bombers already had attacked the Marines defending Midway, and Midway-based bombers had several times attacked the Japanese carriers—without a hit.

Spruance had risked flinging his entire air fleet at the foe, leaving his two carriers largely undefended. His hope was to catch the Japanese fleet as its planes limped back from Midway, out of gas and ammuni-tion. And that's how it worked out. But first, the torpedo planes sacri-ficed themselves. Gay tells the story:

Eventually, after I'd say about an hour in the air, we spotted some smoke on the horizon. . . . We headed right straight for it. And when we got there, we could see they were landing airplanes. The whole premise was to hit 'em before those planes land and refuel. So we started in.

Lieutenant Commander John C. Waldron, leading Gay's torpedo squadron, had planned to link up with dive bombers in a one-two punch. Now he radioed to his men, "Former strategy cannot be used. We will attack. Good luck."

The planes struck from the east, low and slow, stuttering along toward the carrier *Kaga*. Quickly, the Zeros, the Japanese fighters, were on them. Gay, still last in line, could see Torpedo Eight's planes burst into flames, or lose a wing and go cartwheeling into the sea.

Every one of them. If one of them was hit by anti-aircraft fire, it was more or less of an accident. Because it was the Zeros that were shooting us all down. They were coming in from astern, doing a loop, coming in sideways. They were crowding each other to get at us.

Commander Waldron had time to try to jump.

His cockpit filled up with the flames, and he stood up and put his right foot out on the wing before he hit the water. I saw that. When one of those things hits the water, that's the end of it. It's like you throw a can out of a car and it hits the ground. You don't see what happens. . . .It's behind you.

Suddenly, Gay was alone. He tried to remember Waldron's blackboard instructions to ease up to 80 knots and drop to 80 feet, about level with the carrier's deck. Huntington yelled he'd been shot, and Gay felt shrapnel lance his hand.

I picked out a guy on a pom-pom gun up on the port quarter of this carrier, and I made him think I was a kamikaze. I flew right down his gullet, eye to eye. . . . He jumped off that gun just as I went in over his head. . . .

I have never claimed that I even got rid of my torpedo. There's not any logical reason why I shouldn't have. . . . But I'm bouncing around in the anti-aircraft fire so bad I don't know what's goin' on. I've never released 2,000 pounds from the airplane all at one time. It felt like it went at the proper moment, but how the hell do I know?

Gay swung hard right and flew down the length of the carrier to avoid anti-aircraft fire. *They can hit you just as easy goin' as comin'.* But then a Zero picked him off.

The right wing hit first. . . . I'm buckled in, with the water coming up, and that's when I got scared. . . . Bullets are clanging all over the place, but I didn't know how to drown in that airplane. I just got scared.

The ocean bubbled up, red. Gay got a look at Huntington, strapped dead in the back seat as the Devastator sank.

I turned around to see where the Japanese might be. . . . I could see the whole damn Jap navy comin'. So now I'm going to get run over. One cruiser, I could've hit him with a rock.

And then, a wonderful thing.

Out of a high sky came American dive bombers. They appeared just as the last of the torpedo planes was wilting into the sea. The Zeros, skimming the water, were helpless to fend off a high-altitude attack. The torpedo squadrons had died, but they had not died in vain. Gay watched the party as the dive bombers screamed down, totally unopposed.

I saw 'em blow three carriers right out of the water. And that's quite an experience, believe me.

■

It was a complete accident of timing.

Bomber squadrons from all three American carriers had been out at sea for an hour, all looking for the Japanese. Now, at 10:22 a.m., squadrons from the *Enterprise* and *Yorktown* independently had discovered the carrier fleet and had begun to dive.

The historic six minutes had arrived. Lieutenant Commander Wade McClusky, leading all *Enterprise* planes, would combine with Lieutenant Earl Gallaher's squadron to destroy the *Kaga*. Lieutenant Commander Max Leslie of the *Yorktown* would get the *Soryu*.

The *Akagi* belonged to Best. Standing 6-foot-1, with a 28-inch waist, Richard Halsey Best was a Naval Academy graduate from East Orange, New Jersey. He was older than other guys in his squadron. At 32, he had a wife and kid back at Waikiki in Hawaii. He came from the same clan of 17th-century English adventurers in the New World as Admiral Halsey. His father, a Wall Streeter of the '20s, had managed to go bust before the Depression started. At Midway, Best said, "a tremendous bolt of luck" delivered him to the historic place at the historic moment.

When I first saw [the Japanese ships], they were dots on the ocean. When we got a little closer to them, maybe 15 miles, I could see two carriers just off to the left.

Best was ready to dive on the first carrier he saw, expecting McClusky to proceed to the second.

I called McClusky and said, "This is Bombing Six, I'm attacking according to doctrine." But as I opened my flaps, preparatory to pushing over, McClusky came pouring in from on top of me. . . . "Christ, he's jumped my target."

Best pulled up and looked for the next target, seven miles away. Some of his pilots mistakenly had followed McClusky. The remnant now tagged after him as he headed full-throttle for the *Akagi*—flagship of Admiral Chuichi Nagumo, commander of the carrier force and the man who had led the attack on Pearl Harbor.

I used up so much altitude, I had to climb back up to 14,000 feet. I opened my dive flaps right at the top and came right down again—a real roller-coaster ride. For the man in the back seat who goes over that hump, it must be terrific. He's riding backwards.

As he dropped his thousand-pounder and watched the three explosions on deck, Best recalled, he could see the steel deck of the *Akagi* peel and curl like blistering paint. Heading home, he could see a third Japanese carrier taking a pounding. This was the *Soryu*, under attack from Leslie's *Yorktown* squadrons.

It was ablaze from bow to stern, with terrific eruptions of flame and smoke coming out of it. Bang. Bang. Bang. I would say she got 11 or 12 hits on her.

About 11:30 a.m., Bomber Six was back on the deck of the

Enterprise. Best rushed to give a report.

I said there's a fourth Japanese carrier out there. Three are burning, but there's a fourth one to the north. I think we ought to be re-armed and sent out again. Well, hell, we didn't get back to it until 5 o'clock. I don't know what the problem was.

■

A fourth carrier, indeed. Having watched the destruction of the *Kaga,* the *Akagi,* and the *Soryu,* the men of the *Hiryu* lusted for revenge. They soon got it. Onboard the *Yorktown,* Johnston heard them come in straight overhead about noon.

You just stand there and look at each other; you can't see anything. When all the anti-aircraft fire is going off like the hammers of hell, then you know they're after you.

The only fear I had was getting wounded and not being able to get help. Every time I went into battle, I always made sure that I had a nice white hanky in my back pocket. If I got wounded, I could put a tourniquet on my arm or leg or whatever.. . . As far as being killed, it didn't worry me. I don't think it worried anybody. It's like a light bulb. You're OK one minute, and the next minute you're gone.

Three bombs hit the *Yorktown.* The first exploded aft, on the flight deck. The second pierced three decks and exploded deep in the ship's belly. The last exploded 50 feet down in the rag storage area. The ship was dead in the water. Electricity was out. Admiral Fletcher transferred to a smaller ship and turned over command of the entire battle to Spruance.

But then *Yorktown* revived herself. Her crew got the engines going, and the carrier was able to make 19 knots. Had the Navy hit the *Hiryu* without delay, as Best expected, the Japanese fliers may never have had the chance to attack again at 3 p.m. The *Yorktown* might have been saved.

The second wave brought torpedo planes.

Marine Sergeant Kerr, now a retired milkman from Delaware County near Philadelphia, was boss of a three-man crew on a 20-millimeter anti-aircraft gun. He thinks he hit a plane. *I got a good shot anyway.*

He described the battle as a thunderstorm of noise and confusion: *I didn't know what was going on. Nobody knows what's going on. I don't think the captain knew what was going on.*

Then came what Kerr remembers as "a real heavy thud."

Johnston recalled: *Boom!. . .When a torpedo hits, it knocks you on your can; I don't care where you're at. It felt just like it was lifting the ship out of the water.*

The *Yorktown* was leaning badly. Now with two torpedoes in her, she was abandoned. Lines were thrown over the side, and sailors and Marines went down hand over hand. Destroyers smoked back and forth, plucking up survivors.

Three days later, on June 7, the empty hulk would be sunk by a Japanese submarine.

■

One major blow remained. At 5:01 p.m., Best's squadron joined remnants of other squadrons to finally sink the *Hiryu*.

There were many more Japanese ships out there. The Navy got a cruiser two days later. But Spruance chose to break off the fight the evening of June 4. He had won a great victory; he was satisfied and did-n't want to risk a night fight against superior enemy forces. At night, his planes would be of no use to him. He thus escaped a second trap that Yamamoto had set, lying in wait with his battleships off to the west.

The battle—in which 307 Americans and 2,500 Japanese were casualties—was Best's last. He never flew again. A faulty oxygen canister had caused him to breathe caustic soda, and it had damaged his lungs. He spent two years in a Denver hospital.

After the war, he became an executive with the Rand Corp. Now retired to a Spanish-mission-style home in Santa Monica, he reads history and listens to opera.

Gay spent 30-some hours in the water before he was picked up by the seaplane. Back at Pearl Harbor, he had his meeting with Nimitz and quickly became a national hero. He made the cover of Life magazine, and Houston gave him a parade. Now a retired TWA pilot, he frets over America's defenses against a future war.

Making noise for a strong defense—it's his duty, he says. That and remembering those whose bones lie in 18,000 feet of water.

The real heroes died fighting for their country. I'm just the lucky guy who lived through the damn thing and got all the publicity.

7 • WACs and WAVES
July 20, 1942

The day that the first women began training as officers highlighted a debate about American womanhood. And manhood.

July 20, 1992

Before women could be permitted to join the military, Congress, of course, had to have its say.

"Take the women into the armed service? Who will then do the cooking, the washing, the mending, the humble, homey tasks to which every woman has devoted herself?"

Thus spoke a member of the House in March 1942, three months after Pearl Harbor.

"Think of the humiliation!" said another member. "What has become of the manhood of America?"

"This war . . . is not a social event," said a third. "In it, teas, dances, card parties, amusements generally, play little, if any, part."

Once Congress was finished with its debate that May, finally having voted to authorize a Women's Auxiliary Army Corps (WAAC), the bureaucrats got their hooks into matters.

Should the women wear skirts or pants? Carry handbags or shoulder bags? And what about foundation garments? The Army could not require women to wear them unless it issued them. But was it legal to issue garments to women it didn't issue to men?

The battle ran for weeks, with generals, congresspeople, civil libertarians, and fashion designers all putting in their two cents.

Was this any way to run a women's army?

■

Fifty years ago today, July 20, 1942, a group of 440 women from the then-48 states gathered at an old cavalry post near Des Moines, Iowa, to begin training as officers in the WAAC. They were the first of 400,000 women who served in the World War II military, the pathfinders for today's full integration of men and women in the Armed Services.

Betty Berg, of Huntingdon Valley, Pennsylvania, remembers the uniforms weren't ready. Neither, she recalls, were the male instructors. "They didn't know how to treat us. They were scared to death to get near us or touch us."

Though women nurses had served in all wars—and though a few, as in the Civil War, had posed as men to fight—none had ever stood in the place of these women that steamy July on the Plains. "It was so hot," Berg recalled, "that half of us ended up in the infirmary. I think it was 120."

The word *auxiliary* meant that the women were denied equal standing with the men in the Army. That would come a year later when the Women's Auxiliary Army Corps gave way to the Women's Army Corps (WAC). But the WAAC was a start.

On July 30, as the first WAAC officers were in their eight weeks of training, President Franklin D. Roosevelt signed a bill creating a women's service within the Navy—the WAVES (Women Accepted for Voluntary Emergency Service).

The same bill authorized a Marine Corps Women's Service, a name that did not lend itself to a catchy acronym. That was unfortunate because male Marines started calling the women BAMs—broad-assed Marines.

Four months later, the Coast Guard was permitted to get into the act with SPARS—"*Semper Paratus*" ("Always Ready"). That name derived from the Coast Guard motto.

From day one, military women caused a stir. Reporters and cameramen turned out in battalion strength on the first day of WAAC training at Fort Des Moines. The Army counted representatives of 19 newspapers, four wire services, four foreign press associations, six newsreel companies, and two photographic services.

There was a smirking, juvenile quality to some of the coverage that today would be called sexist. Mattie B. Treadwell, the official historian of the women's corps, wrote: "The photographers required the most supervision because of their tendencies toward photographing female underwear or latrine scenes."

Berg said she has no memory of media hubbub. She was too preoccupied with herself. Though a mature 37, married, a Cornell graduate, she felt intimidated by the newness of it all.

"I had no idea of army life at all. Nothing. Nobody I ever knew was in the Army or near the Army."

Berg ended up ranking 50th in her class, "which I thought was pretty good," she said, "because it took me two weeks to find what a PX was and where it was."

Born in Atlantic City, she had grown up in North Philadelphia. Her father, Max, was one of three Bayuk brothers—Jewish immigrants from the Baltics—who founded Bayuk Cigars. Their wrappers included the names Phillies and *Garcia y Vega.*

Berg was 9 when her parents died of different causes. A photo of each rests in a bookcase at the Meadowbrook apartment she shares with husband, also Max.

"It took me a long time to ever get to a funeral," she said there recently. "Or ever to look at a body—you know, when you go up to look at a casket. Couldn't do it."

Her uncle Sam, oldest of the brothers, took her in. She graduated in 1922 from Girls High and went on to Cornell. "My sister was up there," she said, "and I just automatically went."

By the time war arrived, she and Max were living in Bethayres, Pennsylvania. Betty volunteered to chart planes flying over Philadelphia for the Aircraft Warning Service, located on the ninth floor of a building at Broad and Chestnut Streets. One day, the boss asked whether she'd like to join a new women's Army that was going to take over for civilian volunteers.

"I was free. I wasn't working. Max was home, and it was OK with him. He always let me do what I want. . . . I just went."

Eighty of the places in the first class were reserved for Aircraft Warning Service volunteers like herself. The other 360 places were highly competitive.

Thirty-thousand women applied, including about 400 in Philadelphia the first day. They took an aptitude test geared to eliminating 55 percent of them, according to Treadwell. They were interviewed, given a physical, and, if they were lucky, invited back for a second interview. Oveta Culp Hobby, the director of the corps—age 37, mother of two, wife of a former Texas governor—made the final selections herself.

Berg's classmates included a dean, a former sales manager, and several editors. Some had been lawyers, social workers, teachers, even reporters.

"When I went into the Army, I had been out of school for enough time that when I went to classes I had a headache," Berg recalled.

The women were housed in four red-brick barracks, three for whites and one for blacks. "We did nothing together," Berg said. The women assembled on the parade ground at 6, attended classes until 5 p.m., and, after dinner, had a study hour. Before lights out, they washed and pressed their uniforms.

Berg said she found it comical when some 21-year-old lieutenant ran a finger across her locker to check for dust—"young fellows testing whether I was clean or not."

The uniform had turned out to be olive-drab khaki—a skirt with no pleats, shirt with tie, tan oxfords or tennis shoes, rayon stockings (cotton for work), shoulder bag. Foundation garments were issued. The cap was sort of flat, with a long bill. The women called them Hobby Hats.

This being the Army, uniforms seldom fit. The skirts, Treadwell wrote, "were cut as if to fit men's hips, and buckled and wrinkled across the stomach, so that even the slimmest WAAC presented a pot-bellied appearance after she had sat down once."

But that same uniform was a sensation when Berg and three other brand new WAAC officers came back to Philadelphia by train. Berg was in Philadelphia to command a company of 70 to 80 WAACs at the Aircraft Warning Service office, the first WAACs in the city.

"It was unbelievable walking on Chestnut Street," she said. "People would come up and look at you under your hat. . . . I didn't know these people. They didn't say anything. They just wanted to take a good look."

■

Janyce Stovall Taylor, a young graduate of West Philadelphia High, sneaked off to join the Army in June 1943.

"I didn't tell my family I was going because my grandmother and my aunt would have had a fit. They *did* have a fit . . . but there was no point in screaming at me, because it was too late."

Her parents, like Berg's, had died when she was young. She had found the love she needed in a big Virginia family that had branched out to North Philadelphia. Always, there was someone extra—an aunt, a cousin, the cousin of a cousin—at the kitchen table. Her home environment, Taylor said, was "sort of strict." If anything, she needed space.

"I like adventure, I like traveling. That's the main reason I joined the Army. . . . Patriotism I don't think really had a lot to do with it, although my father was in World War I. He was in France."

When Taylor went off for basic training at Fort Devens in Ayer, Massachusetts, she found total segregation—women from men, white women from black women. For a black woman, the Army was a small world indeed.

"I guess we just took it as a normal thing—I mean, segregation. A lot of the girls were from the South and they knew more about it than we did."

Traveling one time by train from Fort Dix to Fort Oglethorpe,

Georgia, she and a group of black WACs were refused the first-class accommodations the Army had booked for them. "When we got on the train, they said they didn't have any available and we would have to wait until we got to Washington."

The black officer in the group knew that if proper berths couldn't be had in New Jersey, they sure weren't going to be available at the gateway to the South.

"She said we weren't going to move. And that train didn't leave Fort Dix until we had our sleeping quarters—first class."

When suppertime came, there was another obstacle—the dining car. It had a curtain that could be drawn whenever blacks sat down. "That way," Taylor recalled, "the whites didn't have to look at you."

But there were 10 WACs and only two tables-for-four behind the curtain. "First, they told us we'd have to eat in two shifts," Taylor said. "And my little lieutenant said we weren't going to do that. . . . She was a gutsy person."

In those days, the Army had a quota for black WACs—10.6 percent, the same as for black men. The WAVES and other women's services took no African-Americans until the last days of the war. But the WAVES were first to integrate blacks and whites. The Army failed in its quota. At peak strength in 1945, about 4,000 of 100,000 WACs were black.

In September 1943, scarcely two months after joining the WAAC, Taylor had had to choose whether to join the new WAC, which offered regular military rank and privileges but also exposed women to court-martial and full military discipline. Berg, wanting to be assured of staying near her husband, opted out. Taylor re-enlisted as a private first class. It gave her the long-sought chance to go to Europe.

A single group of WACs were the only black women to go overseas. The black press and civic groups had pressed the War Department for the move, and early in 1945 the 6888th Central Postal Battalion set sail for England on the luxury liner *Ile de France*. The 800 women arrived in Birmingham to clear a backlog of soldiers' mail. They then moved on to Rouen, France, to clear a backlog there.

Taylor, who now lives in Philadelphia's Mount Airy section, later married a 20-year-man in the Air Force, and they traveled widely. But nothing ever thrilled her like that first trip abroad.

"I used to walk down the street and pinch myself. I just couldn't believe I was in Paris."

■

Once it swallowed the idea of women in uniform, the military had hoped to recruit 1.5 million. Women at first rushed to join, but the enthusiasm ebbed. The reasons are still debated. Certainly, women who wanted to serve their country had opportunities to do so and make more money in defense plants. And unlike men, women were never drafted.

There was another reason, too—a bad rep.

"I think some people thought we were in there to entertain the men, which was not true," said Catherine Corley, of Oaklyn, Camden County, New Jersey, who was in the WAVES.

The notion that WACs and WAVES were sexually promiscuous—a study concluded they were not—became a serious obstacle to recruiting as the war went on.

"Parents weren't permitting their children to go into the service," said retired Air Force Brigadier General Wilma L. Vaught, leader of a foundation that plans to build a $14 million memorial to all women veterans at the gates to Arlington National Cemetery.

"You had a lot of career military men who thought it was just terrible women were in the service. . . . All sorts of terrible rumors get started," Vaught said. "It got so bad that Eleanor Roosevelt and President Roosevelt both got involved."

The actual conduct of military women broke down further barriers to their service. After World War II, it was inevitable that women would gain the full participation—in every role but combat—that America saw in the Persian Gulf war.

By 1978, separate women's services—including Women in the Air Force—had been phased out.

The main role of the services had been to free men for combat. A study of WACs in World War II found that 46 percent had served in administrative capacities, 6 percent in medical roles, 5 percent as drivers, and 4½ percent in supply. Women maintained airplanes, operated radar, and plotted the weather.

Twelve WACs were wounded in action. In the separate Army Nurse Corps, established in 1901 by Congress, 16 were killed in action, 32 were wounded, and 71 became POWs.

Total female casualties were more than 200, according to Women in Military Service for America, the foundation headed by Vaught.

For Berg, now 87, some memories of World War II have faded. Odd details remain sharp, such as her six-digit serial number— "304015," she said without a blink.

"I remember that. I'm the only one in my family with dog tags."

8 • The Eighth Air Force
August 17, 1942

The Wrecking Crew, as it would become known, began its work by striking an offensive blow against the Germans.

August 17, 1992

F or months, they would be the only American troops fighting the Germans in Europe.

Fifty years ago today, August 17, 1942, a dozen B-17 Flying Fortresses took off from an airfield in England on the first U.S. bombing raid of World War II over German-occupied territory. Their target: the railroad yards at Rouen, France. The 10-man bomber crews were the vanguard of the Eighth Air Force, maybe the most romanticized American outfit of the war, the subject of a dozen Hollywood movies from *12 O'clock High* to *Memphis Belle.*

The United States had been at war with Germany for eight months. But fighting had been mostly at sea. The enemy's U-boats had marauded up and down the East Coast, sinking merchant ships, while U.S. attention had been focused on stemming Japanese advances in the Pacific. Now, time had come to strike an offensive blow against the Germans.

But not yet on the ground. It would be three months before U.S. ground troops invaded North Africa; 11 months before they invaded Sicily; 22 months before they landed at Normandy. For now, air attack would have to suffice. The English already were bombing the Germans by night. The Americans now planned to hit in daylight.

"We knew that the future of daylight precision bombing depended on us accomplishing what we were assigned to do on the first mission and subsequent missions," recalled Frank R. Beadle from Marietta, Georgia, who was lead bombardier on the Rouen strike.

47

"The British were betting we would lose a good percentage of our planes on the first mission, because every time *they* sent out an airplane in the day, it got shot down."

To confuse German defenses, a decoy group of six B-17s took off a half-hour before the attack planes. It flew halfway across the English Channel and turned back. As the actual striking force crossed the French coast at 23,000 feet, German anti-aircraft guns sent up bursts of flak.

In the lead plane—later nicknamed the Butcher Shop—the pilot was Colonel Frank Armstrong. Sitting in the copilot's chair, but operating the controls, was Major Paul W. Tibbets, destined to drop the first atomic bomb on Japan.

Hunched in the nose, Lieutenant Beadle, 22, looked through his bombsight and made his calculations. "We had to know the true air speed, the true altitude above the target. We had to know what the weight of the bombs was, what the trail of the bombs would be."

He flipped a toggle switch to let the bombs go. Behind him, the other planes let go on cue. Beadle figured it would take 48 seconds for the bombs to hit.

As they fell, he sang: "I don't want to set the world on fire, I just want to start a flame in your heart."

■

The dozen B-17s of the 97th Bomb Group dropped a total of 352 bombs that day. All planes returned safely. It was the first punch in the nose the United States had been able to give the Germans, whose armies occupied France, Holland, Belgium, Denmark, Norway—indeed, most of northern Europe.

The Eighth Air Force would go on to earn the title of greatest wrecking crew in history. Before fighting was done, it would drop 5,127,244 bombs. The destructive power was equal to 46 of the atomic bombs dropped on Hiroshima and Nagasaki in Japan.

Nearly 300,000 Americans would serve in the Mighty Eighth, biggest of 15 air forces under U.S. Army control. About 17,800 would be killed in battle, a number that approached the nearly 20,000 killed in the Marine Corps. A total of 6,656 planes were lost.

Like most servicemen of his generation, John T. "Jack" Durkin had hardly strayed from his neighborhood, much less gone abroad, when he went to war. He arrived in England at age 18 before Christmas 1944 with visions of Piccadilly Circus and Big Ben. He encountered a cold, muddy airfield where the sun rarely shone.

On only his third mission, his 390th Bomb Group based in Framlingham was sent to bomb the most dreaded target of all: Berlin, the German capital, defended to the teeth by fighters and flak guns.

His pocket diary remembers: *Feb. 3, 1945. God was on our side today. I saw a plane blow up right in front of us. The pieces weren't any bigger than my head. I also saw two other planes go down burning and only saw one chute. The flak was modest and accurate. Boy, arms, legs and assholes were flying in Berlin today. I could hardly hold my coffee at dinner.*

A man might admit fear to his diary, but not to his friends.

"Nobody would say anything," Durkin, now a retired accountant, recalled recently under a patio umbrella at his house in Meadowbrook, Pennsylvania. "I was too macho to say I was scared."

Missions were so dangerous, early on, that if a man completed 25, he could go home. By the time Durkin came along, the loss of bombers had eased somewhat because of better fighter-plane support, and the magic number had been raised to 35.

Durkin was from the Roslyn section of Abington Township, not so far from the Philadelphia suburb where he lives today. "In those days," he said, "I used to come home from school and grab the gun and walk down to the corner and put shells in and go hunting. Pheasants, rabbits."

The Army was looking for young men who could hit a flying target. The B-17s and B-24 Liberators flown by the Eighth defended themselves from enemy fighters by being armed like porcupines with heavy machine guns.

Durkin was made a gunner and was taught how to fire twin .50-caliber machine guns. "The feeling [of power] was awesome; I don't know how to describe it. Just awesome."

A champion wrestler in high school at 127 pounds, he was the perfect size for the cramped ball turret that hung on the belly of a B-17. So he spent his war looking down. "The bombs would drop right in front of me, and I would watch them go down. Probably I was the only one on our plane who could see the bombs hit."

It was an odd way to fight—odder still that air crews, unlike foot soldiers, began and ended their days with hot food and a warm bed on friendly soil. By day, they flew in a world so cold—60 degrees below—that blood immediately froze on contact with any metal surface. The men wore oxygen masks and electrically heated suits.

No. 19. March 18, 1945. Berlin. Today was the roughest mission I have ever been on. I know I will never describe in words the way I felt up there today. Before we got to the target, we were hit by fighters. They shot down two planes out of the formation next to us, then they started after us. . . . The ship behind us got the whole nose shot off. . . . The flak was exploding right under our ship, and sometimes it would lift the tail right up in the air. We nearly got hit by another B-17. . . .

After a mission, combat crews had little to do. They could play ball or drink. A lot drank to drown emotion. Durkin said that, while flying, he would get so angry and frustrated as flak burst around him that he would open up his guns on the ground below.

"I guess you just figure, well, you know, maybe it'll hit somebody in the head."

On his second mission to Berlin, he recalled, "I just couldn't imagine there was anybody alive down there to shoot at us, because the whole city was on fire. I mean, there was nothing but smoke and fire all over the place. You weren't supposed to have terror raids. That was against the Geneva Convention. But it was war. I'm sure we were supposed to be bombing the [railroad] yards. But the whole city of Berlin was on fire."

■

Toward the end of the war, in winter and spring of 1945, the Allies heavily bombed targets in the German city of Nuremberg. John A. Tellefsen, a lieutenant in the Eighth Air Force, remembers it well.

He was on the ground, under the bombs.

A navigator in 96th Bomb Group, he had been a prisoner of the Germans since parachuting from his burning B-17 the previous year.

Also a diary-keeper, he recorded from a POW camp: *No one can truly realize the dread and fear that bombing can cause unless one has been under these conditions.*

Of two particular American raids, he noted: *Both days they came over about 500 strong and dropped all over the city. The flak put up was terrific, and both days I saw a dozen or more ships go down in flames or explode. The boys all did a commendable job, for none came closer than three miles [to the POW camp]. They must have hit their targets, for all night long after each raid gigantic explosions were heard and felt coming from the city. It must have been oil storage, an ammo dump. It was quite an experience to see the planes get hit by flak, and chutes coming out of some, just as I myself had experienced a year before. I truly felt sorry for the boys, but that did them no good.*

Tellefsen, now 70, the retired president of a concrete construction company, counts his wartime recollections among the treasured possessions at his home on a wooded lot in Haverford, Pennsylvania. It is the record of a world that many Americans today have difficulty imagining.

Too often, he said, what today's kids know of POW camps they get from watching *Hogan's Heroes* in endless TV reruns that portray the German captors as fools. "It's a shame if they see that and take it for real instead of a joke."

Like Durkin, Tellefsen remains slim and looks fit, although he walks with the slightest limp, the reminder of a war wound. He is lucky to be alive. Twice, he had to parachute. The first time, shot down on his 13th mission on a February 13, he was fortunate to flutter down in England, where he was helped by a villager out walking his dog.

Thirteen missions later, on April 13, 1944, he was shot down again near Augsburg. The German villagers were not so friendly. He landed hard on a bleeding left foot, shattered by the blast of a 20-millimeter cannon on a German fighter. He found himself surrounded by men and boys with pitchforks.

A farmer held a gun, a Luger. "He was very nervous, you could see him shaking."

Tellefsen, who had had two years of German at Collingswood High School in New Jersey, told them in German that he was unarmed. "No pistol; no pistol," he said, indicating he was unarmed. The prisoner and two fellow crewmen were loaded into an ox cart and taken into town. He eventually ended up at Stalag Luft 3 at Sagan, Germany, where 10,000 American and British air officers were imprisoned.

Mostly, Tellefsen said, he was fairly treated. The kriegies—short for *Kriegsgefangene*, the German word for POW—lived in wooden barracks, received Red Cross parcels, stood for roll calls, performed calisthenics—and killed time. As officers, they were not required to work. But they suffered cold and, sometimes, inadequate food.

The Germans had shot 50 British escapees earlier. Tellefsen still has an orange poster from the camp that warns, in English: "Breaking out . . . is now a damned dangerous act. The chances of preserving your life are almost nil. All police and military guards have been given the most strict orders to shoot on sight all suspected prisoners. Escaping from prison camps has ceased to be a sport."

Said Tellefsen: "I believed them."

Early in 1945, as the Soviet Red Army pressed in, Stalag Luft 3 was evacuated. Ill-clothed prisoners were made to walk 30 miles in a blizzard to a rail head, and dozens fell by the wayside. But because of his foot, Tellefsen was taken by train to Nuremberg. Later, anyhow, he was made to walk to a place called Moosburg. There, Patton's Third Army eventually found him.

"They asked us, 'Is there anything you would like?' We said we'd like an egg. A real egg. . . . Two of us ate five dozen eggs. Fried. Unbelievable. I tasted egg for weeks after that."

■

From its modest beginning, the Eighth Air Force eventually grew into the biggest air armada in history. On D-Day, June 6, 1944, it had been capable of putting up 2,700 bombers and 2,000 fighter planes on a single day.

The American strategy of precision daylight bombing differed from the strategy of both the British ally and the German enemy. British and German airmen did "area bombing." They flew by night and carpeted urban areas with explosives. The Americans, using the superior Norden bombsight, thought they could zero in on a small target—a rail yard or factory—and spare the city around it. Often, that was what happened; sometimes, it wasn't. And therein lies a debate over the civilian casualties. Allied bombing, British and American, is variously estimated to have killed 300,000 to 600,000 civilians.

Temple University Professor Russell F. Weigley, widely considered the leading U.S. historian of the war in Europe, says, "I do think the moral issue has to be dealt with. . . . The people who were supposedly the good guys, who were upholding the values of the Western world, slaughtered large numbers of noncombatants."

Richard P. Hallion, chief historian of the Air Force, says that kind of thinking is pure hindsight. Early on, he said, bombing was the only way the Allies had to slow the German war machine. Later, the Eighth aided Allied armies on the ground, reduced German industry—and brought a quicker end to the war.

Weigley agreed that bombing hurt the Germans but said it only became effective near the end of the war. He said the massive resources applied to the bombing might have been better applied elsewhere.

The Allies never achieved their objective of fully destroying German industry. After the war, the victors discovered factories full of planes and tanks. But precision bombing—by the Eighth in England and the 15th Air Force in Italy—had destroyed oil production. Planes and tanks weren't much use without gas.

For the men who did the bombing, there was only one kind of thinking: Get done and get home.

On April 20, 1945, Staff Sergeant Durkin flew his 35th—and last—mission, a raid on Oranienburg. He closed his diary this way:

We hit a marshaling yard, and it was a very easy target. No flak. There were fighters in the area, but we didn't see any.

Boy, am I glad we are done.

9 • The North African Invasion
November 8, 1942

The landings at Casablanca and Oran would bring triumph and humiliation. To this day, few know the Allies fought the French.

November 8, 1992

G eorge S. Patton seemed to sense, in a general sort of way, that he was destined to become a star. In the days before his troops set sail for war, he embarked on a round of grand farewells.

He paid a call on 82-year-old General John "Black Jack" Pershing, hero of the First World War, who bid him, "Goodbye, George. God bless you and give you victory."

He stopped at the White House and, like some ancient Caesar, pledged to President Franklin D. Roosevelt, "I will leave the beaches either a conqueror or a corpse."

And he went up to West Point to see his son, George, a student at the U.S. Military Academy. The leaves were falling as the two-star general and the plebe walked on the bluffs above the Hudson.

"He came to say goodbye. He said he was going to war, and that was all he could say," his son, now a retired major general himself, recalled. "I knew he was going off to fight the Krauts. I had no idea where he was going to land. It was a closely guarded secret."

Where Patton was going was Casablanca.

Fifty years ago today, November 8, 1942, American forces went ashore in North Africa. Supported by an immense armada, 107,000 Allied troops—84,000 American and 23,000 British—landed on the beaches of Morocco and Algeria.

The place names still resound—Algiers; Oran; above all, Casablanca. Patton was not the man in charge, merely commander of the Western Task Force, one of three invasion forces dispersed over 1,000 miles of coastline. This was the Second Front that Roosevelt had promised to get the United States into the war against Germany.

Hitler himself called it "the largest landing operation that has ever taken place in the history of the world." And it was—then. The invasion was the first wet step on a long road of battle for the U.S. Army that would lead to Sicily, to Anzio, to Normandy, and, finally, to the banks of the Elbe River in Germany itself.

Code-named Operation Torch, the Allied campaign was commanded by Lieutenant General Dwight D. Eisenhower, who had never heard a shot fired in battle and who only two years earlier had been a mere lieutenant colonel.

Over the next five months, his green, ill-trained American troops would experience both triumph and humiliation—the latter coming as a bloody Valentine's Day surprise from Field Marshal Erwin Rommel's famed Afrika Korps. An American general, Ernest Harmon, would say: "It was the first—and only—time I ever saw an American army in rout."

On November 8, as the invasion troops waited to climb down rope nets into landing boats, the United States had been at war for 11 months and a day since Pearl Harbor. But no GI had yet aimed his rifle at a German soldier. The time had now come—or would soon.

First, the Allies had to fend off the French. For it was the French navy that defended the harbors, the French army that manned the barricades.

"Nobody remembers that. I'd say one person in a thousand knows that we had to fight the French," said Max Warshaw, 78, of Columbus, Burlington County, New Jersey, who was wounded by French artillery.

Like most Americans of the time, Warshaw knew vaguely that the Arab kingdoms of Morocco and Algeria were French colonies. That season, *Casablanca* was playing in movie theaters, giving larger-than-life images of a city teeming with refugees from a Europe overrun by Nazis.

German armies occupied Paris and northern France. The south of France was under control of a German-puppet government, with the city of Vichy as its capital. The Vichy government also controlled French colonies in North Africa.

"We figured," Warshaw said, "we were coming to save France."

■

Unlike Patton, Technical Sergeant Howard J. Cain had to wait until he was at sea to learn where he was going. The only stars he was destined for were the Silver Star and Bronze Star, both for heroism. Those would come in an unimagined future—in France after the breakout in 1944.

The graduate of Philadelphia's North Catholic High School had no way of knowing it, but he was going to serve every day of U.S. involvement in World War II. So were most of the soldiers who sailed for North Africa that November a half-century ago—the ones who survived.

Their fate fit a phenomenon of World War II noted by University of Pennsylvania professor Paul Fussell in his book *Wartime*. Even in the Big One, as that war has been called. Only a small percentage of GIs ever saw combat. But those who did mostly saw a lot.

"You were either killed or wounded or driven mad—or replaced—and most of those guys fell into one of those categories," Fussell said in an interview. "By the time they got to Germany, very few of the original were left."

Cain was one of eight men assigned to an armored vehicle. Five did not live out the war. A draftee, Cain had been in artillery training with Patton's Second Armored Division at Fort Benning, Georgia, when the Japanese attacked Pearl Harbor on December 7, 1941. After North Africa, he was in on the Sicily invasion. Then he got his feet wet at Normandy. He fought his way across France, Belgium, and Holland. He was in Germany when war ended in Europe on May 7, 1945.

"I got a big swastika flag as a souvenir," said Cain, now 78, of Ardsley, Pennsylvania.

He and his wife of 50 years, Margaret, had been married just five months when the 35,000 landing troops of Patton's task force departed in secret from Hampton Roads, Virginia, on October 23, 1942.

He was to hit the beach at Fedala, north of Casablanca. On the fateful day, he recalled, "we were awakened by gunfire. . . . Fedala is really a tank town—oil tanks—and some of them were on fire."

Men were lucky if they made it to the beach at all. At Fedala, 262 landing boats—64 percent of the total—were lost. Most of them were swamped by waves. Inexperienced pilots rocked their boats over. Boats landed five miles off-course.

"In our battery, we lost four men from just drowning," Cain said.

It was a good thing the Allies had decided not to invade the German stronghold of Normandy the first time out.

"Oh, yeah, cripes, yes, we'd have gotten murdered," Cain said. "The Germans, that's a damn good army. You know what the British say—you've never fought a war until you've fought the Germans. [The North Africa landing] was a mess because everybody was green troops. For that matter, the command element had never been involved in anything like this."

As soon as he touched sand, a soldier was supposed to move to safer ground. But Cain recalled that all 11 men in his boat had an overriding need: "Because of the nervousness, they all had to urinate."

Two days later, having met no French resistance personally, Cain had moved inland. His commander attended a meeting at 9 a.m. and returned with orders to direct artillery fire at a target on the outskirts of Casablanca.

Cain's battery got off 22 rounds from guns mounted on halftracks, vehicles that had both wheels and treads. And then, suddenly, it was over. The word had come down: "The French had capitulated."

Fighting had been sporadic, and it had ended quickly. But 600 Americans and 700 French had died.

■

Three months later, the front had shifted 500 miles east along the Mediterranean coast to Tunisia. American ground forces still had not fought a major battle with the German army anywhere in the world. That was about to change.

Rommel, who had been in grudging retreat from Egypt after fighting a British army at El Alamein, now suddenly turned around and attacked the Americans in his rear. Private First Class Hale Truitt, 22, of Chester County, Pennsylvania, happened to be in the wrong place at the wrong time.

In the dark hours of Valentine's Day morning, radioman Truitt was part of a four-man observation team in Battery B, 91st Field Artillery, posted atop a treeless mountain in the Tunisian desert. Looking off to the east from Djebel Lessouda, Truitt could begin to see colored flicks of light—red and orange—that indicated a firefight in the distance. With the dawn, Truitt could make out an advancing dust cloud. He could begin to hear the thump of artillery and see the black specks of distant dive bombers. And then, emerging from the Faid Pass—tanks. German Tiger tanks.

The men of Battery B began to shout against the howling wind on their mountaintop. Truitt and his lieutenant got on the radio and broadcast the alarm: Rommel was coming!

The Battle of Kasserine Pass had begun.

"That was our first encounter. We took a beating, yes, we did," Truitt, now 72, remembered. "The Rommel corps had been in Egypt and Libya and all down through there, and they were seasoned veterans. But I'll tell you one thing, our boys fought well. I am proud of them. They did all they could with what we had."

A retired postmaster and real-estate man, Truitt lives in the peaceful horse country of Chester County. To this day, when a thunderstorm rumbles across the green-carpeted valleys, he recalls the sound of war. "My wife will tell you, I like to get in a dark room and stay there."

As Rommel attacked, the First Armored Division had rushed into the breach. But it was no contest. The German tanks' guns were twice the size of some on the American tanks. Scores of U.S. tanks were left burning. Some men got out and ran. Hundreds of prisoners were taken.

"I saw our tanks get direct hits from these big German tanks. . . . You'd see one big flash and then you'd see the black smoke. . . . There was no surviving a direct hit," Truitt said.

The battle was spread out over a hundred miles and went on for 10 days, after which Rommel withdrew, satisfied he had taught the Americans a lesson. World War II historian Stephen E. Ambrose calls it a "mini-Battle of the Bulge."

"At Kasserine Pass, we took a pretty good licking for two days, and we started to dig in," Ambrose said. "Eisenhower made the comment that the American soldier doesn't like to be pushed around. In the end, I think, it was a victory."

Truitt has read the history books. Otherwise, he wouldn't know what happened. He spent several days of the battle on the run with his lieutenant after the Germans cut off their position. Arab villagers finally seized them, exhausted and starved.

"All of a sudden, they come screaming and running for us. . . . I was so weak I could not run. I just looked around and I grabbed a gray stone, and I said to myself, 'I'll take the head off of one of 'em.' "

Truitt must have been struck himself. Next thing he knew, a German doctor was treating his head wound, and another was fixing him scrambled eggs. He was a POW—and would remain one for the duration of the war.

Soon he was interrogated by a German captain. "He asked me if I smoked. And just about then the door flew open with great speed and there was somebody with an Iron Cross here"—Truitt pointed to his throat—"and one on the lapel. The captain said to me, 'Prisoner, I'll see you later.'

"When they left, the guard at the door said to me, 'Do you know who that was?'

"I said, 'No, I don't care.'

"He said, 'Well, that was General Rommel.' . . . I knew he was the Desert Fox. I just never planned on meeting him."

■

The cemetery lies near the site of ancient Carthage, destroyed by the Romans in 146 B.C. It is not as well-known as a similar cemetery above the invasion beaches at Normandy. But 2,841 American war dead are buried there over 27 acres, each under a white marble cross or a Star of David. Names of 3,724 Americans are engraved on the Wall of the Missing.

The American flag still flies in the breeze off the Mediterranean, for this land has been leased forever to the United States. It is a vivid reminder of a campaign most Americans have forgotten.

Although no model of warfare, the campaign achieved its objective. The Axis Powers—German and Italian—were driven from North Africa. In May 1943, Allied forces converged from east and west on the last Axis stronghold in Tunisia; 275,000 prisoners were taken.

Said historian Ambrose: "Militarily, there wasn't much good you could say for this operation. It was a lot of screw-ups—people landing in the wrong place, anticipating the French would lay down their arms and they didn't. . . . You had the terrible spectacle of the Americans and the British fighting their French comrades of the First World War. . . . Everybody was learning."

But learn they did. Never had two nations cooperated so fully in military operations. Bad generals were weeded out, and good ones were found. Eisenhower earned a fourth star; Patton, a third. In the end, the Allies had found the men and tactics that would win the war on the Western Front.

"Out of North Africa," said Ambrose, "came a much better American Army."

10 • The Manhattan Project
March 15, 1943

The U.S. knew an atomic bomb was possible. Now, it was secretly building one. J. Robert Oppenheimer would lead the effort.

March 15, 1993

Fifty years ago today, a tall, storklike figure with a porkpie hat on his head and a pipe in his teeth stepped from the train at a lonely station in the desert of New Mexico.

He was J. Robert Oppenheimer, a brilliant, ego-driven physicist on loan from the University of California, Berkeley, to direct scientific work on the most secret and ambitious endeavor of World War II.

It was March 1943—a desperate moment in American history. The Army was fighting in North Africa and New Guinea, the Navy was up to its mast in the Pacific, and German U-boats threatened to chop the Allied supply line in the Atlantic.

Desperate times called for a desperate venture, and this was it: the Manhattan Project.

Oppenheimer, 38 and among the elite in the world of science, was the appointed leader of 3,000 physicists, chemists, metallurgists, engineers, and technicians who would ride the Santa Fe Chief to a tile-roofed depot with a mud-hole parking lot in Lamy, New Mexico. From there, it was 20 miles north to Santa Fe, then 45 miles more across the Rio Grande, and up switchback turns to a 7,200-foot plateau in the Jemez Mountains, where the military had taken over a ranch school for boys. The place was called Los Alamos. The Army used a code name: Site Y.

The scientists' mission was to make the first atomic bomb.

In Chicago three months earlier, a scientific team led by Italian émigré Enrico Fermi had proved such a bomb was possible. It now fell to Oppenheimer's team to build it. The work would take 23 months, cost $2.5 billion, and employ tens of thousands of people in a dozen states, making it not only a scientific project but a mammoth industrial effort.

In the end, the Manhattan Project would alter not only the course of the war, but of the world. The man in the porkpie hat stepping from a train was leading the way into an awesome and frightening new age.

■

The inhabitants called it The Hill.

For security reasons, no one ever uttered Los Alamos—Spanish for the cottonwoods—when they left that stark, sunlit plateau, covered mostly in Ponderosa pine and sweet-burning pinyon. The site was chosen by Oppenheimer, who came from a well-to-do family and spent summers as a boy in the mountains of New Mexico. He wanted a refuge from prying eyes, far enough removed from any urban area to ease worry about explosive accidents.

Now Oppie, as colleagues fondly called him, was bringing to Los Alamos the greatest constellation of scientific brains in history.

"Everybody says how great Oppie did," said Harold M. Agnew, then a young scientist at Los Alamos. "Well, hell, I think Mother Teresa could have done it if she had just stayed the hell out of the way. It's just amazing who was there. Everybody who was anybody was there."

By Oppenheimer's arrival, the Army Corps of Engineers was hard at work with bulldozers and graders, shaving off great gobs of sandy soil to make way for cabinlike housing and laboratories. It was all slapdash construction, not meant to last much beyond the war. And it didn't. The old Fuller Lodge from the boys' school days still stands. Bathtub Row also stands—a cluster of prewar houses prized by scientists' wives because they had bathtubs, not merely showers. The rest is mostly gone.

Agnew, now 72, of Solana Beach, California, was destined to become a postwar director of Los Alamos National Laboratory, which to this day continues to develop weapons. But in March 1943, he was just "a grunt," a week from his 22nd birthday. His wife, Beverly, was a secretary. Oppie, who left the lab not long after the war and died in 1967, needed Beverly more than he needed him.

He remembered the scene: "It was sort of pandemonium."

When he went to look at his housing unit, he found no doors. But those were great days for Yankee ingenuity. "I borrowed a pickup truck, took the doors off the laboratory where I was working, and took them to my house and installed them."

Laboratories didn't need doors because the scientists had no secrets among themselves. Oppie had insisted on that, despite the Army's inclination to "compartmentalize" research. Oppie said everyone should be free to talk to everyone else.

"You never knew where the good ideas were going to come from," said Raemer Schreiber, 82, who was then a newly stamped Ph.D. physicist from Purdue University.

With few exceptions, the scientists were men, and a significant number of the top men were Europeans who had fled fascism. Fermi, for one, had come to America in 1938. At Los Alamos, he headed a division of deep thinkers. Among the expatriates were a half-dozen Nobel winners or winners-to-be.

The "grunt" scientists were mostly in their 20s. The leaders were older, with wives and children who were accustomed to the social and cultural amenities of university towns.

Kathleen Manley, wife of physicist John Manley, was happy the Army allowed her to ship most of her possessions from Illinois. She arrived in April with a newborn and a three-year-old. "I think I felt less uprooted because I had so many of my own things with me," recalled Manley, who still lives on The Hill. "A lot of people didn't bring anything of that sort."

The well-educated wives quickly formed a school, a choral society, a theater group. Many also had the chance to work for the first time in their lives. Kathleen Manley, who had a background in math, ran problems for the team through an early electric calculating machine.

Mail came to a post office box in Santa Fe. New arrivals reported to a secret office in a Santa Fe courtyard at 109 East Palace, now occupied by shops. Today, the door is blocked. A plaque reads, "All the men and women who made the first atomic bomb passed through this portal to their secret mission at Los Alamos."

Besides scientists, the Army posted about 400 of its troops on The Hill, including a WAC detachment. Oppenheimer may have been in charge of scientific work at Los Alamos, but his boss was Brigadier General Leslie R. Groves, overall head of the Manhattan Project. Groves was obsessed with security. He bent to Oppenheimer's open-door policy within laboratory areas. But he insisted on fences and armed guards all around the area. He liked the location of Los Alamos because it was a natural fortress, surrounded by deep canyons.

The Army bugged the few telephones it permitted at Site Y and opened all the mail.

"They were pretty smart," recalls Robert Porton, then a private in the Army Special Engineer Detachment. "Incoming mail—they opened, read it, resealed it, and sent it on. Outgoing mail—you didn't seal the envelope. It went to the censor; he read it, and if there were things you shouldn't have said, it was blacked out and sent back to you."

The scientists worked hard, often six days a week, but found time to party. Drink was plentiful on a Saturday night. Porton was the drummer in a dance band. He coordinated programs at Theater No. 2, which had a gymnasium, an Army Motion Pictures screen, a chapel, and a dance floor. He also ran the radio station, which broadcast two hours of classical music each night, but never gave out call letters or reported its location. The station often borrowed 78-r.p.m. records from the scientists, Oppie included.

GIs were wont to call the physicists eggheads. It was true that some could appear absent-minded. Agnew tells of Danish Nobel laureate Niels Bohr's leaving a party with the wrong overcoat—Agnew's—and failing to notice that it was several sizes too big.

But Porton said most scientists were "just as normal as anybody."

The Army troops knew nothing of what was going on in the technical area. Porton didn't find out about an atomic bomb until the public did—after the attack on Hiroshima on August 6, 1945.

"We had a very thorough security lecture," he recalled. "They didn't mention atomic. They didn't mention nuclear. They didn't mention anything. They just said that work was going on here that could well shorten the war by at least a year."

■

Almost every other industrialized nation—Germany, Japan, Britain, France, the Soviet Union—had, or would make, a wartime effort to build the bomb.

But only the United States had the industrial capacity to succeed in so short a time, said Thomas P. Hughes, author of *American Genesis: A Century of Invention and Technological Enthusiasm.*

"It is seldom appreciated that the Manhattan Project was a large construction project," said Hughes, a University of Pennsylvania professor. One company alone, Du Pont, put 45,000 people to work building and operating a plant in Hanford, Washington, to make plutonium.

At Los Alamos, the scientists theorized they could make a bomb from either of two radioactive materials: plutonium or uranium. A uranium bomb would be simpler. All you had to do was take one sub-critical mass and fire it from a gun at another sub-critical mass and, boom, you had a super-critical mass. It would explode with the temperature of the sun—millions of degrees.

The problem came in obtaining uranium enriched with the isotope U-235. Nothing in the world was as rare. When Oppenheimer arrived at Los Alamos in early 1943, Groves already had set up a secret uranium-processing plant in the Appalachian hills at Oak Ridge, Tennessee. The guess was it would take Oak Ridge two years to make enough enriched uranium for one bomb—if it could do so at all.

"There were huge factories at Oak Ridge," said Richard Rhodes, author of *The Making of the Atomic Bomb.* "Tons of material would go in. Out would come a few grams of uranium that an FBI agent would slip into a briefcase and personally carry to Los Alamos."

Unrefined uranium was mined from the earth; plutonium was artificial. It existed nowhere until a scientist manufactured it. Still, it was easier to produce than enriched uranium.

By war's end, Oak Ridge had produced enough uranium for a single bomb—the one dropped on Hiroshima. Du Pont, by itself, had produced enough plutonium at Hanford for two bombs, with two more to be ready within weeks. Plutonium's problem was it might not work, after all. The Los Alamos team discovered it could not be fired from a gun; it would pre-detonate and fizzle.

For a time, it seemed there would be no bomb—no uranium bomb, no plutonium bomb. Someone had to find a way to make plutonium work. Here was where Oppenheimer's insistence on free discussion paid off. Seth Neddermeyer, a middle-rank team member from Cal Tech, had an idea.

Why not wrap a ball of plutonium in ordinary TNT? If you ignited the TNT, the blast would compress the ball like a hand-squeeze. A sub-critical mass of plutonium would instantly become a super-critical mass—and, once again, boom!

Agnew: "Seth Neddermeyer had this obsession with the implosion, and he wanted to work on the implosion. Oppie said, 'Fine.' But [Neddermeyer] was really pooh-poohed and ridiculed by the gun people."

It turned out Neddermeyer had seen the light. Implosion was a technical nightmare—about as difficult, a scientist said, as crushing a full can of beer without spilling any suds. It would take the scientists months to figure it out in detail.

But it would work. It was the answer.

■

Fast-forward to July 16, 1945.

The war with Germany was over; the war with Japan dragged on. American planes were fire-bombing Japanese cities. Kamikazes were sinking U.S. ships. The battle for Okinawa had just ended with 32,000 American casualties and many more than 100,000 Japanese killed and wounded.

The U.S. Joint Chiefs were preparing a plan to invade Japan itself—a campaign that could mean a million more Allied casualties. It was still a desperate moment in American history.

At last, the United States was ready to test an atomic bomb. The secret test was code-named Trinity. The Army had chosen a site in an empty desert near the crossroads of Alamogordo, New Mexico. The old maps called the area Jornada del Muerto—journey of death.

The night before, it had rained hard, and the desert had crackled with lightning. The flashes illuminated "the gadget," silhouetted atop a 100-foot steel tower.

It was a plutonium bomb, a fat, aluminum-shelled egg. Wasting the sole uranium bomb didn't make sense. Besides, no one had any doubts that a uranium bomb would work. Doubts about plutonium persisted.

Schreiber was a member of the pit crew. His job had been to help assemble bomb parts. He felt lucky to be a witness to the test, because many scientists waited 300 miles away back in Los Alamos for word on the outcome.

The top men—Oppenheimer, Groves, Fermi—occupied a concrete, earthen-covered bunker 5½ miles from the tower. Schreiber, at the base camp, was 9 miles back.

At 5:10 a.m., a 20-minute countdown began. The tension was touchable. Two years of work had taken a toll. Oppenheimer looked cadaverous; his weight had sunk below 100 pounds.

At 5:29, a rocket fired a warning—one minute. With 10 seconds to go, a gong sounded. Schreiber, as ordered, lay on his stomach, face down, with his feet pointed at Ground Zero. It was still dark. Schreiber could see the blast with eyes closed. He had a piece of welder's glass to shield him from harmful light rays, and after a moment he turned to look.

"It was like the sun came up. You could see the mountains in all directions. . . . And there was this ball of fire. Various colors. Churning. It was enormous. I began to really wonder if it would keep expanding and come out where I was. It was rising and eventually it faded out. . . . By that time, we were all standing up looking at it. And finally we got the shock wave. Not much noise; it was just a poof."

■

Back in Los Alamos, Bob Porton was working at the radio station shortly after noon when 35 or 40 scientists began milling outside the broadcast booth.

"This GI and I looked at each other. I told him on the intercom, 'Boy, something big is happening, but I don't know what it is.' "

The scientists were waiting for the 12:45 news from Albuquerque, where, as Porton remembered it, an announcer reported, "The commanding officer at the Alamogordo Air Base announced this morning that a huge ammunition dump at the base had blown up."

"As soon as he said that, all these scientists smiled, shook hands, patted each other on the back."

That same day, in San Francisco harbor, the USS *Indianapolis* sailed under the Bay Bridge with secret cargo: the lone uranium bomb, nicknamed Little Boy. Although untested, Little Boy was bound for Tinian Island in the South Pacific, where it was to be loaded on a B-29 bomber. Unknown to its 300,000 inhabitants, Hiroshima had a tragic date with destiny.

11 • Meat Rationing Begins
March 26, 1943

Sugar rationing? Sure. Coffee rationing? Can do. But meat rationing? That was too much, and a black market flourished.

March 26, 1993

Americans put up with sugar rationing in World War II. The small sacrifice made them feel patriotic.

Americans put up with coffee rationing. Giving up a second cup for the war effort wasn't all that hard.

Though they grumbled and cheated a bit, Americans even put up with tire and gasoline rationing.

But they most definitely did not put up with meat rationing. It turned them into beasts.

Fifty years ago today, on March 26, 1943, Philadelphia panicked at the mere prospect of meat rationing, set to begin three days hence. All over the region, butcher shops were stampeded. Within hours, every meat counter was stripped bare. Shoppers displayed the herd instinct that had led to the bank runs of the Depression. They feared that if they didn't get there early, the vault would be empty. It became a self-fulfilling prophecy.

By 6:30 a.m., a thousand people were pushing against the doors of the old Lancaster County Farmers Market in the city's Germantown section. The police were called to keep order. The Evening Bulletin reported, "Avid shoppers rushed through the Reading Terminal Market in the center of the city. . . . All stall holders predicted that they would be sold out by noon. None planned to open tomorrow."

Harry G. Ochs 3rd was a kid then, working for his father at the meat market in Reading Terminal that Ochs still runs today. He recalled: "This place was jammed. They came in here and they stood in line, and the lines went outside and down 12th Street. It was really something. As long as we had it, we sold it. When we didn't have it, we closed down. That's the way it was."

Rationing was the greatest hardship demanded of Americans on the home front in the Second World War. With German submarines sinking merchant ships, with factories turning out weapons instead of consumer goods, with armies and allies to be fed overseas, nearly everything was in short supply. Before war's end, the list of products rationed by the Office of Price Administration would run to scores of items, including most foods.

By and large, people were able to grin and bear it. But meat was different. Gallup Polls again and again showed meat was the thing that rankled most.

"We had to have meat. Potatoes, gravy, and meat—that was important in those days," said Evelyn Summers, then a young mother in near-by Lansdale with two small children.

But before families got their meat, the government took its cut—a whopping 40 percent of U.S. meat production. America was not only feeding its own troops; it was also feeding the British and the Soviets, helping to keep them in the war.

By the fall of 1942, meat had begun to be in short supply. In early 1943, the newspapers were full of stories about "meat gangsters" and "meat speakeasies," terms borrowed from the era of liquor Prohibition. On March 11, Pennsylvania State Police stopped traffic at the Delaware line, looking for shipments of uninspected meat. On April 8, a grand jury in Philadelphia indicted 17 people and one meat company for black-market activities.

Agriculture Secretary Claude R. Wickard said "Mr. Black" had become a national scandal, diverting 10 to 20 percent of the meat supply under the counter.

In that era, meat didn't keep, because almost nobody had a refrigerator, just an icebox. Philadelphia had as many as 12,000 neighborhood butcher shops, many of them one-man operations in corner rowhouses.

Motorized meat wagons plied the streets of many towns, just as milk trucks would continue to do for a generation. "People would go out with their platters," Evelyn Summers said, "and come back in the house with the platters full of meat."

Her butcher, Norman K. Nyce, now 89, remembered that sellers, too, had trouble finding meat. "You could get it if you went to the right places," he said. "We got a lot of ours in Lancaster at the stockyard. . . . We did our own slaughtering."

Rationing, combined with price control, was supposed to prevent panic by fairly distributing scarce commodities. It lasted throughout the war. Meats and other rationed foods were sold with two kinds of costs—one in dollars and cents, and one in rationing points.

Every man, woman, and child was issued a book of ration stamps, each marked with a value in points. Blue stamps were for canned, bottled, and packaged foods. Red stamps were for meat, cheese, and fats. Fish and fowl were not rationed, but chicken became scarce as people looked for a meat substitute.

Each person got 28 blue points and 16 red points per week. But the amount of food that amount would buy varied. Point prices changed depending on scarcities. Typically, a pound of porterhouse steak cost ten points; round steak, seven points; hamburger, two points.

You didn't need stamps in restaurants, so people who could afford to eat out could eat more meat. But Mary Jane Freedley of Haddonfield, New Jersey, recalls having to take her food-stamp book with her when she went off to college. "I turned it in so I could eat," she said.

Sometimes there was no meat to be had at any price. "Points are pointless," said an Inquirer headline on March 29, 1943, the day that meat rationing began. Butchers were tempted to withhold meat for favored customers, maybe at an illegal price. The government battled back with appeals to patriotism. On movie screens, at work and on street corners, posters urged shoppers to take a pledge: I pay no more than top legal prices. I accept no rationed goods without giving up ration stamps.

Despite shortages, Americans on average consumed 2.8 pounds of red meat per week in 1943—about their rationed amount, and more than many doctors today would consider healthy. In Britain, people consumed only a pound a week. In Germany, it was twelve ounces; in Italy, four ounces.

But hardship is relative. Americans remembered 1936, the low point of the Depression, when consumption was 20 percent less. The wartime buildup had brought a return of prosperity. A porterhouse steak, a couple of pork chops—these were symbols of having a good job. Rationing seemed a throwback to bad old days.

"The shock of confronting food scarcities in a land of surplus has produced a panic reaction in some quarters," The New York Times commented in 1943, "and now thousands of persons are wondering whether hunger and starvation will stalk wartime America before the year is out."

Ruth Wojtusik, then a student at Philadelphia's Frankford High School, said, "I can remember my mother worrying. There were four of us in the family. My father was a letter carrier, and she always made sure that he got meat—you know, for strength. She wanted to keep him going because he was the breadwinner."

Sometimes, she said, when Dad had meat, the kids had fish, which they didn't like. "We would ask why . . . and he'd say, 'You think meat and it will taste like meat.' "

Meat shortages were greatest in industrial cities such as Philadelphia, which had attracted thousands of workers to its booming shipyards and workshops. Newcomers were most likely to turn to Mr. Black, whose meat was usually uninspected and often past its prime.

Charles H. von Tagen of the Pennsylvania Grocers Association was quoted, "The meat situation here is the worst in the country. It stinks—both the situation and the meat."

Philadelphia, ironically, was one of the biggest meat-packing towns in the East. The railroads brought in carcasses and live animals from the West.

The city had 18 slaughterhouses, according to a contemporary account, and the bellow of cattle or squeal of pigs could be heard in many a rowhouse neighborhood.

Families, too, might have livestock on hand. Charles Blockson, who lived in Norristown, Pennsylvania, said his family raised chickens in the back yard. So did many people in his richly ethnic neighborhood of Fishtown.

"My father and uncle, I recall, had a pig," Blockson said. "They kept it on a farm" owned by the family of present-day Philadelphia City Council President John F. Street. Autumn was killing time, he said. So there was always meat on the holiday table.

Throughout the war, the Office of Price Administration found itself with a credibility gap. It kept insisting that an adequate meat supply was available. Buyers kept asking, "Where's the beef?"

Arthur E. Dennis, a lawyer for Associated Butchers of Philadelphia, estimated in the summer of 1943 that only ten percent of the government-promised beef supply was actually available. A lot of it had been stolen.

Former City Police Officer James N. Reaves, author of *Black Cops*, remembered catching one thief red-handed. "We got information a fellow was taking meat from an Acme market. He was a worker there who worked on Sunday all by himself. So he loaded his car with beef. We met him as he was coming out of the lot at 30th and Walnut and confiscated his meats.

"We made him tell us where he was taking it," Reaves said. "He gave us the names of what we considered some prominent people at that time who were buying it."

Folks whose consciences disdained theft were often not beyond telling a white lie to the ration board. There were 18 boards in the city, made up of respected elders, all volunteers, doing the work of the hated Office of Price Administration. The ration board was like the draft board. It heard all sorts of pleas—and ignored most.

The ration board could grant extra stamps for medical reasons, such as diabetes. In May 1943, one woman was reported to have asked for extra meat because her husband had ulcers. It was pointed out to her that milk was the usual treatment.

"There was a lot of uproar about rationing, but I think on the whole the system worked," said Richard R. Lingeman, executive editor of the Nation magazine, author of a history of the home front called *Don't You Know There's a War On?*

"Meat rationing, I think, did cause the most unhappiness," he said. "But it probably made people healthier. It certainly didn't hurt them."

12 • Civil Defense
June 23, 1943

A taste of what an air attack would be like illustrated the massive effort at home that complemented that of the armed forces.

June 23, 1993

F ifty years ago tonight, the peace of a sticky summer evening in Philadelphia was broken by the rumbling thunder of many airplanes suddenly high overhead. Searchlights revealed a squadron of lumbering, four-propeller bombers.

Then came sirens. All over the dense city of rowhouses, residents drew blackout curtains or doused the lights. In Center City, air-raid wardens blew their whistles and hustled pedestrians into bomb shelters in the basements of office buildings and hotels. Drivers pulled to the curb.

At Shibe Park, a huge candle of light in North Philadelphia, the A's were beating the Boston Red Sox. Suddenly the crowd of 18,000 was plunged into darkness, forbidden even to strike a match. The announcer suggested a song and the crowd launched into "My Wild Irish Rose."

The air raid appeared real enough. Thank God, it was only a drill—the most realistic of World War II. Roaring over a dozen states, from Maryland to New England, squadrons of B-17 Flying Fortresses gave Americans a moment's idea of what the war was like for inhabitants of the bomb-ravaged cities of Europe and Asia.

Except for a few balloon bombs that floated across the Pacific from Japan—in one instance, killing a minister's wife and five children in Oregon—no bomb ever fell on the continental United States in the Second World War. But worry that it could happen never entirely ceased. And civil-defense exercises never stopped.

■

Twelve million Americans served in the armed forces at their peak strength in World War II. Another army of 12 million was officially enrolled in civil defense.

Male and female, young and old, this volunteer home-front army consisted of air-raid wardens, auxiliary policemen, auxiliary firemen, nurse's aides, civilian pilots, airplane spotters, and myriad others—all organized under the federal Office of Civil Defense, nicknamed Ocey-Docey for its common abbreviation, OCD.

Civil-defense activities gave every American a chance to participate in the war effort. Everyone could do something to win the war. World War II was perhaps the last time when the whole country was truly united in common cause.

Millions helped out unofficially.

Naomi Tomlinson of Bristol, Bucks County, north of Philadelphia, remembers that six blue stars hung in the front window of her family's big Victorian house—one for each of her brothers in the Army and Navy, all of whom survived the war. Her father was an air-raid warden and worked at the Fleet Wings plant, which made parts for warplanes. Though a kid in school, Naomi wanted to contribute, too. So she sold war bonds. "I sold the most bonds in Bristol," she remembers, and was given an award at the Bristol Theater.

The term "civil defense" became a very broad umbrella as the war went on. It covered virtually any activity on the home front that seemed good for the country. If you planted a vegetable garden, it was a victory garden. A new style of men's suits that saved on fabric was called a victory suit. For the morale campaign, a local beauty pageant conferred the title Miss Civil Defense. Even physical fitness became part of the war effort.

Sam Evans, then a rising community leader in North Philadelphia, was appointed coordinator of "colored activities" in a national physical fitness program headed by Philadelphia rowing Olympian John B. Kelly. Evans recalls: "That was a part of civil defense; you can't have civil defense unless you're fit, mentally and otherwise."

But the heart of civil defense was still protection against enemy bombing raids, enemy sabotage, even enemy invasion. Almost every neighborhood of every town was organized down to the block level. The man in charge—it was almost always a man—was the air-raid warden. Typically, he was a political committeeman, or maybe a World War I veteran from the American Legion post nearby. His white helmet, flashlight, and arm band were substantial symbols of authority.

The warden's main role, of course, was to respond to air raids. But a good one became everybody's uncle. He patrolled his little turf. He looked in on the sick and infirm. He closed backyard gates. He organized block collections of scrap metal for recycling into weapons. If need be, he issued citations for failure to obey blackout instructions.

"Sometimes you just took a walk, but you were always looking out for anything suspicious," Howard Barnes, 83, an air-raid warden in Philadelphia's Frankford section, recalled.

Barnes patrolled the small area of twin houses around Penn Street, where he lived. "Your area was connected to the next man's," he said. "You would have a boundary line that you would meet on. The other fellows were in whistle-distance if you ever needed them."

He could never quite imagine Nazi armies coming up the Delaware River. "To get to Frankford would take an awful lot of fighting." Aerial bombardment did not seem very likely either, because the enemy had no bomber capable of crossing the Atlantic. But it made sense to be prepared, all the same.

Despite the influx of tens of thousands of servicemen and civilian war-production workers, crime in Philadelphia decreased during the war. In 1943, police investigated 3,820 burglaries, 835 fewer than in 1941. Said Barnes: "Burglars knew they were running the chance of being spotted by an air-raid warden."

Altogether, the war produced an odd mix of emotions. Out of the war fears came a sense of neighborhood peace and security. Grover Driskell, now of Philadelphia's West Oak Lane section, remembers that families were brought together in the same way. Even an air-raid drill could have its cozy quality, for it drew everyone into the same room of the house.

A boy then, he recalls sitting quietly in the dark at home, listening for the piercing whine of falling bombs, but hearing only the soft sounds of breathing and the creaking of the sofa. From the RCA radio, turned down low, came a warm, amber glow. "I wasn't scared. My parents were, maybe, but I wasn't."

■

Immediately after Pearl Harbor, America had panicked.

In Philadelphia, the bridge over the Delaware was closed, lest saboteurs cross the river. Armed guards were posted at defense plants. The entire 4,500-man police force was called to duty until further notice. Next morning, Center City merchants piled sandbags on the sidewalk to protect plate-glass windows. The same day, The Inquirer carried an Office of Civil Defense proclamation that blared in bold type: "AIR RAID INSTRUCTIONS . . . Remain indoors, whether in a home or in an office building . . . Make sure that all lights are extinguished. Turn off all running water, electricity and gas, including the pilot lights of all ranges. . . ."

James N. Reaves, a future city police inspector, then a young patrolman, remembers one day at roll call. "They told us, 'We just got news off the wire that unidentified planes are headed for New York.' Boy, that scared the pants off all of us."

New York Mayor Fiorello LaGuardia, national chairman of civil defense, seemed to panic himself. He called for 50 million gas masks and predicted: "The war will come right to our cities and residential districts. . . . Never underestimate the strength, the cruelty of the enemy. We must prepare for that."

The nerve center of Philadelphia's defense was the John Wanamaker store near City Hall. That was where the Aircraft Warning Service had its offices.

"Wanamakers had the first seven floors, I think, and we were above that," remembers Betty Berg, who headed a detachment of the Women's Auxiliary Army Corps there.

"We had spotters all over the area—people on their back porches, that sort of thing," Berg, now of Huntingdon Valley, Pennsylvania, recalled. "Whenever they saw a plane, they would call in. One engine. Two engines. Headed in such and such a direction. . . . The Air Force could then tell whether the planes were ours or not."

The biggest actual threat to the American homeland was not enemy airplanes but submarines. German U-boats lurked just outside of New York Harbor and all along the Atlantic coastline. Their main target was merchant shipping, and in the first six months of 1942 they sank 492 ships, often within sight and sound of the beach.

Yet this real slaughter caused less panic than the imagined threat of aerial assault. The Navy, true, hid the full extent of the losses. But Samuel Eliot Morison, official naval historian of World War II, called it a scandal that seaside resorts such as Atlantic City failed to black out their lights for months. The glow of the boardwalks silhouetted ships at sea, making them fat targets.

That first season of war, a new arm of civil defense officially emerged. It was the Civil Air Patrol, "the eyes of the home skies." Before long, 100,000 private pilots were flying patrols. Several were credited with sinking or damaging submarines with bombs.

War concerns infiltrated every part of domestic life. On the job, posters warned Americans that only by working harder and smarter could they "zap the Jap." In school, pupils practiced crawling under their desks in the event of air raids.

Mary Jane Freedley, a student at Haddonfield High School in Camden County, New Jersey, during the war, remembers, "I went off cheerfully with several girls on Saturday mornings to scrub someone's basement so it would be prepared for any air-raid casualties."

When rain halted a ball game, the radio announcer was never permitted to state the reason for delay. Giving out weather information might help enemy pilots somewhere out over the sea.

A billboard addressed to women said, "Your home is your post; protect it against air raids." House & Garden magazine advised, "Bedrooms need not go into mourning [during air raids]. . . . Make a blackout curtain by seaming together two pieces of fabric, one black and one to match your curtain."

The Evening Bulletin in Philadelphia ran a feature on how to identify the odor of certain poisonous gases. Lewisite, it said, "smells much like geraniums." Phosgene "smells like green corn or musty hay."

At first, people were really scared. "I was, I know," recalled Dorothy Cunningham of Haddonfield. "Whenever we'd have an air raid," she said, "I'd put my two boys in bed with me, one on each side. And I'd pray, 'Dear Lord, if it's a real air raid, hit the middle of the bed.' "

■

Fifty years ago tonight, as the big air-raid drill was to begin, three gamblers were in police custody at City Hall. They had been brought in from Shibe Park and were about to be searched for loot when the lights went out. The amused Evening Bulletin reported what happened next. When the lights came back after an hour, the searches resumed. The well-dressed gamblers were found to have only a buck or two in their pockets: Further investigation uncovered $3,218 stuck in hatbands, in waistbands, in socks, in shoes. The anecdote revealed the serio-comic nature of air-raid drills a year and a half after Pearl Harbor. As the war progressed and no bombs came, civil-defense alertness waned a little. Some people began to ignore blackout instructions or orders to get off the streets. This laxity was the reason for so realistic a drill on June 23, 1943. It was the first time that real bombers—two squadrons of 12 each—were used. They approached in waves from the south, appearing to fly straight for the Navy Yard. No bombs fell, but for a few moments, at least, many people thought the attack was real.

Charles Santore, 85, a longtime Republican ward leader in South Philadelphia, remembers that the shadowy sight of the B-17s in searchlights was a shock.

"When they came, so many, it looked like they were throwing bombs. . . . The motors from the airplanes, they made so much noise. You could hear women screaming, men hollering—everybody.

"The people were beginning to feel, 'We can't get bombed by the Germans or Japan.' This was mostly to frighten people."

In South Philadelphia, he said, it worked.

13 • The Tuskegee Airmen
July 2, 1943

The black pilots fought the Axis and won. But blacks couldn't miss the irony of fighting Nazi racism while American racism thrived.

July 2, 1993

The little P-40 Warhawks came streaming back over the Mediterranean to a dusty airstrip on the coast of North Africa. The pilots jumped from their planes, their eyes ablaze. They hugged, shouted, and pounded one another on the back.

The men of the 99th Pursuit Squadron had just passed their first test in aerial combat, and one of them, Lieutenant Charles B. Hall, had shot down a German fighter plane in a dogfight.

It was 50 years ago today, July 2, 1943. The fliers had scored not only their first victory over the Axis, but an important triumph over American racism as well. These were the Tuskegee Airmen, the famed black fighter pilots of World War II.

Blacks had long been barred from the Army Air Corps. Then one unit—only one—had been permitted to enter training at Tuskegee Institute, a black school in Alabama. At each step, they had been expected to fail. The Army was just waiting for them to fail.

They'll never learn to fly. . . .Well, OK, they can fly; but they'll never learn to handle a fighter plane. . . . OK, they can handle a fighter; but they'll never stand up to combat. . . .

"When Charley Hall shot down that plane, it was like we all did it," recalls Lemuel Custis, a pilot who celebrated with Hall that day at Fardjouna in the Tunisian desert. Millions of black Americans, rooting for the airmen back home, felt the same way.

■

A fight for freedom, a fight for democracy—that was what World War II was all about. So Americans were told; so they believed.

For black Americans, though, it was a war on two fronts—a fight against one enemy abroad, a fight against another enemy at home: Jim Crow. Jim Crow was the personification of racial segregation. The military of World War II was a Jim Crow institution. Blacks practically had to fight for the chance to fight.

More than one million African Americans were in uniform in the Second World War. But with notable exceptions—the Tuskegee Airmen, the 761st Tank Battalion in Europe, the 93rd Division in the Pacific, and some other units—they were not employed as combat troops.

Blacks had fought in the Revolution, in the War of 1812, in the Mexican War, in the Civil War, in the Indian wars. In the Spanish-American War, they helped take San Juan Hill, though Theodore Roosevelt took the credit. Sent to France in World War I, they fought under French command, in French uniforms, with French weapons, winning hundreds of French medals for valor.

But still, many white officers felt that blacks didn't have the necessities to fight.

For much of the war, the U.S. Marine Corps wouldn't even accept blacks. The Marine commandant in 1942, General Thomas Holcomb, complained that blacks were trying to "break into a club that doesn't want them."

In the Army, black soldiers were confined to segregated units. The majority were in the Service of Supply. After the Tuskegee Airmen, the most famous black servicemen of World War II were truck drivers—members of the Red Ball Express, who under fire supplied Patton's Third Army as it swept across Europe.

If the Army was bad, the Navy was worse. Most black sailors worked as "messmen"—cooks and waiters. They were virtually "seagoing servants," in the words of Bernard C. Nalty, author of *Strength for the Fight: A History of Black Americans in the Military.*

"They were in combat, but they weren't trained to use the weapons," Nalty, a military historian, said in an interview.

George C. Cooper, a member of the Golden Thirteen—the first class of black naval officers, not commissioned until 1944—remembers that he wasn't even given a combat-zone assignment. The Navy sent him home to Virginia to work as a metalsmith instructor.

"There was a tradition in the Navy that said blacks weren't capable of much of anything," said Cooper, now retired from a career as a city official in Dayton, Ohio.

Yet one of the first American heroes of World War II was a black man, Dorie Miller. A cook, he was on board the battleship USS *West Virginia* when it was attacked at Pearl Harbor on December 7, 1941. Seeing his captain wounded, he ran amid bullets ringing off the steel deck and pulled the captain to safety. He then grabbed a machine gun and, having had no training, shot down two Japanese planes.

The Navy at first ignored him, making reference only to "a Negro cook who fired at Japanese planes." Later it awarded him the Navy Cross. In 1943, on Thanksgiving Day, Miller died when his ship was sunk in the Pacific.

He was still a cook.

Most black leaders remained optimistic that the war would bring progress. Like Frederick Douglass during the Civil War, they urged blacks to fight. They imagined that if they fought and fought well, their reward would be greater freedom. Even before the war, the black press had pressured President Franklin D. Roosevelt to open up the Army Air Corps, one of the most prestigious branches of the service, to blacks.

In March 1941, as a result of promises made in the 1940 presidential campaign, the first group of black pilot-trainees reported to Tuskegee Army Air Field. It was called the Tuskegee Experiment.

"It was designed to fail," said Custis, of Wethersfield, Connecticut, a Howard University graduate, one of 13 men in that first class, drawn mostly from the rolls of black colleges. "But we weren't going to fail. We knew if we failed, it would be a setback for the entire black community."

■

Named to command the Tuskegee fliers was Benjamin O. Davis Jr., son and namesake of the most distinguished black man in the Army. The father was the Army's first black general. The son, too, was a pioneer—the first black graduate of the U.S. Military Academy in this century. At West Point, the son had been "silenced," meaning that no other cadet would even speak to him, except in the line of duty. The cadets were trying to make him quit. He refused.

"I was just hard-headed enough to be certain that I wasn't going to permit anybody else to decide what I was going to do."

Now 82, a retired three-star general in the Air Force, Davis lives in a suburb of Washington. He recalled in an interview:

"I had to create in my own mind a psychological ploy that would be satisfactory to me. The one I developed was that these people were a bunch of inferior human beings. If they had any sense or any character or ability, they wouldn't be acting this way. And I convinced myself of that."

After graduating 35th in his class of 276 at West Point, Davis spent five years in the regular army before reporting to Tuskegee. He knew nothing more about airplanes than the rawest recruit. But he was tough, and he knew how to lead. He was 6-foot-2 with a strong chin and a glare that, if turned on full, could cut through armor plate.

Of the 13 pilot trainees in the first class, five would qualify as pilots, a typical wash-out rate. A half-century later, only Davis and Custis are living.

Davis, like Custis, believes the Tuskegee Experiment was expected to fail. "It was nothing but political pressure. Roosevelt wanted a third term. The Army Air Corps bowed to pressure from the White House. That was all there was to it."

Tuskegee Army Air Field was a controversial place, to blacks as well as whites, Davis said. In his autobiography, *Benjamin O. Davis, Jr.: American,* he wrote, "Some black editors railed against Uncle Toms—blacks who were willing to serve in black units and seemed to tacitly support segregation."

The pressure was enormous and came from all sides. Davis discovered he could find some relief in flying.

"You're up there and everything is beautiful. It's freedom beyond all compare. You really are on your own. You demonstrate your own ability in a way that gives you a tremendous self-pride."

Successive classes raised the number of Tuskegee pilots to 23. On April 2, 1943, these pilots, together with the all-black ground personnel, boarded a train at Chehaw, Alabama, and headed for war. Destination: North Africa. By the time they arrived across the sea in May, the last German and Italian forces had surrendered. Next up for Allied invasion was Sicily on July 10.

First, the sea lanes had to be cleared. The Tuskegee Airmen were assigned to dive-bomb an Italian stronghold on the island of Pantelleria. Black newspapers followed closely. On June 19, the nationally circulated Pittsburgh Courier reported, "Our Fliers Help Force Italians to Surrender."

It wasn't until July 2 that the airmen ran into enemy fighters. Lieutenant Hall of Brazil, Indiana, was one of six pilots escorting B-25 Mitchell bombers on a raid over Sicily. Though Hall is now dead, his actions are preserved in this account, taken down on the day of the battle:

"It was my eighth mission, but the first time I had seen the enemy close enough to shoot at. I saw two [German fighters] following the Mitchells just after the bombs were dropped. I headed for the space between the fighters and the bombers. . . .

"I fired a long burst and saw my tracers penetrate the second aircraft. He was turning to the left, but suddenly fell off and headed straight into the ground. I followed him down and saw him crash. He raised a big cloud of dust."

Afterward, a stream of green sedans raised another cloud of dust as they headed out to Fardjouna from the American military head-quarters in Tunis. The brass—Dwight D. Eisenhower, Carl Spaatz, James H. Doolittle—were coming to congratulate the Lonely Eagles, as the papers called the black pilots.

Davis remembers feeling as much relief as elation. "I was very proud—grateful, if you want to put it that way—that we had finally shot down an enemy airplane."

■

The same day that the Philadelphia Independent reported the fall of Pantelleria, the black tabloid carried a story that read, "4-Man Florida Mob Lynches Negro."

The period of World War II was a shameful, rancorous time in American race relations. Black newspapers in the North carried almost weekly accounts of lynchings in the South. There was trouble in Northern cities, too. Two days of race rioting in Detroit left 34 people dead—25 black and nine white.

In 1944, the entire public transportation network in Philadelphia was shut down by a wildcat strike. Workers couldn't get to vital defense jobs. FDR called in federal troops. The reason for the strike: The Philadelphia Transit Co. had put on eight black drivers, and white drivers didn't like it.

Most blacks, as most whites, supported the war. Indeed, it brought immediate economic benefit, as thousands found work in defense plants. The Fair Employment Practices Act, an early piece of civil rights legislation, opened some doors to blacks. W.E.B. DuBois, the most influential black leader of his day, urged blacks to "forget our special grievances" for the duration.

But a few voices urged blacks not to participate in the war. The Reverend Russell C. Barbour, editor of The Voice, a publication of the National Baptist Convention, saw the war as a struggle among colonial powers in which an oppressed people could have no interest. A 1943 story in the Philadelphia Tribune was headlined "Black Pastor Prefers Picking Cotton to Losing Life for British Imperialism."

During the Vietnam War a generation later, Muhammad Ali would say, "I ain't got no quarrel with the Viet Cong." He was echoing Elijah Muhammad, founder of the Nation of Islam, who had said that African Americans had no quarrel with the non-white Japanese. Elijah Muhammad was charged with sedition but acquitted. He was then con-victed on a draft-law technicality and sent to federal prison for four years.

Even blacks who supported the war could not escape the irony of the Army's asking black troops to fight in segregated units to end Nazi theories of racial superiority. Temple University professor Charles Fuller, author of the Pulitzer Prize-winning *A Soldier's Play*, a tale of black life in the World War II Army, notes that black troops "were fighting to save the world from attitudes they came home to find."

Most white Americans, he said, saw no resemblance at all between Nazi racism and American racism.

Most blacks, he said, could not miss it.

■

Lemuel Custis remembers that almost from the moment the Tuskegee Airmen arrived overseas, the German propagandist called Axis Sally was on the radio saying, "What are you black boys doing here? Don't you know what's happening back in America?"

"She was referring to the lynchings and the riots," Custis recalled, at home in Wethersfield, Connecticut. "She'd say, 'Why don't you black boys go home? They don't want you here.'

"We didn't let it destroy our focus. In a sense, it only reflected the general opinion of America anyway. So she wasn't telling us anything we didn't know."

Even after Lieutenant Hall shot down a German fighter plane in July 1943—winning initial congratulations from the brass—the Tuskegee Airmen were still struggling for respect. After a summer in the air, during which no more German planes were shot down, the 99th was in trouble.

Colonel William W. Momyer, commander of the 33rd Fighter Group, said the squadron had "failed to display the aggressiveness and desire for combat that are necessary to a first-class fighting organization." Higher-ups agreed. The airmen were on the verge of being removed from combat and relegated to coastal patrol.

Davis countered that the airmen had done as well as anyone could within the trap of segregation. No experienced white pilots had ever coached them in the tricks of aerial combat, he said. And they had to fly more missions than most pilots, because whites were unavailable as replacements.

A study was ordered. It showed "no significant general difference" in the airmen's performance compared with that of white pilots in the Mediterranean. The Tuskegee Experiment would live on. But it was still on trial. The verdict didn't come in for months—not until two successive days in January 1944, when black American airmen shot down 12 enemy fighters at Anzio.

Custis remembers Anzio well. He shot down one German and helped bring down another. The 99th was then part of the 332nd Fighter Group, commanded by Davis. The group had four black squadrons trained at Tuskegee. Segregation remained the iron-clad rule. The Allies, in a desperate attempt to break out of southern Italy, had landed behind German lines at Anzio. American troops were battling to hold the beach. The airmen formed an umbrella, shielding the troops from diving attacks by German fighters.

"I saw five [fighters] come down on us," Custis, now 71, a retired tax official for the state of Connecticut, recalled.

Other Tuskegee pilots were already engaging the enemy planes. Custis turned and got behind one. His thumb pressed the trigger of his six .50-caliber machine guns.

"When it comes down to crunch time," he said, "many of the things you do are automatic. You almost subconsciously do the right thing at the right time." The German plane tumbled, crashed, and burned.

"As I recall, he didn't get his chute open. I think I saw him trying to. . . . It's a combat situation; it isn't a personal thing. Whoever is doing the right thing at the right time is going to survive."

After their performance at Anzio, the Tuskegee Airmen were given what Davis called "cream" assignments. They would go on to destroy a total of 111 enemy aircraft in the sky and 150 on the ground. They would escort U.S. bombers on missions all the way to Berlin, never losing a single bomber to an enemy plane. At war's end, an additional group of Tuskegee Airmen—the all-black 447th Composite Group—was in training. Anzio had changed everything. "There would be no more talk," Davis said, "of lack of aggressiveness, absence of teamwork, or disintegrating under fire."

■

In some ways, the black leaders who counseled African Americans to fight abroad for freedom at home were proved right. Progress was a bumpy road. But three years after World War II, on July 26, 1948, President Harry S. Truman signed Executive Order 9981:

"It is hereby declared that there shall be equality of treatment and opportunity for all persons in the armed services without regard to race, color, religion or national origin."

It was the first great document of the post-war revolution in civil rights. Today, the military is the most integrated segment of American society. A black man, General Colin L. Powell, has served as chairman of the Joint Chiefs of Staff. Said Nalty: "Jim Crow has been unable to withstand the bravery and dedication of black servicemen and civilians."

14 • The Fall of Sicily
July 10, 1943

Allied forces begin a 38-day assault that some U.S. generals opposed. They said Germany, not Italy, was the main enemy.

July 10, 1993

Shortly after midnight, on the moonlit morning of July 10, 1943, Private Ed Slavin of Philadelphia stood in the doorway of a C-47 transport plane over Sicily, ready to jump into the war in Europe.

He was 29 years old, the "old man" in his outfit of guys 19 and 20. He had volunteered as a paratrooper in the 82nd Airborne Division because it paid more than the infantry—$71 per month, he recalls, compared with $21.

"We were supposed to be shock troops. It means you went in with as many men as possible to destruct the enemy as much as possible. Then get the hell out, quick."

Carrying an M-1 rifle, he leaped. Three thousand other GIs were doing the same. They were supposed to land in four designated drop zones, but they ended up scattered over what seemed like half of Sicily.

"We were not even on the map that we had," Slavin, now of Mantua, New Jersey, remembered. "We were lost, completely."

■

Fifty years ago today, the American and British Allies invaded Sicily. It was their first major landing in Europe in World War II, the opening phase of the Italian Campaign.

In some ways, the whole U.S. Army felt lost in Sicily. America's top generals had opposed the invasion. They had wanted to invade

Normandy right off. Germany, they said, was the principal enemy, not Italy. And the way to beat Germany was to charge across the English Channel and aim straight for Berlin. General George C. Marshall, U.S. Army chief of staff, had also opposed the invasion of North Africa the previous November. He wanted nothing to do with the whole Mediterranean region, calling it a "sideshow" to the main event and a "suction pump" for men and materiel.

But the British were for Sicily. They remembered their disasters of the First World War, their 400,000 casualties at the Somme in France. They dreaded a frontal attack in 1943, preferring a nip here, a nip there.

The decision had to come from the top. Prime Minister Winston Churchill convinced President Franklin D. Roosevelt that Sicily—and all of Italy with it—was the "soft underbelly" of Europe.

And so Operation Husky was a go. Between them, the American and British armies landed 450,000 troops. It was the largest amphibious invasion in history at that time, larger than the North Africa invasion. Today it ranks second, surpassed only by the Normandy invasion on June 6, 1944.

Correspondent Ernie Pyle, viewing the invasion armada from aboard one of the 3,300 ships, tried to give Americans back home a sense of the immensity of the occasion:

"There is no way of conveying the enormous size of that fleet. On the horizon, it resembled a distant city. It covered half the skyline, and the dull-colored camouflaged ships stood indistinctly against the curve of the dark water, like a solid formation of uncountable structures blending together. Even to be part of it was frightening. I hope no American ever has to see its counterpart sailing against us."

■

It took forever to assemble the armada in North Africa. Or so it seemed to Don Evans, a 19-year-old private from Phoenixville, Pennsylvania, in the Second Armored Division.

Shortly after midnight on July 8, Evans was awakened from his bed in Tunisia. At 2:45 a.m., he climbed into a truck for the 40-minute ride to the docks in Bizerte. At 11:30 a.m., he boarded his LST, a big landing ship. The exact times are all written down in his sergeant's log. At 4 p.m., the LST pulled away from the docks. Evans, who only months earlier had been earning 25 cents an hour in a cracker factory, was ready to go into battle.

The LST wasn't. Not yet. It dropped anchor in the harbor and just sat there. For the next 14½ hours, Evans sweated in the summer heat and gagged on the sweet, sooty odor of marine fuel.

"We sat there till the convoy got situated," Evans, a retired forklift operator, recalled at his home near Collegeville, Pennsylvania.

Finally, at 6:30 the next morning, the ship set sail. The men aboard found out where they were headed when each was handed a pamphlet: "Soldier's Guide to Italy."

"We knew we were going somewhere on an invasion, and I thought it was going to be Greece," Evans said.

The convoy sailed east. Early the next day, Evans was off the coast of Sicily, 225 miles away. He could see the mountains rising behind the town of Licata.

"We were standing up on deck, most of us, and kind of looking into the shore. All around, you could see the Navy. We were kind of awed by the number of ships. I heard the anti-aircraft guns go off on some of the other ships, and turned and I saw this German plane coming in."

The German plane was on a strafing attack. Evans saw the "twinkling" of its wing guns. Bullets "skipped off the top of the deck." He ducked down, but looked up in time to see the plane smoking. "He hit the water before he got to the beach. Every naval gun in that flotilla out there must have opened up on him."

Three men in Evans' reconnaissance company had been wounded. And they hadn't even landed yet.

■

Operation Husky called for strict Allied coordination. Problem was, British commanders held little respect for American fighting men based on what they had seen in North Africa. At Kasserine Pass in Tunisia the previous February, the inexperienced Americans had appeared disorganized, shell-shocked. They had since gotten better. But first impressions die hard.

The overall commander of the Sicily campaign was an American, General Dwight D. Eisenhower. All his principal deputies were British. Ike and the British agreed to a plan that subordinate American commanders thought favored the Brits.

The British field commander was Field Marshal Bernard L. Montgomery. His veteran Eighth Army, victors at El Alamein, would land on the eastern end of the island. They would then sweep up the coast to Messina, cutting off the enemy's only route of retreat to the Italian mainland.

The American Seventh Army, under Lieutenant General George S. Patton Jr., would go ashore at three points on the southern coast: Licata, Gela, and Scoglitti. Patton's job would be to shadow Monty's flank, protecting him from any Axis surprises.

The vainglorious Patton resented playing "second fiddle" to anybody in any army, especially the equally vainglorious Monty.

"There was a lot of discord," said historian Carlo D'Este, author of *Bitter Victory: The Battle for Sicily, 1943.*

The result was a race between Patton and Montgomery. After doing as he was told—crawling over the spiny backbone of the island to capture the city of Palermo—Patton would turn east and attempt to beat Montgomery to Messina.

■

Americans would suffer 9,811 casualties in Sicily, including 2,783 deaths. Many would befall Ed Lackman's First Infantry Division, the Big Red One, in the first hours and days of combat.

"We came ashore about 2 in the morning. It wasn't until daybreak that all hell broke loose," recalled Lackman, now retired after 40 years with the Jenkintown, Pennsylvania, post office.

Sicily was defended by about 200,000 Italian troops, backed by 60,000 Germans. An elite Panzer force, the Hermann Goering Division, counterattacked as Lackman and his buddies were trying to move inland from the beach at Gela the first day. The attack began with barrages of rockets fired from mobile launchers called *Nebelwerfers.* The rockets made a terrifying, unearthly howl; GIs called them "screaming meemies."

"Then the tanks came along. . . . A lot of fellows were getting hit. The Germans were trying to throw us back in the sea. The Navy is what saved us."

It was one of the strangest fights of the war—ships versus tanks. From offshore, the Navy opened fire with its big deck guns. Even tanks could not stand up to that. They reacted like mice near a cat.

Lackman, now 70, of Willow Grove, Pennsylvania, said that even for the foot soldier, war is mostly impersonal. "Most of the time when you're firing your gun, you don't see the men you're hitting."

But one time on Sicily was different.

"This one time, things got quiet as we were laying in a ditch. It was hot in the sun and the fellas were sleeping. I looked up and here was this German, maybe 150 feet away, coming right toward us with what they called a machine pistol.

". . . I can still picture him. He didn't have a helmet on. He had one of those peaked caps the Germans used to wear, like in Africa.

"I went down and I grabbed my carbine, and when I jumped up he was maybe 15 feet away. I just, I put every shot into him. . . .It's an instinct. The more bullets you put into him, the less chance he's going to get up. . . . I just knew, if I don't get him, he's going to get me."

■

The Axis had known the Allies were coming. Not the day, not the hour—but coming, for sure. For weeks, the papers in America and Britain had been full of talk about an attack in the Mediterranean region. It was a logical next step after the May defeat of the Axis in North Africa.

On June 8, Churchill told Parliament that an amphibious assault would take place somewhere soon. On June 13, as Allied bombers pounded islands near Sicily, the Philadelphia Record blared in a head-line: "Sicily Next." Yet, come D-Day (as the first day of all Allied inva-sions was named), British troops landed without opposition. So did some, though not all, American troops. Ed Slavin and his company of paratroops ran into only a few enemy soldiers at the outset. Mostly they encountered scared, confused civilians. The Sicilian people, he said, didn't know what to make of the Americans suddenly in their midst.

"One man came out and said, 'Here, cut my hands off—but not my wife's, please.' He had been told that we were unmerciful and that we would cut their hands off."

Everywhere, the Sicilian people were poor. Some were starving. Slavin and another GI briefly became Sicilian heroes when they "liber-ated" a houseful of canned-beef rations for the populace of one village. The beef had been left behind by Italian troops as they fled. An Army major ordered Slavin and his buddy to guard it, since it would be need-ed to feed POWs.

"When he left, a whole bunch of kids and mothers and fathers started gathering around us. They were crying, *Niente mangiare, niente carne, niente latte.* ("No food, no meat, no milk.") I looked at [the other GI] and said, 'Shall we?' He said, 'Hell, yes.' "

So the people were fed. The priest rang the church bell to gather the town. The women lined up and held out their aprons.

"It was better than Christmas," Slavin recalled with a smile. "Then," he said, "we got the hell out of there before the major came back."

■

Patton won his race with Montgomery to Messina. But it was "a hollow triumph," says historian D'Este. When Patton reached Messina on August 17, ending the battle for Sicily in 38 days, the Germans on the island had long since escaped across the Strait of Messina, equip-ment and all.

"They captured the island, but they let the Germans get away," D'Este said. "Every one of those German troops would come back to haunt the Allies" in battles to come on the mainland of Italy.

On July 25, 1943, two weeks after the Allied landings, a coup in Rome had toppled Italian dictator Benito Mussolini. A new government began peace negotiations with the Allies, which culminated in Italian surrender on September 8.

The surrender meant little from an Allied military point of view. The Germans, guests in Italy one day, became an occupying force the next. They would continue to fight in Italy until the very end of the war. General Marshall would be proved right. The Mediterranean was a suction pump.

15 • Italy's Surrender
September 8, 1943

Italian Americans felt caught between love for their homeland and loyalty to the U.S. Italy's exit from the war was joyous news.

September 8, 1993

The first word came from General Dwight D. Eisenhower in a radio broadcast from Allied headquarters in Algiers. It was picked up by the BBC in London and cabled to New York. The wire services clacked it out at 66 words per minute, ringing bells on teletype machines in newsrooms all over America. Within scarcely two hours of Ike's announcement, crowds were dancing in the streets of South Philadelphia.

Italy had surrendered. It was September 8, 1943—50 years ago today. One of the Axis powers in World War II had called it quits. The war suddenly seemed closer to an end.

Nowhere was the news heard with greater joy than in Italian American communities, such as in South Philly. The words *Italy is with us now* appeared on a sign at Palumbo's nightclub. Having their homeland as an enemy had been a great strain for Americans born in Italy or whose parents were born in Italy, who still had aunts and uncles and cousins in Italy.

"The surrender was a great relief," recalled Theresa F. Bucchieri, the daughter of immigrants from Messina in Sicily. "Our boys would say, 'Gee, you mean to tell me that I have to go there and kill my cousin?' How could you kill your relatives?"

Bucchieri, who lived at 21st and Morris Streets, remembered that on her corner "people were dancing with each other, hugging each other, banging pots and pans—you know, like they do on New Year's

Eve. Oh, they were going crazy, kissing everybody. Viva America! Viva Italia! And thanking the Lord, you know."

People thought that, besides sparing Italians from having to shoot Italians, the surrender would spare Italy from further ravages of war. Folks in Italy thought that, too. In Rome, crowds shouted, *"Viva la pace!"*—Long live the peace!

On both sides of the ocean, celebrators went to bed intoxicated with happiness, if not wine. But they awoke to the sobering news that, overnight, American and British troops had invaded the Italian mainland at Salerno—and were in a desperate struggle for survival, not with Italian forces, but with the German troops deployed in Italy. The Italians may have surrendered, but their former Nazi allies most definitely had not.

Warfare in Italy wasn't over. It had hardly begun. The news of the fighting on Italian soil was a great letdown after the illusions of the night before.

■

The Allied invasion of Sicily two months earlier, on July 10, had convinced many Italians that they had to get out of the war—and soon, before the Americans and British made further inroads.

The Fascist Grand Council, Italy's nominal parliament, met in Rome on July 24 to consider the future. Benito Mussolini, Il Duce, the dictator who practically had invented fascism, who had ruled Italy with an iron fist for 21 years, on whom Adolf Hitler had modeled his own rise to power, who had given Italy dreams of a new Roman empire but bankrupted it with war—Mussolini had to go.

The council voted, 19-8, to stand up to him. The next day, Il Duce was summoned by King Victor Emmanuel III, who told him he had been deposed. As Mussolini walked to his car, he was arrested. Marshal Pietro Badoglio, head of the army, was named to lead the new government.

Badoglio announced that Italy would continue, as an Axis partner, to make war alongside Germany. But secretly he opened peace negotiations with the Allies.

The Italians wanted to quit, but they were concerned about the tens of thousands of German troops already in Italy. What would the Germans do if they felt betrayed by their ally? Indeed, Hitler half-expected what Badoglio was up to. Hitler had set up a plan to take over in Rome and disarm Italian troops at the first sign of betrayal.

Badoglio wanted the Allies to invade the mainland—at Rome. His troops, he said, would cooperate by holding the airport and highways around the city. But he wanted assurances that the Allies would land with such power and speed that the Germans would choose to flee, not fight. Italy could then be saved from destruction.

The Allies, after fighting Italians in Sicily, were in no mood to be dictated to. But they had planned to invade the mainland anyway. Why not have inside help?

Ike went so far as to send Major General Matthew Ridgway, commander of the 82nd Airborne Division, on a clandestine mission to scope out the German installations around Rome. He returned with the advice that a paratroop drop was too risky. Any invasion would have to be done the old-fashioned way. That is, troops would have to hit the beaches somewhere and battle their way inland.

Take it or leave it. That's what Ike told Badoglio. The Italians decided to take it.

On September 3—the very day that a diversionary British force crossed over from Sicily and landed on the toe of the Italian boot—the Badoglio government agreed to capitulate. The surrender would be announced—and become effective—on September 8.

The Italians didn't know it then, but September 8 would be the eve of Operation Avalanche, the main Allied invasion in the Gulf of Salerno, 150 miles to the south of Rome.

Public announcement of the surrender was to be made in Italy at 6 p.m., local time, on the 8th. Ike would simultaneously put out the word from Algiers. By then, Allied invasion fleets from Sicily and North Africa would be well on their way.

■

World War II was trying enough for any American. It was especially trying for immigrant Americans from countries at war with the United States. The five million Italian Americans were almost all first- or second-generation. More than Germans and Japanese, they tended to maintain close ties with the old country.

"It wasn't until after the Second World War that they came and stayed permanently," said Dr. Tito A. Ranieri, 81, of Haverford, Pennsylvania, an authority on Italian settlement in the Philadelphia area. "Before the Second World War, most of them would come here to work for a few years and go back. Then they'd come again."

The agony that the war brought was illustrated by a story in June 1943 out of Providence, Rhode Island. For years, an immigrant named Vincenzio Gaudio had been trying to get his son Luigi to join him in America. That month, he showed up—as a prisoner of war. The father got a letter from the War Department that the son was at a POW camp in Colorado Springs, Colorado.

After Pearl Harbor, America had panicked at having so many

Germans, Japanese, and Italians in its midst. On December 8, 1941, immigrants from the Axis nations were classified as enemy aliens. Only the Japanese—clearly for reasons of racial prejudice—were interned wholesale. But many hundreds of Italians and Germans were arrested and confined at least briefly.

Italian Americans went out of their way to prove their loyalty to the United States. They joined the Army, the Navy, the Marines; they bought war bonds; they gave blood.

Joseph P. DeMarco of Drexel Hill, Pennsylvania, a Salerno campaign veteran, said that when the Army drafted him, it asked, "How would you feel about fighting against Italians?" He answered, "Well, I'm an American Italian, so I got to do what I got to do."

The Italian-language press in America had supported Mussolini in the '20s and '30s. Dictator though he was, he had improved the Italian economy, lifted the nation's morale—made the trains run on time, as was often said. "Mussolini originally wasn't bad; he really tried to pull Italy up," said Elba Farabegoli Gurzau, 84, of Philadelphia, who traveled to Italy during the fascist period. "Then Mussolini was sort of drawn into the Hitler camp, and he started doing things he shouldn't have done."

After Pearl Harbor, Italian Americans dropped Mussolini like the proverbial hot potato. Pro-Italian, anti-fascist—that was how they saw themselves. In October 1942, U.S. Attorney General Francis Biddle lifted the Italians' enemy-alien designation.

"We were very happy when [the Allies] went into Sicily because we were all anti-fascists," said Bucchieri, who has lived in South Philadelphia all of her 81 years. After the invasion, she recalled, her parents sent "CARE packages" to the relatives in Sicily.

When word came that the Badoglio government had surrendered, it was as if a steam valve had suddenly released the pressure that had been building for years.

"It was a great relief for us . . . because of the tensions within ourselves," recalled Bishop Louis A. DeSimone, auxiliary bishop for the Roman Catholic Archdiocese of Philadelphia.

Bishop DeSimone had grown up in Bridgeport, Pennsylvania, an industrial town on the Schuylkill that had a large Italian community.

"Both my parents were from Italy," he said. "I sympathized with the good people over there." He had been in North Africa as a soldier before the Italian surrender, and, he recalled, "We were in an awkward position. . . . We were considered an enemy of our patrimony, of our own heritage, of our own people."

Now that conflict was over. *"Dio benedica l'America,"* the crowds shouted in South Philadelphia. "God bless America."

■

On board a cruiser sailing for Salerno, Staff Sergeant Frank T. Neutts of Carbondale, Pennsylvania, wasn't thinking about being an Italian American or any kind of ethnic American. He was thinking about being a target for a bullet. Like all soldiers on the eve of battle, the men of the 36th Infantry Division were in a quiet, contemplative mood as the invasion fleet pushed on. It was a perfect late-summer evening.

Before the war, the 36th Division had been the Texas National Guard. Now only about half the members were Texans. The division would be the first American troops on the beach. They didn't know it, but their landing would be the bloodiest yet in the war.

"We were at sea when it was announced that the surrender had taken place," Neutts, a son of Italian immigrants, recalled. The news came over the ship's loudspeaker. "Well, naturally, everybody let go—shouting, hollering, whooping it up."

The soldiers deluded themselves just as the folks back in South Philadelphia deluded themselves. They reacted as if the surrender meant there would be no more fighting in Italy. They were forgetting the Germans, who had been alerted to the invasion fleet and at that moment were cleaning their guns for battle in the hills above Salerno.

"We knew there was no heart in the Italians to fight Americans," said Jerry A. Padovano, 74, of Toms River, New Jersey, another Italian American. "We were happy about them giving it up, so to speak. We certainly didn't want to kill our own people."

But the brass knew better than to celebrate. They knew the Germans were there waiting.

"We all started cheering and everything," said Pasquale T. Carlo, 73, also of Toms River. "But the people in charge said, 'Don't get your hopes up.' They knew."

The American forces landed at 3:30 the next morning. They would suffer 3,500 casualties at Salerno. A German counterattack would almost repel them into the sea. It was the start of a campaign on the Italian mainland that would go on for close to two years and end in a virtual stalemate, eclipsed in importance—but not in blood—by the fast-moving war in northern Europe.

In the end, much of Italy would be destroyed.

16 • How 'bout them Steagles?
Fall 1943

The war took a big toll on manpower in the NFL, so the Pittsburgh Steelers and the Philadelphia Eagles merged for a season.

October 26, 1993

Only a world war ever produced a football team as odd as the Phil-Pitt Steagles.

It was 1943, the middle of World War II. Most healthy young men were in the military, many off somewhere in Italy or the Pacific. The National Football League was struggling to survive a severe manpower shortage. Good prospects were draft material, all right, but not for the NFL.

President Franklin D. Roosevelt, a fan of the New York Yankees, had declared that professional baseball should continue, war or no war. The national pastime, he said, was essential to morale on the home front. Americans, he thought, "ought to have a chance for recreation and for taking their minds off their work."

But football? FDR had nothing to say about football.

The war had interrupted pro football from its outset. Pearl Harbor Day was an NFL Sunday. Many a cabinet member, general, and admiral had heard the news of Japan's attack at Washington's Griffith Stadium, watching the Philadelphia Eagles lose to the Redskins, 20-14.

By then, the 1941 season was ending. In 1942, 10 NFL teams were able to limp along. Come 1943, 50 years ago this fall, the player scarcity had reached a crisis. The Cleveland Rams folded for the duration of the war. The Eagles and Pittsburgh Steelers didn't have enough players, either.

Elmer Layden, the league commissioner, urged the Eagles and Steelers to merge for that one season, splitting home games between the two cities, which were separated by a 300-mile ride on the Iron City Express. The hybrid would be a two-headed monster, co-coached by Philadelphia's lean Earle "Greasy" Neale and Pittsburgh's fat Walt Kiesling, both future Hall of Famers.

The players would wear the Eagles' green-and-white jerseys. But what would the team be called? Steelers-Eagles was the unimaginative choice. Fans came up with a catchier name. Thus were the Steagles born.

■

Jack Hinkle was classified as physically unfit for military service. But that didn't stop him from playing halfback for the Steagles.

"I was in the Air Force, and I was discharged because of ulcers," Hinkle, a second-team all-pro that season, recalled from his home outside Norristown, Pennsylvania.

Playing a pro sport didn't excuse a man from Uncle Sam's draft. He needed a deferment—or a discharge—for that.

Tommy Miller, an end, "he was in the Navy preflight program, and he had a crack-up, and they discharged him because of an injury that he had," Hinkle said. "He came back and played pro football at left tackle."

Edgar Michaels, a guard, "he couldn't hear," Hinkle continued. "He was practically deaf in one ear because he never wore a helmet. So he couldn't have gotten in the service, anyhow. Then Ray Graves, who was our center, he had one ear. . . . We called him Floppy."

Players who had flunked draft physicals were classified 4-F. Others were 3-A, deferred because they were married and had dependent children. Some were actually in the service, stationed nearby. They played soldier all week, then football on the weekend. The largest number of players earned deferments by holding jobs classified as essential in defense plants in Philadelphia, where the Steagles were headquartered. They could work by day and still practice from 6 to 9 each night.

Because of the manpower problem, the NFL owners had considered junking the 1943 season. Instead, the league cut the roster limit from 33 players to 28. (Today's NFL teams dress 45 players on game day.) At the first Steagles workout in July, even 28 players seemed optimistic. Only 19 showed up.

"It's a good thing we merged with the Steelers, or we wouldn't have had a team," Hinkle said.

On the field, rosters might change from week to week. For a player who stayed with the team, it was a chance to demonstrate talent that otherwise might have gone overlooked.

Take Hinkle. Described in press accounts as "a fine, good-looking chap, broad-shouldered, slim-hipped," he was 6-foot-1 and 215 pounds, as big as most NFL linemen. He had always been a blocking back, both at Syracuse University and in the pros. With the Steagles, he got a chance to carry the ball.

He ended up leading the league in rushing, though he never got official credit for it. Bill Paschal of the New York Giants won the rushing title with 572 official yards in nine games, one more yard than Hinkle had.

The problem was, Hinkle recalled, that the statisticians had missed a 47-yard run he made against the Giants early in October. Usually, he wore the number 43. But his jersey had ripped, and that day he was wearing, coincidentally, the number 47. The jersey change may have caused the confusion.

On Tuesday after the game, statistics were posted at practice. Even though Hinkle's 47-yard run had been noted in The New York Times, "my longest gain was down as 20 yards," Hinkle said. "I should have pursued it, but I didn't. . . . Stats didn't matter as much in those days."

Though Hinkle played eight years in the NFL, he never again had such a rushing season.

■

The Chicago Bears—the dominant team of the era—were preseason picks to win the championship. Art Morrow of The Inquirer pointed out that they had an edge that applied only in wartime—"more married men than most squads."

But nothing was certain in that season of jumbled rosters. The Steagles opened with a 17-0 victory over Brooklyn's football Dodgers, a Saturday-night affair before 11,131 fans at Shibe Park. Pro football's second-class status as a spectator sport was evident in the press coverage. The Sunday Inquirer played up the Penn-Yale game. The Evening Bulletin, which had no Sunday edition, gave the game a single paragraph on Monday.

The Steagles won their second contest, 28-14, over the Giants, amid signs of disorganization. They set an NFL record for fumbles: 10 in one game. After that, they dropped two ugly games, giving up a total of 90 points.

To Philadelphia fans, the team began to look like the same old Birds, who hadn't had a winning season in 10 NFL campaigns. But the Steagles weren't dead. Far from it. It just took time to blend two teams under two coaches.

Francis Joseph "Bucko" Kilroy, described in a press guide as "240 pounds of red-headed fighting Irishman," was a rookie tackle that season while simultaneously in the Navy College Training Program, better known as V-12. He remembers that Neale and Kiesling couldn't have been more different as men and coaches.

Kiesling, he recalls, was enormous—well over 300 pounds. Neale was lean and elegant, not at all the figure his nickname suggested. He had earned that as a kid when, after calling another boy "Dirty," the boy had retaliated by calling him "Greasy."

A superb athlete himself, Neale had been both a pro football player and major-league baseball player. As a Cincinnati Red, he hit .357 in the famous 1919 World Series, the one tainted by the Black Sox scandal.

"Greasy had a sense of humor, and he was a confident, upbeat guy," Kilroy, now vice president of the New England Patriots, recalled. "I wouldn't say Kiesling didn't have a sense of humor, but he was more serious."

It was lucky for the Steagles that the coaches had different interests. Neale was mostly offense-minded, a proponent of the new T-formation, first used in the pros by George Halas of the Bears. Kiesling was a defense guy.

Like most players of the day, Kilroy went both ways. He played offense and defense, and could observe both coaches closely. He called Kiesling "an innovator . . . the guy who started the basics" of the Eagles' championship defense later in the '40s. But it was Neale, he said, who altered the game. He picked up Halas's T-formation from film of Bears games and massaged it to perfection. Between them, Halas and Neale "opened up the offense" and "really made" pro football a spectator sport, Kilroy said.

■

Early in the 1943 season, the whole NFL got a scare when the War Manpower Commission announced that it was investigating the Bears' roster for possible draft fraud. The question was whether Bears who had obtained draft deferments because of their work in defense plants were really war workers, first, and football players, second. The test was money: In which job did they earn more? Fortunately for the NFL's image, the Bears were low-paid. Most of them earned more in the factory. It would have been a public-relations disaster for professional football to appear to be cheating on the war effort.

All over the league, salaries were as low or lower. NFL players were seen as ordinary Joes, even if they weren't G.I. Joes. That helped alleviate the anger that occasionally arose in public over their draft status.

Of all professional sports, it was baseball that took the most heat. It was simply a bigger sport; the public cared more about it. Some of the biggest stars of major-league baseball were booed at one time or another. Allie Sherman, then a rookie backup to Steagles quarterback Leroy Zimmerman, recalls occasional resentment from football fans.

"There were local tensions, wherever the cities were," he said. "Sure, you had people who were objecting. . . . Why is my son in? Or my nephew in? And why isn't this guy in? He's healthy. . . . You know how people are in time of war."

Sherman would become head coach of three Giants teams that played for the NFL championship in the '60s. Neale called him "the best football mind I ever coached." But in 1943, with the Steagles, he was paid exactly $75 a game. Because of a perforated eardrum, a result of childhood scarlet fever, he was classified 4-F and didn't need a defense job. But he took one anyway in the off-season, working at the as a welder. Like other unmarried Steagles, he lived during the season at the 600-room Hotel Philadelphian, at 39th and Chestnut Streets. He remembers that his roommate, tackle Eberle Schultz, kept his beer cold on the windowsill. Sherman, at 5-foot-10 and 160 pounds, was the smallest man on the team, while Schultz, 6-4 and 250, was the biggest.

"Greasy was a very frugal guy," Sherman recalled. "He was always giving you a lecture. 'Don't call from your room; call from the pay phone in the lobby. . . . And I suggest you eat at the Horn & Hardart. It's the healthiest food, the best food, and it's certainly less costly.'

"So we took him up on it. And then we had a run of diarrhea."

■

One season the Steagles lasted. But what a season it was.

Neale and Kiesling were able to meld the Steagles into an effective team. Going into their final game, which they lost to the Green Bay Packers, they had a chance to tie for the Eastern Division title. As it was, they finished 5-4-1.

In 1944, the last full year of war, the Eagles were again able to go it alone. The Steelers merged with the Chicago Cardinals. That team was so bad, 0-10, that the writers called it the Car-Pitts—the carpets—because everybody walked all over it.

But the Eagles were putting together the nucleus of a fine football team. In 1944, the Eagles went 7-1-2. By 1947, they were playing in the NFL championship game. And in '48 and '49, they won it all, twice. No other Eagles team has ever won back-to-back championships.

"The old Steagles, that's where a lot of it started," Hinkle said.

17 • The Battle of Tarawa
November 20, 1943

**A tiny Pacific atoll was home to a key Japanese air strip.
For the United States, it was a step toward Japan.
It was a costly victory.**

November 20, 1993

You might need a magnifying glass to find Tarawa Atoll on a globe. It's a dribble of sand just a pencil tip above the Equator, all but lost in 64 million square miles of Pacific Ocean.

Sitting around the Tarawa lagoon, like table guests, are two dozen tiny islets. The largest is Betio, hardly two miles long and a half-mile across. In the fall of 1943, it may have been the most heavily fortified place on earth. On this little lump of coral was an airstrip. The Japanese needed it to protect their outer ring of sea defenses. The Americans wanted it as the first steppingstone in their campaign of island-hopping across the Central Pacific. The commander of the Japanese garrison had boasted that a million men couldn't capture Betio in a hundred years.

The U.S. Marines would take it in just 76 hours—but at a nightmarish cost.

Fifty years ago today, on November 20, 1943, the battle of Tarawa began. Of all the beaches bought with Marine Corps lives in World War II, Tarawa's may have been, inch for inch, the bloodiest.

To conquer a sand spit of 291 acres, 1,085 Marines and 30 Navy personnel died. On the other side, the Japanese desire never to surrender—combined with the Marines' desire not to take prisoners—produced casualties that were even more horrifying. Of several thousand Japanese, only 17 lived through the battle.

Tarawa remains legendary for blood and courage within the ranks

of the Marine Corps. But what survivors remember is the smell: the sickly sweet stench of literally tons of human flesh, rotting in the equatori-
al heat.

"I'll never get rid of that smell. Never," said Perry F. Grisdale, now
69, of Norristown, Pennsylvania, a machine-gunner at Tarawa.

■

Private Grisdale arrived on Betio beach dragging a dead Marine
under his arm. It was after 9 on a white-sky morning, the start of three
days in hell. Grisdale was 19 years old, still baby-faced and chubby. He
would later write to his mother, "This was the first time I ever seen a
man cut in half. And one of my buddies got his head blown off by a Jap
shell. The place was like a butcher shop with legs, arms, heads and half
of bodies flying around."

The battle for Tarawa promised to be simple and brutal, a case of
kill-or-be-killed. "One side was going to prevail, and the other side was
going to be wiped out," said retired Colonel Joseph H. Alexander,
author of a 50th-anniversary Tarawa study for the Marine Corps
Historical Foundation.

Naval bombardment was supposed to soften up Betio before the
troops went in. Rear Admiral Howard Kingman, in charge of gunnery,
boasted confidently to fellow brass hats, "Gentlemen, we will not neu-
tralize Betio. . . . We will obliterate it."

At 6:22 a.m., three battleships, four cruisers, and nine destroyers
opened up, carpeting the island with high explosives for 90 minutes.
Then came strafing and bombing attacks by Hellcats and Avengers
from the aircraft carriers *Essex, Bunker Hill,* and *Independence.*

But as the Second Marine Division started toward shore, it quickly became apparent that the Navy had failed. The Japanese were dazed
but not done. That was because over the previous months, Japanese
engineers aided by hundreds of Korean laborers had constructed elab-
orate defenses on Betio. Mammoth coastal guns now anchored Betio's
artillery defenses. Trenches were laid out like the black keys on a piano,
arranged so that a bomb or shell practically had to drop on a defend-
er's head to kill him.

In addition, the engineers had built dozens of sand-covered
machine-gun pits that resembled ant hills. The Japanese command post
was in a concrete blockhouse with walls five feet thick. And so, the
moment the Marines started in, they were hit with a typhoon of fire.

The Marines attacked in waves, 300 yards apart. The first three
waves consisted of amphibious vehicles called amtracs. Eight of the 87
were knocked out by enemy fire before they reached the beach.

Then it was Grisdale's turn.

"I figured, I'm dead," he recalled recently.

His Third Battalion of the Second Marine Regiment was to be carried in as far as possible by Higgins boats, then dropped in the surf. But the brass had miscalculated the tide that washed over the coral reef. The Higgins boats scraped bottom while they were still a half-mile offshore. Grisdale and the others had to jump into chest-deep water, right there, and start to wade in. They were easy prey for the Japanese gunners.

As Grisdale remembers it, just two of 40 men in his Fourth Platoon of L Company made it ashore unhurt. His company commander, Michael P. Ryan, now a retired major general, said in an interview from California that losses were not quite that high. But one-third of the men in the whole Third Battalion were killed or wounded in the first two hours of battle.

The battalion's target was Red Beach One on the northern side of the Betio islet. Ryan, then a major, had witnessed the destruction of the amtracs. He looked to his right and saw a single Marine scuttle over a sea wall that the Japanese had built as a defensive measure. He pointed: "Let's try there."

Grisdale plodded forward, but it was slow going in four feet of water. On his right shoulder, he carried his squad's .30-caliber machine gun, which weighed 28 pounds. In his left hand he held his .45 above the water. Machine-gun bullets skittered all around him, making little geysers of water.

As No. 2 gunner in his squad, Grisdale had to keep close to the No. 1, Howard Hirst of Monson, Massachusetts, who toted the tripod.

"Me and my No. 1 gunner, we were more or less off to ourselves," Grisdale, now a retired construction worker, said. "I didn't like to be in a group because they can get too many of you at once that way. We got across this sandbar. A Jap machine gun was firing down on the sandbar, and the Marines were piled up all over the place. . . . We got another 50 or 60 yards, and a sniper got [Hirst]."

Hirst yelled out one word. "Grisdale!"

"I turned around and put my left arm around him and got him ashore. But he died on me. There was a lieutenant there on the beach. He didn't know what to do. He looked around and said, 'Anybody with you left?' I said, 'I don't see anybody left.' I had no tripod, no ammunition, no nothing. So he told me, 'Leave the machine gun here and take this carbine.' "

The lieutenant thrust the weapon at Grisdale, then ordered him to leap over the sea wall and go find a Japanese machine gun that had been creating havoc. "Today," Grisdale said with a smile, "I'd tell him to go do it himself." But over the wall he went. "That's when I seen my squad leader. He had his stomach all ripped open. . . . I ran up this trench toward where I heard the noise coming from. All this time I was running, I could see the sand turning up where the bullets were hitting."

Suddenly, a hand reached out and yanked him by the collar.

"Where are you going?" It was Major Ryan.

"I said I was supposed to find where the fire was coming from. He said, 'We know where it's coming from. Get down.' "

■

By nightfall of Day One, 5,000 Marines were ashore, 1,500 of them dead or wounded. They clung to the fringe of sand along the northern side of the island. The question was, could they hold on long enough for reinforcements to arrive?

Ryan's men held an isolated pocket on the extreme right of the Marines' lines. His men held the beach itself and a sand rise behind it. Any Marine who lifted his head above that rise risked losing it.

Night passed. For some reason, the Japanese did not counterattack. In the morning, Ryan's men spread out and cleared their end of the island—Green Beach, it was designated—to prepare for a landing by First Battalion of the Sixth Marine Regiment.

■

Enter Major William K. Jones.

Jones and his 800-man battalion came ashore in rubber boats, paddling carefully through a minefield in the shallow water over the reef. They almost made it without a scratch, but then one of two amtracs they had brought with them hit a mine and exploded.

The Sixth Marines had been held in reserve to go to the aid of either the Marines on Tarawa or the Army troops that had landed the same day on another of the Gilbert atolls, Makin. The fierce Japanese defense of Tarawa called for relief there.

"Jones's landing on the evening of [Day Two] was the turning point of the battle," said historian Alexander. His men were the first to land, fresh, without major casualties.

Ryan shook hands with Jones on the beach and showed him the lay of the land. The stench gripped Jones immediately. Now a retired lieutenant general, he recalled the story of one man at Tarawa who had jumped into a hole to escape shelling—and had found himself among dead, decomposing Japanese.

"It just smelled so terrible that he finally couldn't stand it," Jones said at his home in Alexandria, Virginia. The man jumped out and ran back to the Marine lines, risking death rather than smell that smell.

As Ryan and Jones talked, it was past 6 p.m., and darkness was again looming at the equator. Colonel David M. Shoup, the overall Marine commander on Betio, reached Jones by radio and ordered him to pass through Ryan's lines at daylight and attack the Japanese flank.

At 8 a.m., Jones's men were up and moving. The terrain was flat, with underbrush and heavy sand. It wasn't at all like the thick jungle that Jones remembered from Guadalcanal a year earlier. The stands of coconut palm trees were as thin as hair on a balding man's head.

The Marines moved forward quickly with M-1 rifles, crouching behind two Sherman tanks. Machine-gun bullets came at them from everywhere, but they rarely saw any Japanese. The enemy kept out of sight, hidden in "pillbox" fortifications.

Digging them out was dirty business.

"We had a system," Jones said. First, the tanks would try to blow open a hole in the pillbox. Then a Marine would throw in a "satchel charge" of 50 pounds of TNT. Next came the flamethrower teams.

"They would run up there and stick their flame in the aperture to try to kill any remaining Japs. . . . We didn't take any prisoners. We didn't try."

His men were suffering heavy casualties, too. "Some of my platoons were commanded by sergeants or even corporals because I lost a lot of officers."

By 3 in the afternoon, the attack had petered out in the heat. The Marines had progressed a mile along a path between the surf and the airstrip.

Over on the other side of the island, Marines in other battalions held a similar line. The remaining Japanese were now isolated in a slim finger of land.

One more day; that was all it would take. Then the Marines would have the battle won. But first would come one more night—and the long-awaited Japanese counter-offensive. It would fall across Jones's depleted lines and nearly break them.

About 8, the Japanese made a probing attack, feeling for weak points in Jones's line. The Marines beat them off, reloaded and waited for more. They knew it would come.

"Marines, we come to drink your blood."

Jones remembered: "Those that could speak English would yell that to scare us. . . . The Americans would be yelling back in English, 'Screw your emperor.' The Japs probably didn't understand a lot of it. All it did was make 'em madder."

Jones's Marines were hardly more than kids, mostly 17 and 18. Many were high school dropouts, and Jones recalls that a disproportionate number seemed to be from the rural South.

"I was a young man myself; I was only 27. I was going to do the best job I could. . . . I felt very strongly about all these young men I was responsible for, because they all had mothers and fathers. I knew that they were wild youngsters. They were at the stage of their life that they thought nothing could destroy them."

In the deep dark after midnight, the main attack of the night played out. The Japanese rushed through the lines with bayonets on their rifles and jumped into the holes of individual Marines. The combat was hand to hand in those cases. Mostly, though, the killing was done with machine guns, hand grenades, and howitzers.

"At daylight," Jones said, "I walked the lines. I had tears in my eyes because I saw all these dead Marines. Many of them I had known for a long time. . . . We had held the line, however, and had not let them go through the line."

■

Now it was Jones's turn to sit back. The Third Battalion, Sixth Marine Regiment, came up from behind him, passed through his lines, and, in a few hours, mopped up the remaining Japanese forces.

It was over. The Americans had won their precious airstrip. From that foothold they would launch attacks on the Marshall Islands, closer to Japan. From the Marshalls they would jump to the Marianas, and from the Marianas to Iwo Jima and Okinawa. By the summer of 1945, when the atomic bomb ended the war abruptly, only one leap would have remained—invasion of Japan itself.

When news of Tarawa casualties reached the United States at Thanksgiving 1943, there was a storm of outrage. For the first time, military censors permitted the public to see newsreels of bloated, dead Americans floating in the surf. Thirty-four hundred dead and wounded! For an island no one had ever heard of! Somebody had to be to blamed! Indeed, the generals and admirals had made mistakes aplenty. A Newsweek report soon after the battle foreshadowed history's judgment:

"Many factors contributed to the heavy Marine losses on Tarawa. They included the failure of naval and air bombardment to knock out enemy fortifications, poor soundings of the lagoon, and possible faulty coordination of the operation with the tide. But the thing that stuck in most people's minds was the fact that many of the Higgins landing boats piled up on the submerged reefs, making it necessary for the troops to wade 300 or more yards under murderous fire."

That judgment took nothing from the heroism of the Marines. Major General Holland M. Smith, looking at Japanese fortifications after the battle, said, "It looks beyond the realm of human possibility that this place could have been taken."

18 • The Stage Door Canteen
From June 1942 through the war

For the man in uniform, this was the place for a free show, some free food, and the sight of a pretty woman. But only the sight.

December 21, 1993

For 1,129 consecutive evenings during the Second World War, it was the best free show in town.

All the biggest names played the Stage Door Canteen when they came through Philadelphia: Frank Sinatra, Duke Ellington, Abbott and Costello, Helen Hayes, Lucille Ball.

The only patrons admitted were servicemen, and the only ticket they needed was their uniform. They came in battalion strength, thousands a week. For the World War II man in the military, the No. 1 place to go in Philadelphia for a free sandwich, a dance with a pretty girl, and maybe the chance to meet a star was the Stage Door.

Part no-booze nightclub, part cafeteria, part dance hall, the canteen was located in the pipe-infested basement of the proud old Academy of Music. Out on the corner of Broad and Locust, a sailor on leave from the Navy Yard could surely find a faster crowd. The bars were available, and he might meet a "victory girl" or a "khaki-wacky" teenager, identifiable by her bobby socks, saddle shoes, and easy virtue.

Inside the grand orchestral hall—through the glittering lobby and down 17 steps—scores of "junior hostesses" in frilly dresses and aprons tried to show the boys a good time, too, but in a more wholesome, more gracious way. They'd serve up coffee, do the jitterbug with them, and listen as they talked about home.

Today, a half-century later, few physical traces of the canteen remain, just remnants of murals painted on the dark basement walls.

But the Stage Door lives in many a memory as a flashback to a cohesive time in the city, when it seemed that everyone was either in uniform or seeking ways to buck up those who were.

"Oh, it was absolutely such fun; it was thrilling," recalled Bernice Sherman Mann, now of Palm Beach, Florida, who twice was voted Miss Stage Door Canteen by the soldiers, sailors, and Marines.

"They were just lonely boys and wanted somebody to talk to, and a dance was even better. The girls never dated the boys. If they ever did, they were not permitted to return as hostesses. . . . I guess they didn't want any broken hearts, and they didn't want any girls taken advantage of.

"It was a different time, such a different time."

■

They all did their part, the Biddles and the Dorrances and the Kents. When it came to the war effort, it was everyone's duty to pitch in, Philadelphia's society crowd included. The Stage Door was their pet project—theirs and that of hundreds of other patriotic folk from Rittenhouse Square and Chestnut Hill, Melrose Park, and the Main Line. Each week, 2,800 volunteers helped out somehow.

Socialite Peter A.B. (Pete) Widener II bused tables and, once at least, was tipped a nickel. Harriet (Mrs. Upton) Favorite, the board president, was photographed down on all fours working with a stiff scrub brush and a metal bucket.

"The social people worked very hard on it, yes. But there wasn't any snobbism, none at all," said Gloria Braggiotti Etting, the Stage Door's publicist.

Plans for the canteen began three months after Pearl Harbor. It was modeled on the soon-to-be-famous Stage Door at the 44th Street Theater in New York, subject of a hit song, "Stage Door Canteen," from Irving Berlin's all-soldier revue, *This is the Army*. Later would come a film called *Stage Door Canteen*.

By war's end, five additional canteens had opened across the United States—in Boston, Cleveland, Newark, San Francisco, and Washington—and two had set up shop overseas—in London and Paris. The West Coast crowd, led by Bette Davis, got into the act with a Hollywood Canteen.

In Philadelphia, as elsewhere, the Stage Door was sponsored by the American Theater Wing led by Broadway angel Antoinette Perry, who gave her nickname to the Tony Award. It was not associated with the USO.

In May 1942, four local daily papers ran shots of society leaders scrubbing, painting, and sweeping in the basement of the Academy. Art director Emlen Etting painted ballet murals and got other artists to do murals. Thirty businesses and wealthy people agreed to rotate donating the food or the money to buy it.

On June 20, opening night, more than 400 servicemen showed up. By July, the average was 600 a night; by August, 800. On September 1, upwards of 1,300 went to lay eyes on film goddess Hedy Lamarr, who was in town for a war-bond drive. Ironically, Bernice Mann recalls, Lamarr was a disappointment. "She was very standoffish and didn't smile a lot." But Paulette Goddard—now there was a movie star the boys loved. "She was down to earth and very friendly and very warm."

Jimmy Cagney chatted and ate a sandwich. Bill "Bojangles" Robinson tapped out a dance. Eleanor Roosevelt shook hands all around. Then there were the vaudevillians and stars now mostly forgotten—Constance Collier, Larry Adler, "Judy Canova and the rest of the Earle Show."

The entertainment ranged from the lowbrow to the high, from spinning-plate acts and trained seals to violinist Yehudi Menuhin and, as The Evening Bulletin put it, his "$50,000 Stradivarius."

The servicemen loved it. And they were, indeed, men. Women in uniform—WACs and WAVES and such—eventually had to open the Service Women's Club at 254 South 15th Street, for there was no place for them at the Stage Door.

An official history of the American Theater Wing explains, "Service women were not permitted in the canteens in America because the Wing could not permit any romance in the canteens."

The official history also says that the Wing was a pioneer in racial desegregation. But it's hard to find an African American man in the old photos, except maybe an entertainer.

In September 1942, at the Philadelphia canteen, the big to-do was about a lesser matter—dancing. L'affaire jitterbug, The Record called it.

"The people who run the canteen are polite and socialite, and nobody wanted to name names," the newspaper said. But "somebody" had issued an edict banning the racy jitterbug. And when the executive committee, headed by banker R. Livingston Sullivan, reinstated the dance, it was Jane (Mrs. John D.M.) Hamilton who resigned.

All she said publicly was, "There are some people who just don't work together. And Mr. Sullivan and I simply don't get along."

The Record, in an editorial, added caustically: "If the social front committee members want to get their pictures taken in connection with their high patriotism, they may do this if they do not get in the way of the fighting men."

■

Free food, free entertainment—that was sure to appeal. Free hair-cut, free movie ticket, free long-distance phone call. At Christmas, carols and a small gift. The Stage Door offered all of that and more.

But the big attraction was, without any doubt, girls, girls, girls.

"A lot of Uncle Sam's uniformed boys," The Bulletin said at the outset, "are going to see for themselves that Philadelphia's girls are as pretty as advertised."

Strict rules were put in place: "Don't wear slacks, or sweater and skirt. Don your most feminine, fluffy clothes. . . . Mustn't spend too much time with any one man or group. . . . Mustn't leave the canteen with any man or meet him outside in the vicinity of the canteen."

Junior hostesses wore red-white-and-blue aprons; food hostesses wore white. Heels; no flats. "Captains"—matrons, usually—inspected grooming and attire.

The girls turned out by the hundreds, every night, 5 to 12. Most had brothers, boyfriends—even husbands—in harm's way. Most appreciated the chance to feel they were contributing something, too.

Hope Montgomery Scott of Villanova, Pennsylvania, could never forget that her brother-in-law, Warwick Potter Scott, was a Japanese prisoner in the Philippines. He would eventually die a captive.

She couldn't help him, she recalled, but she could cheer other boys, the ones in the here-and-now at the canteen. "It was mostly Navy people and Merchant Marine," she said. "They were awfully nice fellas. They had been out on the seas for a while and had come into Philadelphia harbor. They were awfully glad to be with people for a while, friendly people."

Hope Scott had been the inspiration for Katharine Hepburn's free-spirited, independently minded character in the stage play and film *The Philadelphia Story*. She wasn't hesitant to break the canteen rule against outside socializing.

Two of the boys, she took home. They became lifelong friends of hers and her husband's.

"I was quite circumspect, oh, certainly. I'd have them out to lunch and meet them at the train [in Villanova]. One of them, I remember, I met with a horse and buggy because I had to keep the gas. . . . He was very surprised. He had never driven with a horse, ever."

Besides working at the Broad Street canteen, the hostesses and entertainers regularly took their show on the road to military hospitals in the area, most often to Valley Forge General Hospital, where so many of the war's worst burn cases were treated. In fact, the canteen continued in business for a year after the war as a balm for wounded vets.

Hostesses recall that servicemen seldom, if ever, got out of line with them. "It was like a big family," was how Bernice Mann put it.

But Gloria Etting remembers one incident in which a sailor, if not out of line, was certainly an out-and-out liar.

It was late in the war. Horror stories about cruel treatment of POWs had been filtering back from the Pacific, and this sailor indicated he couldn't talk. He wrote on paper, as Etting recalled it, that "the Japs had cut his tongue out."

The actress Celeste Holm was in town, starring in a local production of *Oklahoma*, the big hit musical of the war period. "She took pity on this poor fellow," Etting said, "and danced with him and gave him a ticket for the show.

"I sat next to him at the theater. He didn't say one word. Never spoke. I gave a party after the performance, and he came. Celeste Holm came, too. . . . I gave him a lot to drink. I had vodka and scotch and everything else."

The house had a sofa without a back that rested against a wall. A bit tipsy, the sailor rocked back and hit his head.

"Ouch!"

"Well, that did it," Etting said. The Shore Patrol took the guy away. That was one sailor they never saw again at the canteen.

19 • The Anzio Landing
January 22, 1944

The mission was to stop the Germans in Italy. A bold landing was followed by an order to stop. Historians say it was a bad decision.

January 22, 1994

The invasion began as a great success. A few startled Germans either gave up or were killed. By nightfall, the Americans and British had landed two divisions.

Boldly, the Allies had sneaked behind the German lines in Italy. The place was the seacoast town where legend says the emperor Nero fiddled while Rome burned: Anzio. It was January 22, 1944—50 years ago today.

The invaders next planned to seize two inland highways and capture the hills beyond. A German force facing another Allied army, 60 miles away at Monte Cassino, would be boxed in. The objective was to break a deadlock in the Italian theater. As a bonus, the Allies hoped to capture Rome.

But then U.S. Major General John P. Lucas gave an order that has remained in question for a half-century. He called a halt to wait for reinforcements.

To German Field Marshal Albert Kesselring, it seemed a miracle, a chance to recoup. As Allied troops stood and waited—"We were just hanging around," recalls the Reverend Alex Dryden, an Anzio veteran—German tanks raced to contain the invaders. Soon it was Germans who had captured the highways and hills, and the Allies who were trapped.

The Allied invasion, after its quick start, thus collapsed into a stalemate. For four long months, the two armies remained in each other's grip. On each side, men turned into moles, burrowing into the earth for escape from artillery and air attack.

Anzio turned into a battle unlike any other in World War II, a throwback to the frostbite and the lice, the muck and the misery, of the trenches in the First World War, a time of cold and sickness, of prolonged boredom broken only by moments of terror.

■

Before settling into a stalemate, the two forces first had to test each other's strength. The Allies, in the last days of January, tried to punch through the German fence around them. They failed miserably. The Germans then launched a major counterattack.

Lucas by then had six divisions ashore, three British and three American. Five were at the front. In reserve was the 45th Infantry Division, made up mainly of National Guardsmen from the Southwest. Lucas now threw them onto the spear-point of the German attack.

"Time and again," wrote war historian Carlo D'Este, "the men of the 45th fought back against overwhelming odds."

Nobody in the 45th Division faced longer odds than Second Lieutenant Jack C. Montgomery of Oklahoma on the morning of February 22, two weeks into the German offensive. A platoon leader, he was dozing in his foxhole before light when his sergeant nudged him. Out on the flat, nearly treeless landscape, "the Krauts" were making noises that indicated preparation for an attack. He grabbed an M-1 rifle and stuffed his pockets with hand grenades.

"Cover me," he said.

Montgomery couldn't know it, but he was about to earn the Medal of Honor, his country's highest award for gallantry. The enemy, he would discover, had set up positions about 50 and 100 yards from his platoon. Beyond those, at maybe 300 yards, the Germans occupied a farmhouse.

"I just went up there to kind of make a reconnaissance, to see what there was," Montgomery, 76, recalled at home in Muskogee, Oklahoma. "And I guess I had a chance [to do more]."

Crawling unseen through a gully, he came upon a group of a dozen Germans with four machine guns and a mortar. His Medal of Honor citation says he then "climbed boldly onto a little mound." He recalls only standing up behind a bit of brush. In any case, as the citation records, he "fired his rifle and threw his grenades so accurately that he killed eight of the enemy and captured the remaining four."

Did he realize, he was asked a half-century later, that he was exposing himself to fire?

"I probably did. . . . I didn't think that I was going to get killed. I thought I might get the hell shot out of me, but I didn't think I was going to get killed."

He sent the prisoners to the rear. Returning to his platoon, he discarded the heavy M-1 and picked up a light, rapid-fire carbine and loaded up on more hand grenades. He told his sergeant to radio for artillery fire on the farmhouse. Then, again by himself, he went forward.

At the University of Redlands, in California, the 135-pound Montgomery had played baseball and football. In gridiron terms, he now ran down the right sideline and cut deep across the middle. There, he encountered a second bunch of Germans, armed with two machine guns.

The citation declares: "He attacked this position with such fury that seven of the enemy surrendered to him, and both machine guns were silenced. Three German dead were found in the vicinity later that morning."

This time, Montgomery didn't go back. "I just motioned for [the captured Germans] to go on down the road." He continued toward the farmhouse. It was fully daylight now—gray and cold, "muddy and sloppy."

The artillery crashed down on the house. Suddenly, Germans started streaming out, hands up. Montgomery, "unafraid of treacherous snipers," as the Medal of Honor citation notes, ran to assemble them. By now his platoon of about 20 men—reduced from 40 after months of combat in Italy—was coming up behind him. Unsure whether the house was empty, Montgomery sent a squad around back to look. The Germans had, in fact, all given up.

In all, 32 Germans surrendered that morning to one 26-year-old American. Eleven Germans were dead. Decades later, the events remain as much a mystery to Montgomery as anyone. Maybe it was the sheer audacity of Montgomery's charges. "Maybe," he says, "they were ready to give up. . . . I didn't talk to them, didn't try to talk to them."

That night, Lieutenant Montgomery's war came to an end. A German shell landed just a few feet from him, and shrapnel ripped into an arm, a leg, and his chest. His fingers ran over his body, trying to distinguish between mud and blood. He would either die or go to the hospital, a good soldier's only escapes from perpetual combat.

"I was laying there. I thought, now I can rest."

■

By the end of February, the German counter-offensive had petered out. The Allies clearly weren't going to be pushed back into the sea. But the Germans weren't going anywhere, either. The Anzio battlefield became an exhausted stalemate.

Axis Sally, the English-language German propaganda broadcaster, began calling the Allied beachhead "the largest self-supporting prisoner-of-war camp in the world."

For the rest of the winter and through March and April, neither side was capable of a major attack. Anzio became a long-range artillery duel, a clash in which the Germans had a decided advantage because of their hold on the Alban Hills.

In daylight, the Germans could spot almost anything that moved, and they usually took aim at it. They had 372 artillery pieces, according to historian D'Este, ranging from many "88s" to two massive railway guns, which were hidden in tunnels and rolled out when ready to be fired.

One of the railway guns—nicknamed Anzio Annie by GIs who suffered from it—was such an engineering marvel that a victorious U.S. Army later shipped it home to Aberdeen Proving Ground in Maryland for study. There it sits today, a 230-ton museum piece, capable of firing a quarter-ton shell 31 miles from its 70-foot barrel.

The Allies resorted to living in holes. "Nobody ventured above ground in the daytime," remembers Father Dryden, now a Roman Catholic priest, provincial archivist for the Pallottine Fathers at Pennsauken, New Jersey.

At Anzio, Father Dryden was a machine gunner in the 45th Division's cavalry reconnaissance troop. When his outfit went to the front, the cooks, naturally, started to set up a kitchen. "The Germans right away were able to detect it," he said, "and they killed four or five of our men."

That was the last of the hot meals for a while.

Typically, two or more men shared a "dugout." The sandy soil was easy to dig through. But the water table lay only a few feet down. Trenchfoot, a condition resulting from exposure to the cold and damp, became rampant, just as in World War I.

By day, there was little to do but hunker down. Paperback novels became as useful a currency as silver. Food came in a can. No one bathed, except from his helmet. The lice had a bloodsucking feast. Sleep, when it came at all, was fitful. Men developed the vacant, baggy-eyed look perpetually worn by Willie and Joe, popular "dogface" soldiers created by cartoonist Bill Mauldin in Stars and Stripes.

Most actual fighting during the long period of stalemate took place at night, when a front-line soldier didn't dare light a cigarette for fear of snipers. Father Dryden and his recon troops were ordered to infiltrate German lines and try to take prisoners. He remembers that he learned to say *"Haende hoch!"*—"Hands up!" Getting back through the American lines was often as hazardous in the dark as crossing enemy lines.

The rear echelon, miles back in Anzio and adjacent Nettuno, was-n't much safer from artillery than front-line troops. Both towns were lit-tle by little reduced to rubble. War correspondent Ernie Pyle noted that, at Anzio, "people whose jobs through all the wars of history have been safe ones were as vulnerable as the fighting man. Bakers and type-writer repairmen and clerks were not immune from shells and bombs. Table waiters were in the same boat."

Even hospitals weren't immune.

"If you talk to any of the men that were on Anzio," recalls Ramona Music McCormick, then an Army nurse from Chicago, "they will always tell you that the one place they never wanted to go to was the hospital. Because we were right in the middle. We used to get everything. They'd bomb, shell. They did everything."

McCormick, now of Macungie, Pennsylvania, near Allentown, said she isn't sure the Germans ever actually meant to hit the hospital tents, which were marked with big red crosses. But it happened often enough that the hospital area began to be called Hell's Half Acre. A college nursing graduate, McCormick arrived ashore with the 94th Evacuation Hospital on March 27. The staff included 240 enlisted men, 40 male officers, and 40 female nurses, all officers. They could pack up, move, and set up again in 36 hours.

She worked in the "sawbones department," meaning surgery. The nurses lived four to a tent, a little ways off from the hospital tents. The mud, she recalled, would "suck your boots off." The setting was a lot like *M*A*S*H.* If surgery was going on when an attack fell, there was nothing to do but keep operating. McCormick said she would take a metal basin and place it over an anesthetized patient's head.

Soldiers suffered terribly from the fighting, she said. She recalled one poor man whose jaw had been blown off. "His tongue had nothing to support it, and it was lying on his open neck. . . . This fellow, he want-ed a cigarette so bad. Some of the guys, they lit up a cigarette and blew smoke in his face. That was the best they could do for him. He couldn't inhale. He had nothing."

Altogether at Anzio, 7,000 Allied soldiers were killed. An addi-tional 36,000 were wounded, and 4,000 were hospitalized with sickness.

As time wore on, McCormick said, "I realized I was so full of anger. . . . I wrote a letter to my dad and I said, 'I am so tired of seeing parts of men.' I said, 'I want to see one whole, healthy man.' "

■

The costly stalemate could not go on forever. In May, the Allies attempted a breakout. The plan called for a one-two punch from the

Allied forces in Italy.

At Monte Cassino, the U.S. Fifth Army had faced the German 10th Army across the Gustav Line for months. Difficulty in cracking the line had been the reason for Anzio in the first place. Now another try would be made. The attack began May 11.

The Fifth Army broke through and pushed to link up with the Anzio forces. On May 23, the Anzio forces delivered the second blow, code-named Operation Buffalo. The Germans there "collapsed like a house of cards," D'Este wrote in his book *Fatal Decision: Anzio and the Battle for Rome.*

But then, once more, an American commander called a halt. This time, it was Lieutenant General Mark Clark, Fifth Army commander. His motivation wasn't the caution that had stopped Lucas in January. His critics say it was a big ego. Clark wanted to personally liberate Rome, ancient capital of conquerors.

It had begun to appear that the fast-moving Anglo-American forces in Operation Buffalo would reach Rome before he could, coming up from the Cassino front. He feared that the British would hog the credit. So he halted Buffalo, which had been a stampede, and launched Operation Turtle. True to its name, Turtle inched along. His decision was "one of the most misguided blunders" made by an Allied commander in World War II, D'Este said in an interview from Massachusetts.

Rome was taken, eventually, but at a cost of more lives—including American lives—than should have been necessary.

On June 5, riding in a jeep through a throng of cheering, kissing, flower-throwing, wine-toasting Italians, Clark entered Rome at the head of an American column. The headlines were all his.

For a few hours.

The next day, June 6, 1944, the Allies invaded the Normandy coast of France in the greatest military venture in history. Clark's fleeting Roman triumph was all at once swept aside.

20 • Kids on the Home Front
Through the war years

Even America's kids had jobs to do. And it may have been the last time that Americans were unified.

April 6, 1994

Shortly after Japanese planes bombed Pearl Harbor, plunging the United States into World War II, Ray Doyle of Philadelphia enlisted in his country's defense—as a can-smasher.

It was important work for a five-year-old.

"We collected tin cans and stamped them—crushed 'em, flattened 'em—and piled them up in the local air-raid warden's garage," Doyle, now a professor at nearby West Chester University, recalled. "We were told that we were helping to build weapons."

All over America, from 1941 to 1945, kids contributed to the war effort. They gathered and bundled newspapers. They carried kitchen grease to the butcher shop to be turned into glycerin for gunpowder. They saved their pennies to buy war savings stamps at school.

Today, millions of people in their 50s and 60s remember World War II as a rare and thrilling time, in which children felt as worthy as adults. In many ways, despite the distant threats and fears of a global war, it was a great time to be an American kid. Small ones did what small ones could do. Older ones took on more mature roles. Paul Jepson, as a 15-year-old Senior Scout, was assigned by civil defense officials in Haddonfield, New Jersey, to spot enemy bombers should they fly over town on the way to hitting Delaware River shipyards.

He worked two hours each Sunday night, paired with a graying World War I veteran from the American Legion. Their post was up in the press box at the high school football field. "I remember the code name of the location was Eugene 8. You picked up the telephone and the first thing you said was, 'Eugene 8.' . . . It seemed pretty important at the time."

Jepson, now a retired New Jersey treasury official, also recalls getting off early from school some afternoons to cut hay on South Jersey farms, a task made necessary by a shortage of adult labor. "The farmers would come in their trucks, right in front of the school."

The war effort brought out the best in most folks, children included.

"Kids really did contribute; they got into it a hundred percent," says William M. Tuttle Jr., author of the recent book *Daddy's Gone to War*, a look at childhood on the home front.

Tuttle, a University of Kansas professor, was himself a child of war. "Kids certainly had nightmares about invading Japanese and Germans," he said in an interview. "But they had no doubt who was going to win. . . . They felt they were on the right side, the side that God was on."

"All of us," Tuttle said, "think we are members of a special group, a special generation."

■

In 1942, J.B. Lippincott Co. of Philadelphia published *A War-Time Handbook for Young Americans*, something of an army training manual for small fry.

"Every real American boy and girl," writer Munro Leaf began, "wants to do his or her share to help win this war and help bring it to an end just as soon as we can.

"Any person who tells us that this war isn't any of our business doesn't know what he's talking about. This war is just as much our job as it is that of any grown-up in the country."

It was a message that children everywhere were getting.

No child—and no contribution—would be too small. Even the littlest member of the family could help by being cheerful, Leaf wrote. Fathers and mothers would be working harder than ever, and they'd need a little peace and quiet. "Remember, it only takes one noisy, quarrelsome, grouchy brat to spoil a home."

Making the bed would be a help, too. And picking up clothes. It was all part of the war effort—or so children were told.

Playwright-screenwriter Charles Fuller, author of *A Soldier's Story*, was a preschooler in North Philadelphia during the war. He remembers some moments as almost magical.

During air-raid drills, he said, every apartment in the Weldon Johnson Homes where he lived would turn out its lights. Shades would be closed, and children would be ordered away from the windows. Fuller recalls sneaking to the window and glancing out. All he could see was the flickering white light of the air raid warden's flashlight—"walking down the street as if by itself, suspended in air."

School was the main place where children learned the responsibilities of being patriotic young Americans. Nothing was more patriotic than raising money to pay for tanks, jeeps, and airplanes. This was done through the sale of war bonds—or, in smaller denominations, war stamps. Schools held bond drives.

In 1943, the Hamilton Disston Public School in Northeast Philadelphia became the first elementary school in the area to "buy a bomber," The Evening Bulletin reported. The pupils had sold $150,000 in bonds, going door to door in their Mayfair neighborhood.

Out on the Main Line, six-year-old Judson Vosburg of Strafford Elementary School was lauded in 1944 for having peddled $1,718 in bonds, more than all the rest of the children in that school combined.

Today, Vosburg, a banker living in Berwyn, Pennsylvania, says he can't remember why he was so successful. Maybe it was because the neighborhood was new and there weren't many children. "I didn't have much competition."

He remembers clearly the day that a sailor came to school and told how he had been saved from drowning by a life-jacket filled with milkweed pods—"you know, that fluffy stuff that blows around." The kids in Strafford had been collecting milkweed for life jackets, and they could well imagine that they had saved the sailor's life.

■

Despite memory's warm glow, the war was tough on family life. Right after Pearl Harbor, courthouses all over America witnessed a flood of young couples hurriedly applying for marriage licenses before the men had to go off in uniform. Nine months later came a boom of babies born to absent fathers.

Older brothers and uncles went to war by the millions. After 1943, fathers were drafted. By war's end, 183,850 Philadelphians alone were in the armed forces.

Children whose fathers did stay home were often uprooted. Big-city jobs lured families away from farms and small towns.

"Well more than 30 million people moved from one place to another. Some people moved several times," Tuttle, the professor, said. "It was very hard on kids."

Cities became overcrowded. The housing shortage was "especially pronounced for African Americans," said Karen Anderson, a University of Arizona professor who has studied the wartime family. The cities tried to confine new black residents to old segregated areas.

Mothers, too, left home—to take men's places in mills and shops.

"Most moms who worked were moms of school-age kids," Anderson said. "Mostly, the kids were cared for by other relatives, probably Grandma."

Newspapers and magazines were full of alarming stories about the rise in juvenile delinquency and teen sexual promiscuity. "Victory girl" was the name given to the young "pickups" who gave the soldier boys a memorable sendoff.

Anderson contends that the amount of delinquency was overstated. There may have been some increase in teen sex, but that, too, was mostly talk, she said—a guilt-trip laid on working mothers.

The war stirred up passions of many kinds. Charles Blockson, 7 years old when Pearl Harbor was attacked, remembers that the war taught him early lessons in racial hatred. In Norristown, Pennsylvania, where he lived, there was a store owned by a Japanese American. The owner was tormented terribly, he recalled. "His son committed suicide because of the harassment. They were called 'dirty Japs.' . . . It was the same kind of bigotry that we were used to as African Americans."

■

"The entire student body of the Bartram High School—approximately 3,000 boys and girls—was sworn into the High School Victory Corps this morning . . ."

So read a short article in The Evening Bulletin in November 1942. At that time, Victory Corps units were being formed in nearly every high school. The kids got an arm band and, maybe, a cap.

On their own, high schoolers searched for ways to prove their patriotism. At Dobbins Vocational School in North Philadelphia, they wrapped "writing kits"—note pads and pencils—for soldiers. The girls added a red lipstick kiss to each package.

Children couldn't donate blood, but they could ask adults to do so. At Olney High, two girls canvassed their neighborhood with the pitch: "Would you give your blood to save a serviceman's life?" Fifty people pledged in one night.

At Bristol High in Bucks County, Ralph Ratcliffe's shop class made partitions for the draft board office in town. He was a member of the school Booster Club, which collected scrap metal of all kinds—pots, pans, toasters, bedsprings—for recycling into weapons. "You can't believe what it was like in those days," Ratcliffe, now a retired mailman, recalled. "That was the last time that America was really together."

The war rushed many children into adulthood. One million fewer were in high school than before the war. Some joined the Marines; some worked in the factories, which were starved for labor. In many states, child-labor laws were relaxed.

Thomas Dawson, at 16, came up from a farm on the Eastern Shore to work at the Philadelphia Navy Yard in the summer of 1944. He rented a room on his own.

"I do remember collecting scrap metal and such," said Dawson, now of the city's West Oak Lane section. "But I was of the age and place where I was doing real work."

Perry Triplett, a retired construction inspector from the LaMott section of Cheltenham in Montgomery County, didn't need to join the Victory Corps. Instead, at 15, he lied about his age and joined the Pennsylvania State Guard. The State Guard, he recalls, replaced the Pennsylvania National Guard, which had gone to fight in Europe. He trained Tuesdays and Thursdays, and got paid for it.

"There was a need out there, and it was better than the Boy Scouts. We were two or three steps ahead of the Boy Scouts. You could carry a gun, and you could fire it."

■

There was no American Anne Frank. No kid in America disappeared in the Holocaust. None was bombed, as in London, Dresden, or Hiroshima. None starved, as the thousands did in Leningrad.

Millions of kids died in the Second World War, but they were kids from other lands.

"I remember being very scared as a child, frightened that possibly the Germans or the Japanese would come. I remember that was something that bothered me as a 12-year-old," said Pat Gilbert of West Grove, Chester County.

During the war, she lived nearby, in Upper Darby. Her oldest brother, Dick, was in Europe, and her mother often cooked dinners for foreign sailors docked in Philadelphia. They would tell tales of being torpedoed at sea.

But, somehow, still, the war seemed far away.

"It was a time that I'm glad I lived in," she said. "Even though it was a war, we were able to be children."

One of the stranger domestic results of the war was the creation of the Steagles, a one-season merger of the Philadelphia Eagles and the Pittsburgh Steelers. Jack Hinkle (center) was rejected by the armed forces but played for the Steagles. *Courtesy of Jack Hinkle*

Japan's December 7, 1941, attack on Pearl Harbor cost America much
of its air strength - on the ground. This was the destruction at Wheeler Field.
National Archives

J. Robert Oppenheimer with the remains of the tower on which the test atomic bomb had been mounted. He and Brigadier General Leslie R. Groves covered their boots to avoid picking up radioactive dust. *National Archives*

The Tuskegee Airmen, the famed black combat pilots, are honored in the Pittsburgh Courier (left) and upon completion of training (below). *Jonathan Olson (top); collection of Lemuel Custis (bottom)*

I CAN
I CAN
ALL CAN
HELP

FOR
PREPARED TIN CANS
ONLY

Philadelphia youngsters help the war effort, collecting cans for scrap metal to be turned into weapons. *The Evening Bulletin*

Two days before the start of meat rationing, throngs of Philadelpians mobbed the meat counters at the Lancaster County Farmers Market in Germantown. *Temple Urban Archives*

Japanese Americans, freed from internment camps, load their belongings en route to jobs at Seabrook Farms in New Jersey. *Philadelphia Inquirer*

General Douglas A. MacArthur wades ashore at Lingayen Gulf in the Philippines in January 1945. At his left, wearing pistol, is Roger O. Egeberg, MacArthur's physician and aide. *Associated Press*

After suffering an injury and eight months in German captivity, Army Sergeant John Morelli celebrates V-J Day on Philadelphia's Market Street. *Philadelphia Inquirer*

Howitzers shell German soldiers in 1944, weeks after the Allied invasion, near Carentan, France. *National Archives*

The most famous image of World War II, Joe Rosenthal's classic photo of flag-raising at Iwo Jima. *National Archives*

U.S. troops go ashore at Normandy, France, after the initial D-Day landings. It was the beginning of the end for Nazi Germany. *National Archives*

Italian Americans rejoice in the streets of South Philadelphia
upon learning of the surrender of the Italian government.
Many had felt conflicting loyalties. *Philadelphia Inquirer*

Two-year-old Robert W. Kelly, a flag-waving paper collector, during a salvage drive in Philadelphia. *Temple Urban Archives*

The eight black trolley operators whose promotions by PTC led other workers to shut down the system. The strike was a national embarrassment. *Courtesy of SEPTA*

The Eighth Air Force made some of the earliest strikes against Germany. John Tellefsen (second from right in bottom row) was shot down twice. *U.S. Army Air Forces*

21 • D-Day
June 6, 1944

It was the biggest invasion in history, and both sides knew that the outcome of the landing would likely be the outcome of the war.

June 6, 1994

Gene Cook parachuted behind enemy lines in the dark, breaking his ankle in the tumble. He remembers "a tremendous amount of ground fire—it looked like the Fourth of July."

Leonard Lomell scaled the hundred-foot rock cliff of Pointe du Hoc with rope and grappling hook. He remembers looking back across the English Channel and seeing "ships as far as the eye can see—thousands, literally thousands."

Vincent Bognanni waded in at Omaha Beach, where a thousand men would be cut down before their boots dried. Amid the din of battle he remembers the surreal sound of a popular song, *"Besame Mucho"*—"kiss me a lot" in Spanish—playing from a record on his stranded landing boat. "We're lying there on the sand and getting raked by machine guns, and we're hearing this song. The next thing—boom!—the boat gets hit and blows up."

Each man understood that this was a day history would remember. It was June 6, 1944—50 years ago today. Operation Overlord—the D-Day invasion of the Normandy coast of France—was underway.

It was the start of Western Europe's liberation from four years of Nazi military rule. It opened the long-awaited Second Front in Europe, a means of squeezing Germany between the Soviets in the East and the Anglo-American armies in the West.

With 5,000 ships and boats crossing the channel, 11,000 aerial sorties overhead, and 154,000 men going ashore by foot, parachute, and glider, D-Day was the greatest invasion in history. And the D-Day troops were merely the vanguard of legions that would eventually total 3 million.

Each man had been handed his personal copy of a message from General Dwight D. Eisenhower, supreme commander of the joint U.S., British, and Canadian enterprise: "Soldiers, sailors and airmen of the Allied Expeditionary Forces—You are about to embark on the great crusade. . . . The men of the free world are marching together to victory. I have full confidence in your courage, devotion to duty, skill in battle.

"We will accept nothing less than full victory. Good luck! And let us all beseech the blessings of Almighty God upon this great and noble undertaking."

This clearly was going to be the decisive day of World War II. "The tide has turned," a confident Eisenhower told the troops going in. But if the invasion was repulsed, the Allies would need a year to marshal forces for another try—if, indeed, they dared try at all.

The German commander of the defense of France, Field Marshal Erwin Rommel, also knew the Allied assault would have epic proportions. Rommel had concluded that the Germans could not resist the Allied tide once it was ashore. The war, he had told subordinate commanders, would be won or lost on the beaches.

■

That the Allies planned an invasion was hardly a secret. They had been amassing troops for two years and now had 1,100 encampments in England, a presence that hadn't entirely escaped German notice. The Americans alone had 20 divisions in England; the British, 15; the Canadians, 3. The Free French and Free Poles each had a division that would land sometime after D-Day. Eisenhower joked that the British isle might sink.

The only questions about invasion were where and when.

In response to the Allied buildup, the Germans had installed a 2,400-mile coastal chain of concrete fortifications, artillery emplacements, land mines, trenches, barbed wire, and tank obstacles virtually across Europe, from Norway to the French border with Spain. In France alone, they had stationed 59 divisions and a million men.

The Germans had long figured that the most likely place for an invasion was at Pas de Calais, well to the east of Normandy. There, the Allies would have the shortest jump across the channel—just 21 miles, compared with about 100 at most points in Normandy. But the Allies kept the Wehrmacht guessing by bombing coastal installations across the entire front.

As for timing, the Germans knew that in previous invasions in the Mediterranean, the Allies had come at dawn on a rising tide. It seemed probable they would do so again. That left open only a few days in any month.

The first week of June seemed to fit the Allies' needs. But a severe storm in the first days of June convinced the Germans that invasion was impossible. Rommel felt enough at ease to go home to Germany for his wife Lucie's birthday.

Indeed, the Allies had set the invasion for June 5, then cancelled it because of the weather. The infantry was already aboard ship and steaming for France when the order came to turn back.

But the British had better forecasts for the English Channel than the Germans did. Group Captain J. M. Stagg of the Royal Air Force predicted a pause in the storm from the afternoon of the 5th to the evening of the 6th. After that, more storms.

If Stagg turned out to be wrong and the storm persisted, Overlord could founder. But the next chance to move wouldn't come for two weeks, and then there wouldn't be enough moonlight for the airborne troops. Waiting until July was unthinkable.

"OK," Eisenhower decided early on June 5, "we'll go."

The Germans and British had been at war since September 1939, the Americans since December 1941. The Luftwaffe had bombed London and Coventry; the Allies had leveled Hamburg and Munster. The Kriegsmarine had battled the Royal Navy and U.S. Navy in the Atlantic. The Wehrmacht had collided with Anglo-American armies in North Africa and Italy.

But all those were preliminary bouts. Now came the main event.

William Watmuff remembers a feeling of bravado as swarms of C-47 transports took off close to midnight on June 5 to deliver the parachute jumpers to France.

"We were flying over, everybody's happy, saying, 'We're going to get these Nazis, and what a great surprise it's going to be for them,'" Watmuff, who lives in Drexel Hill, Pennsylvania, in suburban Philadelphia, recalled.

The Allies' plan was fairly simple. They would attack with six infantry divisions—three American, two British, and one Canadian—under the overall command of British Field Marshal Bernard L. Montgomery. The invaders would push inland across a 59-mile front, spread out, and link up. The British hoped to capture the city of Caen, while the Americans aimed toward Cherbourg.

The job of the airborne troops was to prepare the way. They would go in at night, hours ahead of the infantry. By parachute and glider, they would magically appear behind enemy lines, seize key highways and bridges, and sow confusion.

Watmuff was a private first class in the 490th Quartermaster Unit, attached to the Ninth Air Force. He was dropmaster on his plane, meaning it was his job to signal to paratroopers on board when it was time to jump. "I'd stand in the door and, if anybody freezes, I'd kick them out."

All was calm, Watmuff recalls, until the first C-47 Dakotas crossed the French coast, droning noisily at low altitude. "Then all hell started breaking loose."

As anti-aircraft shells exploded around the plane, Watmuff looked back at the paratroopers, faces blackened with grease. He could see fear in their eyes. "They were scared, but at the same time they were gung-ho—very much so."

Knocked around by anti-aircraft bursts, pilots panicked. Airplanes went off-course, and the paratroopers from the American 101st and 82nd Airborne Divisions ended up scattered over the Norman countryside. Men got hung up in trees, landed on roofs, drowned in marshlands.

Somewhere in the sky, 18-year-old Private Cook of the 506th Parachute Infantry Regiment of the 101st Airborne prepared to jump, too.

Outside, the night was illuminated with a dazzling display of ground fire. Cook remembers that the bullets piercing the thin sheet metal of the airplane rattled like pebbles or "peas dropping in a pan."

A group of "pathfinder" parachutists was supposed to have lighted the designated drop zones. But Cook's C-47 was miles off-course. At 1:35 a.m., he recalls, he leaped into blackness.

It was a short drop, "maybe like 275 feet," said Cook, now of King of Prussia, Pennsylvania. "I was in the air less than 20 seconds, I think."

His left ankle snapped when he hit the ground. "You kind of hit before you expect to, and then it's too late." He cut off his chute with his knife and tried to find a hedgerow for cover. There was no one in sight, American or German.

"It was about three hours, I think, before I found anybody," Cook said. "I was just wandering around. . . . Everybody ran into a cow or two. That scared the hell out of us. You hear a sudden noise in the night and you don't know what the sound is."

The 23,000 Allied airborne troops had already accomplished one of their goals: sowing confusion. They were so widely scattered that the Germans couldn't tell where to strike back.

The Allies added to the confusion by dropping hundreds of life-like dummies rigged with firecrackers that went off when they landed.

After the initial waves of paratroopers came gliders, which could deliver fighting men in bunches—and also bring in heavy equipment. They flew too low to be detected by German radar and, without engines, were virtually silent.

Flight Officer Jay Kattelman, now of West Philadelphia, piloted a British-made Horsa glider with two dozen Americans, a jeep, and a howitzer. He remembers that everything seemed to go wrong as soon as he crossed the coastline, towed by a British bomber.

His landing zone was supposed to be lighted, but he couldn't see it. As he swooped into a turn, a blast ripped off the left wing. The canvas-and-wood glider spun in a circle and plunked itself down in a cemetery in the town of Ste.-Mère Église.

The paratroopers poured out of holes in the canvas. Kattelman grabbed his M-1 rifle and ran for a ditch. French citizens were firing at the Americans from their stone houses. "I guess they were afraid not to help the Germans. The invasion looked like such a farce."

For the rest of D-Day, airborne troops fought in scattered actions. On the eastern flank, the British seized and held bridges over the Orne River and Caen Canal. In the west, the Americans captured Ste.-Mère Église, then found themselves fighting off a savage counterattack.

∎

As the paratroopers fought for their lives, the men of the Fourth Infantry Division were still asleep or drowsing aboard ships crossing the channel.

William Clayton of Hatfield, Pennsylvania, remembers that he slept little. There was simply too much to think about, too many airplanes rumbling overhead. "The guys were kind of quiet—you know, not kidding around like they usually do."

Clayton's Third Battalion of the Eighth Infantry Regiment was aboard the USS *Bayfield*, flagship for the assault on Utah Beach—code name for the westernmost of the five invasion beaches. The Americans would tackle Utah and Omaha Beaches; the British, Gold and Sword; the Canadians, Juno.

Well before dawn, Clayton remembers, the Fourth Division was roused and sent to breakfast. "They had sausage and bacon and eggs, but I wouldn't take the sausage, because I was afraid I'd get sick on the boat."

Soon the 26-year-old Clayton was climbing down a cargo net into a 36-foot boat with a ramp in front called an LCVP, which stood for "landing craft, vehicle and personnel." The water was rough, but Group Captain Stagg had been right: The weather had let up.

Unlike the Marines who had assaulted beaches in the Pacific, the

Army soldiers were not all volunteers. And while many Marines were vir-
tual kids—17 or 18—Army soldiers were mostly in their 20s, or older.
"We had guys 38 when we hit the beach," Clayton said. "They said,
'What are we doing here?' "

The division had been in training back home and in England for
two years, far longer than most, but had never been in combat.

At 5 a.m., as the massed landing boats churned toward the shore,
the vast naval armada opened fire on the German defenses. No one
who witnessed that display of firepower ever forgot it.

"Awesome is the word I would use," said Larry Flanagan of East
Norriton, Pennsylvania, who was in the same company as Clayton. "I'll
tell you, the Navy sure earned its keep that day."

About 6:30 a.m., as units began to land on the beaches, Clayton's
boat struck a sandbar. The ramp fell and the men charged out. After a
few steps, the water suddenly got deep.

"One guy, I remember, was up to his eyeglasses," said Clayton.
"We'd lift him up and say, 'Breathe!' He'd take a couple steps and we'd
lift him up again. That's how he got in."

The German fire at Utah Beach wasn't as intense as expected.

The channel current and smoke from the naval bombardment
had thrown the Fourth Division a mile off-course. It was probably a
lucky break. At the spot the division was supposed to land, the Germans
had two heavy guns. Here, they had none.

Brigadier General Theodore Roosevelt Jr., son of the hero of San
Juan Hill, sensibly dismissed any idea of rectifying the mistake by moving down the beach.

"The war," he said, "starts here." He walked up and down with a
walking stick and a pistol, shooing the men inland, up and over the
small sand dunes.

On D-Day, there would be fewer than 250 casualties on Utah
Beach.

■

Casualties would have been a lot higher if Army Rangers hadn't
disabled German artillery guns pointed at Utah. It was "the most dangerous mission on D-Day," said General Omar Bradley, commander of
American ground forces.

The Rangers were the U.S. counterparts of the British
Commandos, men specially trained to carry out surprise raids. Their
job was to attack a high promontory that gave the Germans a commanding view of the channel, plus miles of beach. On it, the Germans
had built huge gun emplacements protected by domed concrete
bunkers with walls several feet thick.

This was Pointe du Hoc. The Allied air forces had bombed it for months. All they appeared to have accomplished was to create a moonscape. The bunkers still stood.

The Rangers would have to climb the sheer face of a cliff that rose a hundred feet above the water. Then they would have to get inside those bunkers and destroy the guns by hand.

Len Lomell, a former Golden Gloves welterweight, was one of 225 men in the Second Ranger Battalion assigned to land at the base of the cliff, shoot up rocket-propelled grappling hooks, and climb to the top.

As a first sergeant in D Company, Lomell was an acting platoon leader. Now a retired lawyer from Toms River, New Jersey, he remembers: "As the ramp went down and I came charging out, I got machine-gunned in the right side. . . . It swung me around, burned the hell out of me. It went right through fat or muscle. It did not hit any bone; it did not hit any organs."

Lomell kept going. Climbing the cliff under fire would have been difficult under any circumstance. But the Rangers were soaked from the channel waves, and the ropes were slippery.

The months of Allied bombardment gave them some help: It had gouged out footholds in the rock. "My guys were up there in 5 to 10 minutes from the time the ramp went down, all 22 of them," Lomell said.

Shell craters then provided some shelter as the Rangers dodged from one hole to another, closer and closer to the artillery. But casualties mounted.

The Germans appeared to be gophers. "We'd go after them and, suddenly, they'd disappear," Lomell said. "Then they'd pop up behind us and shoot us in the back." It turned out that the whole area was a warren of holes and tunnels. Finally, the Rangers reached the gun emplacements. What they found were not gun barrels but decoys.

"I saw a telephone pole sticking out—two of 'em—and nothing inside," Lomell said. "We had fought our way through the Germans—and nothing."

They had expected big German 155s—guns with six-inch bores—on Pointe du Hoc. "We said, 'Well, they've got to be in an alternate position somewhere.' "

The Rangers were also supposed to capture a road that ran behind the point. Lomell's men took off in that direction and set up a roadblock. He and Staff Sergeant Jack E. Kuhn, now a retired police chief of Altoona, Pennsylvania, then broke away from the others and crept down a farm road to see if they could find the guns.

They poked their heads through a hedgerow and, lo and behold, there the guns were—five of them, hidden in an apple orchard. Other Rangers, all under command of Colonel James E. Rudder, had been looking, too. "We just happened to be the lucky ones on the west flank that found them," Lomell said.

Now they took action that would earn Lomell the Distinguished Service Cross and Kuhn the Silver Star. They set out to destroy the guns all on their own.

The only Germans they could see were a ways off to the left, where an officer was addressing them from atop a truck. While Kuhn covered him, Lomell darted to the first gun emplacement. He ducked silently into the bunker. The gun appeared not to have been fired; the rounds of ammunition were stacked in neat rows.

He opened a Thermit grenade—a mixture of finely granulated metal that melted at high heat when exposed to air—and set it on the gun's traversing mechanism. The Thermit grenade was designed for this sort of sabotage. It made no noise or smoke, but acted like solder, fusing the gun parts together. The weapon was effectively destroyed. For good measure, Lomell smashed the sight with the stock of his submachine gun, wrapping it in his jacket to muffle the impact.

He ran to a second gun emplacement and did the same thing. Then, out of Thermit grenades, he retreated to Kuhn's hiding place. The two men ran back to their platoon at the roadblock, gathered more grenades, and returned to the orchard.

Once more, Kuhn stood guard and once more Lomell ran silently to sabotage the artillery. The German soldiers were still off to the left, still having their meeting. One by one, Lomell destroyed the remaining three guns.

He and Kuhn then beat feet out of there. By 8:30 a.m., the pair had accomplished the Rangers' main objective on D-Day: The guns of Pointe du Hoc were out of action.

■

At that hour, Omaha Beach was under siege. Hundreds of bodies lay on the strip of sand. The survivors of the initial assault waves huddled, terrified, against the base of steep bluffs, out of the line of fire. High above them, on the grassy top of the slopes, German guns dominated the scene for miles.

Of the estimated 10,000 American casualties on D-Day, which included 2,900 deaths, nearly one-third occurred at Omaha Beach. The Americans there landed right in the teeth of German strength.

Four decades later, General Bradley would write in his autobiography: "Omaha Beach . . . was a nightmare. Even now it brings pain to recall what happened there on June 6, 1944. I have returned many times to honor the valiant men who died on that beach. They should never be forgotten. Nor should those who lived to carry the day by the slimmest of margins. Every man who set foot on Omaha Beach that day was a hero. . . .

"Omaha Beach remained a bloodbath for too long," he wrote. "Six hours after the landings, we held only 10 yards of beach."

Taking Omaha was the job of the American Fifth Corps, made up of the First Infantry Division, an outfit in the regular Army known as the Big Red One, and the 29th Infantry Division, a National Guard unit from Maryland and Virginia.

The official history of the 29th Division tells the story of Company A of the 116th Regiment, which lost two boats before reaching shore: "The dropping of the ramps seemed to set off the automatic weapons on the bluffs. The boats at once came under a deadly crossfire of machine guns, and the first men attempting to descend the ramps were riddled with bullets. Order was instantly lost, and the long-rehearsed unloading plans were abandoned. Men went over the sides of their boats, plunging into the water to avoid the fire. . . .

"Men who had reached the beach unhurt found their position on the wide, exposed sands more dangerous, and ran back into the water up to their necks for concealment. . . . The men in the water had abandoned their arms and had thrown off their helmets to keep from drowning. The company's combat effectiveness was almost zero and all thought of moving forward was abandoned."

Bernard S. Feinberg, now a retired dentist from Long Branch, New Jersey, was a captain in the medics attached to the 116th Regiment. He arrived on Omaha a little later, but still within the first hour.

"I'll tell you how lucky our boat was. Every boat was opened up by fire except ours. . . . We were able to put our ramp down and walk ashore."

The dead and wounded, he said, were "all over the joint." The unhurt were congregated against the base of the bluff. "We were pinned down for about five or more hours. If the tide were coming in instead of going out, we would have been drowned."

Reinforcements were coming. At midmorning, Private Vincent Bognanni of South Philadelphia was still on his boat out in the channel with the 115th Regiment of the 29th Division, waiting to go in.

He remembers: "Our captain gets us together and he says, 'I've got this communiqué . . . At 6:30 this morning, elements of the 16th Regiment of the First Division and elements of the 116th of the 29th Division landed at Omaha. There were heavy casualties. . . . They're still on the beach and they're being slaughtered.'

"We're thinking, 'Great, and we're next.' "

Once ashore, the 115th joined the huddled masses against the base of the bluffs. But gradually men began to fight their way upward through the sea grass, dirt, and rocks. The more experienced First

Division made headway. So did the Rangers and groups of men from the 116th.

Feinberg recalls seeing Brigadier General Norman Cota, assistant commander of the 29th Division, calmly tapping men on the shoulder: "C'mon, why should we die here? Let's go up there and die."

Retired Army Major General Albert H. Smith, a captain in the First Division on D-Day, remembers that what motivated men to stand up and run into enemy fire was not patriotism, not really.

Men fight, he said, to save face with their buddies—not the Army, not their division, not their regiment, not their battalion, not even their company. They fight for guys in their squad, the ones they eat with, smoke with, get drunk with.

"They certainly don't fight for medals."

Bognanni said that in his sector, designated Dog Red, the soldier with the minesweeper—the man who was supposed to find a clear path up the slope—refused to budge.

"We're arguing with him, and Al Ungerleider, our platoon leader, comes up and says, 'What's going on?'

" 'This guy says he doesn't want to go up; it's suicide.'

"So Ungerleider says, 'If he doesn't do what you tell him, shoot him and take his equipment.'

"We wouldn't have done that, probably. We'd just take his equipment. But he thought better of it, and the next thing you knew he was going up there."

The American Army was back on the offensive.

■

News of the invasion broke like a clap of thunder in the States. Because of time-zone differences, even morning papers were able to get out "extras" on June 6.

Factory whistles blew, cars honked. President Franklin D. Roosevelt came on the radio. He said he had known the previous night, while announcing the fall of Rome to Allied forces, that troops were already crossing the channel in another, greater venture—a success, "thus far." He asked the nation to join him in a prayer:

"Almighty God—our sons, pride of our nation, have this day set upon a mighty endeavor, a struggle to preserve our republic, our religion, and our civilization—and to set free a suffering humanity."

But the enemy is strong, he warned. As Roosevelt spoke, the outcome was still in doubt. The Germans had been slow in reacting to the invasion. Rommel had departed for Germany early that very morning, for June 6 was Lucie's birthday. He was home at 6:30 a.m. when he got word that a fleet was right on the Normandy coast. He got in his car and raced back.

In Rommel's absence, reports of the airborne landings had reached his boss in France, Field Marshal Gerd von Rundstedt, who by 4:30 a.m. had concluded that a landing was underway. Rundstedt telephoned army headquarters in Berlin, requesting Adolf Hitler to release a powerful force of German tanks held in reserve inland.

But Hitler was sound asleep, and no one dared wake him. It wasn't until 4 p.m. that the tanks got orders to move—and by then the British and the Americans were strong enough to hold. All day and evening, the battle went on.

Private Cook, hobbling on his broken ankle, linked up with other lost jumpers in the town of Ravenoville. "When I first went into the town," he said, "I went in very carefully—there were some dead Americans already in the road." For much of the day, he battled the enemy from house to house. That night, the Americans were pushed back to the outskirts of town by Germans who were themselves being driven back from Utah Beach.

Out among the fields and hedgerows behind Pointe du Hoc, Sergeant Lomell and his fellow Rangers were also under siege as D-Day ended. Starting about 10 or 11 p.m., Lomell remembers, the Germans launched three counterattacks against their isolated position. "They had us on the ropes," he said. But the Germans then withdrew.

Above Omaha Beach, the Americans had finally pushed inland. Once they got above the bluffs, Private Bognanni said, the worst was over—for D-Day at least.

"June the 6th was more a day of confusion than anything else. It really was a whirlwind day," Bognanni said. "You really didn't realize how big this whole thing was. You're a little guy in one little area, and all you're thinking is, 'I got to survive this thing.' "

On D-Day, the Allies fell far short of their objectives. The Americans held on to Ste.-Mère Église, but failed to make much headway toward Cherbourg. The British and Canadians, who had hoped to advance 30 miles, couldn't come close to Caen, six miles inland.

The Allies had a foothold; that was all.

But they would not let go.

22 • The Transit Strike
August 1, 1944

Philadelphia became a national embarrassment when white workers shut down the system because eight blacks were promoted.

August 1, 1994

It was a clear day, not particularly hot and sticky for the first of August. William Barber rose from bed, washed, and put on a clean white shirt and tie. He doesn't remember whether he ate. "A lot of times you lose your appetite when you're excited about things."

It was Barber's first day as a trolley operator for the Philadelphia Transportation Co., forerunner of SEPTA. He left the house by the screen door and walked to catch the No. 43 trolley, which ran on Haverford Avenue and would take him to the car barn at 59th and Callowhill Streets.

"Nothing was running," he recalled. Eight or 10 other riders were waiting at the stop. There were rumors of a strike. Barber went back home and turned on the radio.

That was how he learned that all across the city, transit workers had walked off their jobs. They were protesting the promotion of eight African Americans who had passed exams to become trolley operators—the first ever in the City of Brotherly Love. They were striking, Barber realized, because of him.

Thus began the most important Philadelphia story of World War II. It was 50 years ago today, August 1, 1944.

The wildcat walkout shut down a city that boasted that it was the workshop of democracy. A million riders were stranded, unable to get to factories and shipyards. War production in Philadelphia nearly stopped. After three days, President Franklin D. Roosevelt ordered in thousands of troops with rifles and bayonets to get the wheels rolling again. It was close to martial law.

All because eight black men were chosen to run trolleys.

■

Barber was supposed to report to work at 8 a.m. He figured he might as well go. It was a good walk, 22 blocks. Two other men from among the eight new operators joined him as he reached the Callowhill barn. A white crowd was out front.

Across the way, a black crowd had emerged from homes to watch the scene. There was tension in the air, but nothing happening. Barber and the two other men looked at one another.

"We didn't know if we should go over there or not, because we might run into some trouble. 'I don't mind trouble,' I said."

They crossed toward the white crowd and, as Barber recalls, "the Red Sea parted." One striker said, "Go ahead. Go on in. Nobody's going to bother you."

The door was locked; they knocked.

"The superintendent, he came to the door. We told him who we was. 'Come on in.' "

Other black operators had been assigned to other depots. Barber and his companions, Lou Thompson and Rufus Lancaster, were told there'd be no work that day. But they would get their pay. All they had to do was sign a voucher, and then they could go home. The next day, and for days after that, they would repeat the whole routine. Go to work, sign the sheet, go home. Barber and the other new drivers were now spectators to the most dramatic event of their lives.

Mayor Bernard Samuel feared street violence. At 3 p.m. on the first day of the strike at PTC, he ordered bars closed. That night, a ball game at Shibe Park between the Phillies and the Chicago Cubs was cancelled "in order to avoid the dangers incident to the assembly of any large crowd," as The Inquirer put it.

Because of wartime rationing of gasoline and tires, relatively few Philadelphians drove cars. As a symbolic gesture during the strike, the mayor had his chauffeur pick up hitchhikers on Broad Street.

Employers did what they could to get their people into work. The Navy Yard, which employed 45,000 people, brought in buses from other Navy facilities in the East and had them make the rounds of South Philadelphia neighborhoods, where many of its workers lived.

From its first hour, the strike was recognized as a threat to national security. Only the day before, the War Manpower Commission had issued an order requiring employees in 35 industries in Philadelphia and Camden to put in six-day workweeks. This was seven weeks after the

D-Day invasion, and the war was reaching peak intensity. August 1 happened to be the very day that Lieutenant General George S. Patton Jr. took over the Third Army and began his race of tanks across France. The demand for weapons and materiel was never greater.

Army and Navy representatives went to the car barns with company officials and appealed to the pickets' sense of duty. The 6,000 strikers had no elected leaders, only ringleaders. Their union, the Transport Workers Union, opposed the walkout. In fact, the TWU, an affiliate of the liberal Congress of Industrial Organizations, had just won a contract guaranteeing non-discrimination on the basis of race.

Barber remembered: "The union tried to get them to go back to work, but they refused."

Months earlier, the TWU had won an inter-union election for the right to represent the workers. TWU officials said the ringleaders of the walkout were disgruntled bosses of the old union.

A committee of strikers said the issue in the walkout wasn't race; it was a question of seniority. The PTC, they said, planned to grant the eight black men seniority on the basis of time with the company, not time as operators. That meant they would "bump" operators who had been on that job longer but had less time with the company.

Jules Widetsky, a white PTC employee during the war years, remembers that such "bumps" could mean the difference between getting a day's pay and not getting it.

Widetsky said he himself was not on strike. His entire repair shop was shut for vacation. But he was an "extra man" as an operator at one point in his career. He recalled having to report to the car barn each day, and then wait to see whether someone was late or called in sick.

"That was the whole issue," he said. "It was not racial."

Barber said that when the strike ended and he was finally permitted to work, he did, in fact, go to the bottom of the operators' seniority list. "I was an extra man for about six months." He said he thought that was the plan from the start.

The company's attitude was harder to peg. The PTC initially had defied an order from the federal Fair Employment Practices Commission to take on black motormen, as operators also were called. It had surrendered only when the United States threatened to draft its employees, who as "essential" war workers were draft-exempt. Many Philadelphians surmised that the company was secretly rooting for the strikers.

The longer the strike lasted, the more Philadelphia became a national embarrassment.

Sam Lo-Maglio of Rochester, New York, a soldier fighting in France with the 29th Infantry Division, read about the strike in the Army newspaper Stars and Stripes. He wrote home from a foxhole:

"Now that is something!! . . . What is wrong with some people in America? Can't they understand anything? . . . I wonder what Private John Smith or Private John Doe lying along a French road in a pool of his own blood would say if he could speak? . . . They have given their lives, and for what!! You might say for nothing—for that is what it amounts to when you read about what some people are doing at home."

Something had to break, soon.

On the evening of August 3, at the close of the third day of the strike, Roosevelt authorized the Army to take physical control of the transit system's 1,932 streetcars, 564 buses, and 59 trackless trolleys, plus the Broad Street Subway and Market-Frankford Elevated. Suburban trains were not affected by the walkout.

It wasn't clear how the Army planned to get vehicles running. It did not have enough trained men to run a vast system. Major General Philip Hayes, in charge of the Third Service Command, issued a last appeal for the strikers to return to work, once more appealing to patriotism:

"Production of radar equipment, heavy artillery, heavy trucks, incendiary bombs, flame throwers, and many other critical items needed by our fighting men is being held up because of the inability of Philadelphia war workers to get to their factories and workbenches.

"Our chances for speedy victory are being lessened by this tie-up. Our troops—some of them the sons and brothers of Philadelphia transit workers—will have to pay the price in increased casualties unless this threat to production is removed immediately."

If the carrot didn't work, the government had a stick—elimination of draft deferments. In addition, the Justice Department vowed to jail strike leaders under the Smith-Connolly Act, aimed at breaking wartime strikes in essential industries. This time, the pressure was unbearable. The strikers remained publicly defiant one more day, but let it be known privately that they wanted to return to work. One obstacle remained: They feared that as they drove their vehicles through black neighborhoods, they'd be assaulted.

That problem, real or imagined, was something the Army could solve.

On August 5, a Saturday, 5,000 troops from the 102nd Infantry Division—passing through Fort Dix, New Jersey, on their way from Texas to the fighting front in France—were diverted to Philadelphia. Other units, including 3,000 men of the 78th Infantry Division at Camp Pickett, Virginia, were also called in. It was a massive show of force to let everyone know that the government was in charge. The troops' job: to stand guard on public transit.

Maurice Mulhern, now of Glenolden, Pennsylvania, was a native Philadelphian among the troops from Fort Dix. He remembers pitching camp in Philadelphia's Fairmount Park and spending his first night on the El platform at 63rd and Market Streets. The next day, he spent 16 hours riding the No. 13 trolley, which ran back and forth from Center City to Yeadon, Pennsylvania.

The troops were welcomed with open arms by nearly everyone, everywhere. The city seemed vastly relieved that someone—anyone—was in charge. The mood was almost festive.

"When I rode the 13 car, I think I must have had a hundred bags of sandwiches and cakes," Mulhern said. "Every block, somebody gave you lunch. I could have fed the whole division."

■

By Monday, the transit system was back to normal. After a week and a half, the Army pulled up tent stakes and left town. Strike leaders were, indeed, arrested and jailed.

And eight African Americans began work as trolley operators.

It was an important victory for civil rights in an era when many public places in Philadelphia were segregated—if not by law, as in the South, then by social pressure and custom.

Barber, now 75, remembers going into a bar near the old Arena on Market Street after boxing matches there. At first, the bartender would ignore him and his friends. If they stood there long enough, they could get a drink. But as they left, they'd hear the crashing sound of their glasses being broken.

The Unique movie house on Haverford Avenue, he recalls, had a section of 20 or 30 seats in back roped off for black patrons. "Once that was filled, no more blacks could get in there."

The Leader theater, at 41st and Lancaster, restricted African Americans to the balcony, he said. At the Linton's chain restaurant in University City, he said, blacks knew better than to take a seat. Instead, they'd go to the back and order out. "They didn't have to say that to you. You automatically knew it. That's what the policy was."

So it didn't surprise Barber that some white Philadelphians resisted riding with a black motorman.

He remembers one woman, in particular. She got on without looking at him. But when his black hand reached to take her fare, she recoiled. She said, "Oh, no! I don't ride with niggers." Then she threw her coins on the floor and got off.

That was a half-century ago. His children and grandchildren hardly believe the stories, Barber said.

Not too long ago, he was in a poolroom and met a member of the Tuskegee Airmen, the famed World War II pilots who proved to America that black men could fly in combat, the ultimate test of an aviator.

"We was just talking, in general, then somebody told me, 'You know, he's one of them guys that was a pilot.' I told him I was one of the first black guys that went on the trolley."

During the war, African American leaders had talked of waging a Double-V Campaign—victory for freedom abroad, victory for freedom at home.

The motorman and the airman—each was a pioneer, one on the fighting front, one on the home front.

"Yeah, I guess," said Barber. "In a way."

23 • The Liberation of Paris
August 25, 1944

When the Americans marched into Paris, the Germans had already fled. So everybody partied. But the war wasn't over yet. Not hardly.

August 25, 1994

"It felt like the war was over."

That's how Richard W. Baker of Wildwood, New Jersey, remembers the joyous scene in Paris 50 years ago today as Allied troops—French and American—crossed the River Seine to drive out the Germans. The American Fourth Infantry Division, in which Baker was a private, came inching across the bridge, rifles and reflexes at the ready, looking up at windows, scanning rooftops for snipers—prepared to duck into doorways and start shooting.

But here came the ordinary people of the city, a flood of men and women and children, laughing and weeping, holding out wine and cognac. "*Les Americains! Les Americains!*" they shouted. "*Merci! Merci!* Sank you! Sank you!"

Except for scattered holdouts, the Germans had withdrawn before the Allies arrived—first a French division, then the Americans, via different routes.

It was August 25, 1944. Paris was liberated.

The bloody campaign that had begun on the beaches of Normandy 11½ weeks earlier had reached a climax. The capital of France, under the Nazi boot since 1940, was free at last. *Vive la liberté!*

For Baker, who had come ashore on D-Day at Utah Beach, the reception in Paris was beyond imagination. All pretense of a military operation quickly dissolved as the Parisians overwhelmed the Fourth

Division columns of men and vehicles.

"They had glasses. They would put the wine into the glass and you would drink it. And the next person would give you some bread and cheese or some kind of meat. The next person would hug you or kiss you and hand you a flower. Then you'd go a little farther and you'd get a little more booze and some more bread and cheese."

"The kids would keep asking, 'Gum? Gum?' Or, 'Chocolate?' What we had we were passing out. And cigarettes—they wanted cigarettes. We were giving the French cigarettes, and they were giving us wine."

For one glorious moment, the war seemed long ago and far away.

■

General Dwight D. Eisenhower, the Allied commander, had wanted to bypass Paris.

After the American breakout from Normandy on July 25, the Germans had been giving ground rapidly, fighting and retreating, fighting and retreating, back, back toward the Rhine River. Every man whom Eisenhower sent to liberate Paris was one fewer to trap the Germans before they could organize a strong line of defense beyond their own border.

Lieutenant General George Patton's Third Army was now making history with the speed of its drive across open French countryside. Every resource that Eisenhower could muster had to go to Patton, or to his counterpart in the U.S. First Army, Courtney H. Hodges, or to the British and Canadians advancing toward Holland.

"At that moment," Eisenhower wrote in his memoir, *Crusade in Europe,* "we were anxious to save every ounce of fuel and ammunition for combat operations, in order to carry our lines forward to the maximum distance, and I was hopeful of deferring actual capture of the city, unless I received evidence of starvation or distress among its citizens."

The French, however, couldn't wait.

On August 19, the French Resistance came out from hiding and captured the police headquarters. Guerrilla fighters began ambushing German soldiers. Citizens built barricades of furniture and tree trunks across intersections. Gasoline bombs were thrown at German tanks, and paving stones were ripped from streets to be hurled as missiles.

By nightfall, at least 50 Germans were dead. Many more civilians had become casualties.

Major General Dietrich von Choltitz, the German commander, was at a loss what to do. He could see a full-scale uprising developing, but most of the troops that might have been at his disposal already were gone from the city—off fighting the Allies at the front.

He was under personal orders from Adolf Hitler to destroy Paris—

bomb it, burn it—when he could no longer hold it. Yet he was reluctant. He did not want to be remembered as the man who destroyed what might be the world's most beautiful city.

With help from an envoy of neutral Sweden, Raoul Nordling, Choltitz arranged a truce to buy time for most of the rest of his forces to leave the city. Still, street fighting continued.

Charles de Gaulle, leader of the Free French, who weeks earlier had been received in Washington by President Franklin D. Roosevelt as de facto leader of a French government-in-waiting, pleaded with Eisenhower to send aid to the Resistance fighters.

"In this matter," Eisenhower later wrote, "my hand was forced by the action of the Free French forces inside Paris."

The French Second Armored Division of General Jacques Leclerc, the only large French army contingent available, was given the honor of liberating the capital. The division was 120 miles from Paris when it moved out at dawn on August 23.

The advance went slower than planned, with more German resistance than expected. General Omar N. Bradley, in charge of American ground forces, grew impatient with the French and ordered the U.S. Fourth Division to take off for Paris, too.

On the night of August 24, a small contingent of Leclerc's soldiers finally reached the city and drove all the way to the Hotel de Ville—the city hall—before backing off. Next morning, both the Americans and the French entered Paris in force. By lunchtime, after a brief firefight, Leclerc had accepted German surrender from Choltitz.

Baker remembers, "All the bells were ringing."

A draftee from the West Oak Lane section of Philadelphia, he had just turned 23. He was an ammunition bearer in a heavy-weapons company of the 12th Infantry Regiment, and already had been wounded once in battle. He would leave the Army with two Purple Hearts and a Bronze Star for valor.

The partying went on all day while the soldiers struggled to do their jobs. Officers continued to issue orders, and scattered gunfire could still be heard in the city.

That night, the Americans dug their foxholes in the Bois de Vincennes, a wooded park on the southeastern edge of the city. Some were joined by young women of Paris.

"We were supposed to stay in the foxholes because of the snipers that were still in town. They didn't want anybody getting shot. And all the civilians had to be off the streets from dusk until dawn—which happened. There were no civilians out on the street or anything. But when dawn came, all the women were hopping out of the foxholes and going home."

The American troops spent one more night in Paris, during which a few German planes bombed the city—a reminder, Baker thought, that the war really wasn't over.

"Then we were right back in combat."

■

While the Fourth Division was in battle, somebody had to march with French units in the big parade around the Arc de Triomphe and down the Champs Élysées planned for August 29.

Lucky guys, those men of the 28th Infantry Division. Though they had nothing to do with liberating Paris, they got to enjoy the rewards.

"Some said we didn't deserve it," said Harold J. Camisa, who was a staff sergeant in the outfit. "Maybe we didn't."

The soldiers of the 28th wore a dark-red keystone patch on their left arms, signaling the division's history as the Pennsylvania National Guard. But by 1944, they were a blend of men from all over the country. Camisa, then as now, was from Bloomfield, New Jersey.

Eisenhower hadn't wanted to send a U.S. division to parade in Paris, either. But again his hand was forced. De Gaulle, who entered the city on August 26, was by no means secure as leader of the French. The Resistance had been divided into two groups—Gaullists and communists. The communists still hoped to challenge for power.

De Gaulle wanted the parade to celebrate. He also wanted a show of Allied force to cement his authority and keep order. He feared a return to the civil warfare that had swept Paris in the 19th century after the Franco-Prussian War—the last time German troops had occupied the French capital.

Thus did the 28th Division get a taste of the wine and cognac the Fourth had enjoyed.

After his initial resistance to taking a U.S. division out of combat, Eisenhower found a way to justify the move when he realized that the 28th could just as well march through Paris as around it on its way to a new position at the fighting front.

"Because this ceremonial march coincided exactly with the local battle plan," he wrote, "it became possibly the only instance in history of troops marching in parade through the capital of a great country to participate in pitched battle on the same day."

The 28th Division was a relative newcomer to the war. It had landed well after D-Day and hadn't been introduced to combat until July 31. Since then it had been "mopping up," as the Army called it—eliminating pockets of Germans still fighting west of Paris after the bulk of their forces had retreated east.

Late on the evening of August 28, the entire division of 15,000 men was put on canvas-covered trucks and driven all night in a downpour. The morning of parade day, they found themselves in the Bois de Boulogne, a park on the western edge of Paris.

"They told us to shine our shoes and make sure everybody shaves," Camisa said. "I'm looking out through the trees, and over there I see all these tall buildings. I say, 'Hey, what the hell's going on here? Where are we at?' And a guy yells, 'Hey, Camie, we're in Paris.' That's the first time I knew."

Frederick Hooven, of Radnor, Pennsylvania, then a first lieutenant from St. Albans, New York, remembers: "The interesting part of the Bois de Boulogne was that the French Second Armored Division had all their tanks parked in the woods . . . and they had their pup tents pitched alongside their tanks. And there was a Frenchman and a female in every one of them as we passed by."

The rain had stopped and the sun had brightened as the 28th moved out. From side streets, the division flowed onto the tree-lined parade route, where the troops marched 24 abreast, cheered by thousands of people.

After the war, when the United States issued a postage stamp commemorating the Army's contribution to victory in World War II, this was the scene chosen—a photograph of the 28th Division marching in Paris by Peter J. Carroll of the Associated Press. So the Army Air Forces wouldn't feel left out, an artist put in planes overhead.

The column split in two as it went around the Arc de Triomphe, where de Gaulle, Leclerc, Bradley, Hodges, and the division's own commander, Brigadier General Norman D. Cota, awaited on a hastily built reviewing stand. The 56-piece Keystone Band played full blast as the soldiers turned heads and saluted the generals.

"It was a thrill; you felt like the war was all over," Hooven said, expressing a common sentiment. "I mean, here we are—we've got Paris, the Germans are on the run. Little did we know what was to come."

After the division passed the Place de la Concorde, the end of the Champs Élysées, Hooven's 109th Regiment continued down the Rue de Rivoli.

"From that point on," he said, "the parade kept getting shorter, from the rear up, because the French people were grabbing GIs out of the ranks. Of course, the GIs weren't fighting them off."

Camisa, a squad leader in the 112th Regiment, ducked out of the line of march and headed for a café.

"There was all the beautiful French girls in there. We're sitting on their laps, kissing 'em. They're giving us cognac. . . . Man, it was great."

■

The fun was over too fast.

No one could know it, but nine months of war were yet to come before Allied victory in Europe. Still ahead for the men of both the Fourth Division and the 28th Division lay the brutal combat of the Hurtgen Forest and the Battle of the Bulge.

Camisa, who became a prisoner at the Bulge, remembered these events one recent sunny day as he sat on a park bench in his home town. Across the way, a bronze plaque at city hall contained the names of 177 Bloomfield men killed in World War II.

In front of him lay a photo of the 28th Division march in Paris.

"Most of these fellows," he said, "became casualties. Believe me, most of them."

24 • Conscientious Objectors
Through the war years

This was the "good war," and it was a difficult time to be a pacifist, even in Philadelphia with its deep Quaker history.

October 7, 1994

Like thousands of men later on, Richard Collins Baker of Haverford, Pennsylvania, wanted nothing to do with the Army. It was the autumn of 1941. America wasn't yet at war, but dark clouds loomed. Baker, 32, had received an induction notice from his draft board. A Quaker pacifist, he believed that war was killing and that killing was indefensible. So he refused to cooperate in any way. Wouldn't even fill out the draft board's questionnaire. They threatened him with jail. He persisted. Eventually, he was tried and convicted as a draft resister. His sentencing was scheduled for a Monday—December 8, 1941.

Bad timing.

When Baker arrived in Philadelphia federal court that morning, the city was ablaze with war hysteria. The day before, the Japanese had attacked Pearl Harbor. Soldiers stood guard on the Delaware River Bridge in case the Japanese tried to cross from New Jersey. Sandbags were stacked on sidewalks to protect store windows from imagined bomb blasts. Men by the hundreds were rushing to enlist.

Now Baker stood to face the bench.

"This man," said Judge J. Cullen Ganey, "has refused to obey the laws of his country and has attempted to set himself above the will of the majority. He therefore is not entitled to any leniency as far as I can see."

Baker, 84 now, remembers that the prosecutor had told him privately, "You ought to be shot."

Ganey wasn't that harsh. He sentenced Baker to prison.

"A year and a day," said the judge.

■

It wasn't easy to object to the "good war." It put a man far out of step with the vast majority of Americans, who felt that stopping Hitler and Mussolini and Tojo was worth the cost of killing.

A few men didn't care how the majority felt. Among them were many Philadelphia-area Quakers, together with Mennonites, Brethren, and Jehovah's Witnesses. They felt called to duty by a higher authority: their conscience, which told them that war was immoral, no matter how evil the foe.

Of the 34 million men who registered for the draft in World War II, only 72,354 applied for exemption as conscientious objectors—COs, as they called themselves.

That was just a fraction of one percent of the draft-eligible population—at first, men aged 20 to 36; later, men 18 to 37. During the unpopular Vietnam War, five percent would apply as COs.

Before Pearl Harbor, most Americans opposed U.S. involvement in what was then a European and Asian war. Pearl Harbor brought the war home.

"This wasn't a war, presumably, where you could make a very good moral case to stay out," said Albert Keim, a scholar on conscientious objectors who teaches at Eastern Mennonite College in Harrisonburg, Virginia.

Yet most who opposed the draft never saw a jail cell. For that to happen, a man practically had to thumb his nose at the draft—as Baker did.

There was a legal way out: Civilian Public Service (CPS).

Most conscientious objectors were willing to accept conscription into CPS work camps. Some planted trees in national forests. Others became smoke-jumpers, fighting fires out West. Some helped build the Skyline Drive and Blue Ridge Parkway in the mountains of Appalachia. Some worked at the psychiatric hospital at Byberry in Northeast Philadelphia.

But Baker couldn't bring himself to do any of those things. It would still have been helping the war effort, he thought. It simply freed other men to go off and fight.

"That's just playing into the hands of the people who are doing the killing. It was just an addition to the war nonsense," Baker, now living in Boyertown, Berks County, Pennsylvania, said recently.

One-third of the men who started out wanting to be COs eventually went into the Army in noncombatant roles, such as in the Medical

Corps. Another one-third failed the military physical, so the Army didn't end up wanting them anyway. Only about 12,000 entered Civilian Public Service. Baker was one of 6,116 who ended up going to jail. Most of these were Jehovah's Witnesses, who refused to apply for CO status or to perform civilian service.

After serving nine months in the federal prison in Danbury, Connecticut, Baker was paroled. Though educated at Haverford College in entomology, the study of insects, he later worked mostly as a farmhand. Though he received an unsolicited pardon from President Harry S. Truman after the war, he wasn't sure he wanted it—not from a government that had sent millions of men to war.

"I didn't know whether that was an insult or not. If they didn't have any more sense than to [go to war], it showed they didn't have the sense to discriminate between a person who deserved to be pardoned and one who didn't."

■

Civilian Public Service was a new idea, born out of the bad experience of World War I.

In the First World War, Quakers, Mennonites, and Brethren—members of what have been called the historic peace churches—had two options: the Army or jail.

Those who chose the Army came face to face with sergeants who often called them cowards. Many were permitted to work in kitchens, weed flowers, or do other noncombatant work. But if they refused to do that, they were often dumped into camp jails, where they were fed bread and water in solitary confinement.

Their churches did little to help guide them. "The burden was left on the young men. The elders let them down," said Keim, author of the book *The CPS Story.*

After the war, Keim said, both the government and the peace churches decided to find a better way. The churches drafted a proposal that eventually worked its way into the Selective Service Act of 1940.

Section 5(g) read: "Nothing contained in this act shall be construed to require any person to be subject to combatant training and service in the land and naval forces of the United States who, by reason of religious training and belief, is conscientiously opposed to participation in war in any form."

The emphasis was on religious training and belief. Pointedly left out was anyone who objected to war on philosophical grounds, such as poet Robert Lowell, who refused to serve "as a matter of principle" and was sentenced to a year and a day in jail.

Major General Lewis B. Hershey, head of Selective Service, was

willing to go along with the peace churches. But he didn't want just anyone to be able to claim he was a CO. An applicant had to write a statement of his beliefs and show they came from his upbringing in the
church.

Hershey also didn't want the public relations problem of seeming
to coddle conscientious objectors, Keim said. So he got the peace
churches to agree to finance the Civilian Public Service camps themselves and run them under loose government supervision.

Of 11,996 men who enrolled in Civilian Public Service, 5,830 were
Mennonites (including Amish) and 1,353 were Brethren (many from
old German settlements in Lancaster County and elsewhere in
Pennsylvania). Many of the 951 Quakers also were from Pennsylvania,
as well as New Jersey and Delaware, all of which had been settled by
Quakers as far back as the 1680s.

For Francis G. Brown of Downingtown, Pennsylvania, civilian service was ideal—a way to do something for his country without laying
aside his beliefs. He spent the winter of 1941-42 at Buck Creek Camp in
North Carolina, surveying the boundary of the Blue Ridge Parkway. He
later was posted as a firefighter near Lake Tahoe in California, then
worked as a milk tester in Connecticut.

"We were under conscription. We weren't free . . . but it was a great
experience," said Brown, who is now retired as general secretary of the
Philadelphia Yearly Meeting of the Religious Society of Friends, a
Quaker governing body.

A 1939 graduate of Haverford College, a Quaker school, he could
trace his Quaker roots in Pennsylvania back to the time of William
Penn, himself a Quaker.

When Brown received his draft notice, he sat down and wrote:

"My beliefs upon which I claim exemption stem from a very fun-
damental religious principle. . . . There is something of God in every
man. I believe that all men, viewed thus, are infinitely precious and are
therefore entitled to be treated with respect. . . . War submerges the
good in men and brings out fear, hate, and distrust. . . . Therefore, I
affirm that all war, whether offensive or defensive, is morally wrong."

Downingtown was a Quaker community, and he had no trouble
convincing his draft board of his sincerity. The hardest thing, he
remembers, was not joining in a common cause. His own brother had
decided that defeating fascism was reason enough to join the Navy.

Brown believed in the injunction not to resist evil, but to overcome evil with good. Today, at age 77, he's frankly not sure how Hitler
could have been stopped short of war. But that doesn't mean he's
changed his mind about war.

"World War II ended Hitlerism, but it was just the beginning of
Stalinism. . . . While it destroyed Hitler, it unleashed this guy that was

equally brutal—Joseph Stalin. So even the supporters of World War II can't claim—as people said about World War I—that it made the world safe for democracy."

■

The Jehovah's Witnesses of the world took a position of neutrality in World War II. "What we do in this country is the same as we do around the world," said Bob Dailey of Kennedale, Texas, who went to prison as a draft resister. "A lot of religions have different positions in different countries, but ours is the same worldwide."

In Hitler's Germany, a Witness was required to wear a purple triangle stitched to his lapel, just as a Jew had to wear a yellow star. Thousands of Witnesses perished in the Nazi death camps.

In America, Witnesses incurred public wrath by refusing to salute the flag. In Texas, three schoolchildren were arrested for refusing to say the Pledge of Allegiance. It took a 6-3 ruling of the U.S. Supreme Court to affirm their right not to do so.

Draft-eligible Witnesses who resisted induction into the military were often sentenced to longer terms in jail than other offenders—five years, in Dailey's case. Partly, that resulted from prejudice against Witnesses in many communities. Partly, too, it resulted from the Witnesses' refusal as a group to cooperate with the government. By cooperating, Quakers, Mennonites, and Brethren had been able to tailor a program to their liking.

Rather than seek exemption from the draft as conscientious objectors, Witnesses asked out as ministers. Every member considered himself a minister of Jesus, one who worked many hours each week spreading the faith, often door to door. But their definition of minister wasn't the same as the government's, which understood a minister as a person set apart.

Bob Dailey got his draft notice when he was 18. He was then living in Dallas with his sister. Their parents were Presbyterians from Ohio, but his sister had started going to a Kingdom Hall of Jehovah's Witnesses. He began going, too. Soon, he recalls, he had entered the Pioneer Ministry, to which he was expected to devote 100 hours per month. "I was just doing odd jobs to support myself."

He told this to the judge at his trial. He also told the story of Jesus's arrest in Matthew 26, of how a disciple had reached for his sword and had cut off a man's ear. "Then Jesus said to him, 'Put your sword back into its place; for all who take the sword will perish by the sword.' "

The judge wasn't impressed.

"He just told me I was yellow—that I had a yellow streak down my back a mile long, something like that."

Dailey was sent to the federal prison in Texarkana, Texas, where he met other Jehovah's Witnesses.

"Some of the prisoners there would look down on us because we wouldn't fight for the country—men who had broken all kinds of laws. I thought that was amusing."

On Christmas Eve 1992, a half-century later, President George Bush included Dailey's name on a list of pardons. Next day, the papers all focused on the pardon for former Defense Secretary Caspar W. Weinberger, who had been caught up in the Iran-contra scandal. Dailey didn't hear about his own pardon until a friend said: "Hey, you're in the paper."

He was glad someone finally had recognized that he never belonged in jail.

"I was never a coward."

25 • MacArthur Returns
October 20, 1944

The legendary general erased the humiliation of fleeing the Philippines by wading ashore and declaring, "I have returned."

October 20, 1994

As he stood on the deck of the cruiser USS *Nashville*, waiting to set foot again in the Philippines, General Douglas A. MacArthur must have thought back to that humiliating day 31 months earlier when he had sneaked away from the islands on a torpedo boat, leaving behind his 12,000 men to be killed or captured by advancing Japanese forces.

There had been whispers that MacArthur was chicken. Nothing could be farther from the truth. This was the same man who had charged into machine-gun fire in World War I, who twice had been recommended for the Medal of Honor. He had fled from Corregidor, yes—but only after he was ordered to do so by President Franklin D. Roosevelt, who insisted he save himself to fight another day.

"I shall return," MacArthur had vowed.

Now, at last, the time had come. It was October 20, 1944, 50 years ago today. The reconquest of the Philippines—U.S. colonial territory since the Spanish-American War but lost to the Japanese soon after Pearl Harbor—had begun.

It was a big step on the road to conquering Japan itself, made even bigger by the fact that on October 23, 1944, three days later, it ignited the largest naval battle in history—the final destruction of the Japanese navy at Leyte Gulf.

America—and MacArthur—had come back with a massive force: the Sixth Army, 200,000 men strong, backed by the Fifth Air Force and two Navy fleets with a combined 35 aircraft carriers, 12 battleships, 28 cruisers, and 150 destroyers.

In the Normandy invasion four months before, the United States had landed five divisions on D-Day. MacArthur would land six on Day 1 at Leyte Island in the central Philippines.

The first waves of troops already had pushed inland against light resistance when a small landing boat sidled up to the bigger *Nashville* and took MacArthur aboard. The boat plowed toward the beach, the ramp clanged down, and MacArthur sloshed ashore, his khakis wet up to his knees. Roger O. Egeberg, his personal physician and aide-de-camp, recalls that MacArthur's hands shook later as he stood in a warm drizzle to deliver a radio address from the sand. "This meant so much to him," Egeberg remembered. "He felt so badly about having been driven out of the Philippines."

MacArthur's voice was a growl as he began: "People of the Philippines, I have returned. By the grace of almighty God, our forces stand again on Philippine soil. . . ."

■

He was the Army's most famous figure in the long fight against Japan in World War II, a brilliant and charismatic leader who often seemed larger than life. Back in Washington in 1942, the Joint Chiefs of Staff had wished that MacArthur had said, "We shall return," not "I." But that wasn't his way.

Son of a Civil War hero, first in his class at West Point, commander of the famed Rainbow Division in World War I, Douglas MacArthur once had been the Army chief of staff himself. General Dwight D. Eisenhower, now the supreme Allied commander in Europe, had been his aide.

MacArthur stood over six feet tall and bore the profile of a Roman emperor. Usually dressed in a plain uniform with an open collar, he crowned his head with a massive peaked cap that became his trademark, along with dark glasses and a gigantic corncob pipe.

Egeberg, who became close to MacArthur, says he was really a shy man, who in a struggle to overcome shyness could appear to be haughty.

"He was proud," Egeberg said, "but not arrogant."

MacArthur was 61 when Pearl Harbor came along. His forces in the Philippines were attacked on the same day, December 7, 1941, and he, too, had been caught off-guard.

He had expected help from the States, but little came, and by April of 1942 the Japanese had captured nearly 70,000 U.S. and Filipino troops on Bataan. Remnants of his forces had retreated to the fortress of Corregidor, where they held out until May, two months after

MacArthur's departure.

Criticism of MacArthur was more whispered than spoken. The newspapers painted him as a hero, though the reporters who covered him were divided in their opinions, says historian D. Clayton James, author of the three-volume biography *The Years of MacArthur*.

"Some of them thought he was a hero," James said in an interview, "and some thought he was a flamboyant egomaniac."

President Roosevelt gave him the Medal of Honor—an award for valor above and beyond the call of duty that he probably had deserved in World War I but that now seemed a gesture. General George C. Marshall, MacArthur's only boss in the Army, hoped that the medal would "offset any propaganda by the enemy directed against his leaving his command."

Starting from Australia, MacArthur fought back toward the Philippines for almost three years. His New Guinea campaign showed genius. Instead of hitting Japanese strongholds head-on, he leapfrogged from weak spot to weak spot.

Though he deserved a lot of credit, he sought even more. He began issuing questionable casualty reports. After the war, a historian added up his reports and found he had claimed to have killed 150,000 to 200,000 Japanese, while losing only 122 Americans.

The Marines grew infuriated that, seemingly every time they led the assault on some Japanese-held island in the central Pacific, suffering awful casualties, MacArthur would issue a press release bragging about how low his losses were.

The Marines and the Navy waged one war against Japan in the central Pacific, while MacArthur waged another in the southwest Pacific. Each theater of operations demanded the lion's share of resources.

In July 1944, Roosevelt traveled to Pearl Harbor to mediate. Admiral Chester W. Nimitz, commander in the central Pacific, proposed bypassing the Philippines and, instead, attacking Taiwan, then called Formosa. It was closer to Japan.

MacArthur wanted the Philippines for a host of military reasons. But he also saw it as a matter of loyalty to the Filipino people, who had been loyal to the United States during the fighting in Bataan and Corregidor, and who were now organizing guerrilla bands to aid in the promised return of the Americans.

"And besides," said Egeberg, "he loved the Filipino people and they loved him. There was an emotion."

MacArthur won the debate. Formosa was called off; the invasion of the Philippines would go ahead.

■

Aboard ship the night before the landing, MacArthur wrote out his speech. It would take him only two minutes to read, but he worked on it and worked on it. Egeberg, now 90, a retired assistant U.S. health secretary living in Washington, says that his one claim to fame was getting MacArthur to change a line. The general, Egeberg remembered, was planning to say something about a return to normalcy in the Philippines after the Japanese were driven out. He wrote, ". . . and the tinkle of the laughter of little children shall again be heard in the streets."

"And I said, 'You can't use that.' We were sitting in his cabin, and he said, 'Why?' And he looked hurt.

"I said, 'That's an old cliché.' I'm not sure it was, but it had the ring of an old cliché."

MacArthur glared. He looked at another of his aides, Larry Lehrbus, for his reaction, but Lehrbus's face was blank. He started to defend the line, then stopped, and crossed it out.

There was no question that MacArthur would say the words "I have returned." To this day, Egeberg defends the general's decision to use "I" in his original promise.

"He knew what they were saying about him—that he should have said 'we.' . . . But he knew the Orient. He knew that if he said, 'The United States is coming back,' the Filipinos wouldn't feel that was very much. If he said, 'Our army will return,' maybe they would have thought that was more.

"But when MacArthur said, 'I shall return,' the Filipinos believed him. And that's why he said it at the time. That was the Oriental way. You believed the man—if you had some evidence to believe him— rather than the country or the army."

The next day, Egeberg rode with MacArthur in the landing boat. His boss had given him a job: to stick close to Philippines President Sergio Osmena, who was going to address his people on radio after MacArthur finished. Osmena was a civilian, the general told him, and might panic if he heard gunfire at close range.

The famous scene of MacArthur trudging through the water came about by accident, according to D. Clayton James, the biographer. MacArthur's critics later charged that it was staged; it wasn't. MacArthur had changed into a fresh uniform and had no intention of getting wet. But the boat was too big to ride up onto the beach. So he had to walk.

Later, when MacArthur saw the photograph, which ran in virtually every newspaper back home, he recognized the heroic image it conveyed. From that time on, whenever he went ashore in an invasion, he had his boat stop short so he could wade.

As MacArthur hit Red Beach at Leyte—one of the bigger of about

7,100 islands in the Philippine archipelago—he was only a few hours behind the 24th Infantry Division, which by then was battling scattered Japanese forces a few hundred yards inland.

MacArthur and Osmena sat around for an hour before the microphone was ready to beam their messages back to a ship and, from there, to the world. By then, light rain had started.

As his physician, Egeberg knew that MacArthur had a hand tremor, which appeared "only in times of great tension or emotion." It appeared now.

"Rally to me!" he told the Filipinos. "Let the indomitable spirit of Bataan and Corregidor live on. As the lines of battle roll forward to bring you within the zone of operation, rise and strike! . . . For your homes and hearth, strike! In the name of your sacred dead, strike! . . . Let no heart be faint. Let every arm be steeled. . . ."

■

The Japanese, too, had expected MacArthur to return. They hoped to win the battle for the Philippines not so much on land as at sea. Their plan called for the Imperial Navy to ambush MacArthur's troop transports near the beach.

Admiral Soemu Toyoda dispatched three fleets to the Philippines, two from Japan to the north and one from Borneo to the south. After three years of war, they were all Japan had left. Toyoda was willing to risk everything to defend the Philippines, which were vital to Japan's defense of its home islands.

MacArthur's ultimate fate was thus in the hands of the U.S. Navy. If the Navy couldn't keep his supply line open, his troops would be wiped out, sooner or later.

After his radio address, MacArthur returned to the *Nashville*. Troops were still pouring ashore a couple of days later when Vice Admiral Thomas C. Kinkaid, commander of the Seventh Fleet, told him that the *Nashville* would have to sail off to fight.

The general, Egeberg recalls, was so excited that he momentarily forgot himself. "That'll be great," he said. He had never witnessed a naval battle.

"Kinkaid," Egeberg said, "straightened himself out and said: 'No, I'm afraid you can't go. . . . I have to go there, but I shall not take the risk of you coming.'

"MacArthur looked disappointed, but then he said, 'You're right.' "

Of the two U.S. fleets on hand, Kinkaid's was weaker. The bigger Third Fleet, with 16 fast carriers and six new battleships, was led by the daring Admiral William F. "Bull" Halsey Jr.

Knowing Halsey's reputation for taking risks, Toyoda laid a trap for him that nearly turned the battle in Japan's favor.

Leyte Gulf was really a series of battles over four days and hundreds of miles. It opened on October 23 when U.S. submarines spotted the Borneo fleet. The subs sank two cruisers and damaged a third, but the fleet kept going. The next day, Halsey's carrier planes attacked the same Japanese force and sank a battleship. But still the Japanese kept going, heading toward the San Bernardino Strait north of Leyte.

Meantime, Kinkaid's forces discovered and destroyed one of the two fleets sent from Japan. Sailing far south of Leyte, this Japanese force had attempted to swing back north through the Surigao Strait. There, it ran right into Kinkaid's battleships.

But the battle wasn't over yet. Now came Toyoda's trap. The bait was the second fleet sent from Japan, a weak force of old aircraft carriers without aircraft. It was a decoy to lure Halsey away from the San Bernardino Strait. And it worked. When the Borneo fleet sailed through the strait, ready to descend on MacArthur, only Kinkaid's small escort carriers stood in the way.

Fred DiSipio, now 68, a record promoter from Cherry Hill, New Jersey, remembers looking out from the USS *Gambier Bay* and seeing nothing but pagoda-shaped masts on the northern horizon.

"Halsey took the bait and left us stranded," DiSipio said. "The battle boiled down to six small carriers, five destroyer-escorts—and the whole damn Japanese fleet."

Shells began raining on Taffy 3, the name of the small carrier group. Rear Admiral Clifton Sprague ordered his ships to lay down smokescreens, launch planes, and hope for the best. They fought valiantly for as long as they could.

The *Gambier Bay* soon was afire and sinking.

DiSipio spent five nights clinging to pieces of the shattered flight deck. Two of 18 men on his makeshift raft were eaten by sharks, he said, and others died of exposure. Some grew mad and swam off to "imaginary islands."

But it wasn't in vain. Having swept aside Taffy 3, the Japanese suddenly had turned away. Maybe they were confused. Maybe they knew reinforcements were on the way. Whatever, they'd had enough. In total, the Battle of Leyte Gulf cost the Japanese four carriers, three battleships, 16 cruisers, and 14 destroyers, along with as many as 10,000 sailors.

DiSipio remains understandably proud of the Navy.

"If it wasn't for what we did," DiSipio says, "they would have gone right up to the beach and blasted every ship—every troop ship, every hospital ship. And they would have massacred every soldier."

■

On land, the real battle didn't begin for almost a month. The Japanese, taken by surprise, took that long to recover well enough to put up stiff resistance.

Like the fight between the Germans and the Americans in far-off Italy, the battle for the Philippines would end only when the war as a whole came to a close. MacArthur kept pushing the Japanese into smaller and smaller corners, but they never really gave up.

After Leyte Gulf, the Imperial Navy was a non-factor in the war. "That really put the finish to the Japanese fleet," said military historian Stanley L. Falk, author of the book *Decision at Leyte.*

In the end, the recapture of the Philippines was America's costliest campaign in the war against Japan. More than 13,700 Americans were killed and 48,000 wounded. Japanese casualties over nine months of fighting numbered in the hundreds of thousands.

Over the whole scene stood the towering figure of MacArthur— symbolized by the powerful image of his wading ashore at Leyte.

Even that became a source of controversy. After landing at Red Beach with the 24th Division, he tried to show solidarity with each of his other divisions by going ashore at their beaches on each of the next three days. Soldiers who saw the second- or third-day landings didn't believe that he had ever landed on the first day. Rumor spread that the famous October 20 photograph was a fake.

"I don't know of any commander in World War II who had been bashed as badly as MacArthur has—and I think quite undeservedly," said James, his biographer. "He had flaws, but he was brilliant." MacArthur died in 1964.

To the ordinary soldier, the general was a walking legend, like him or hate him.

Edward H. Voves Jr. of Northeast Philadelphia, an Army Air Forces corporal in the Philippines, remembers the thrill of merely catching sight of MacArthur on an airfield tarmac.

"He had that pipe and everything," Voves recalled. "Some people used to say, 'I think he sleeps with it.' "

26 • The Growler
November 8, 1944

It was the end of the line for the Growler, a sub in the Pacific war. Its demise was preceded by many triumphs—and a legendary quote.

November 8, 1994

"Take her down."

Those words, shouted by Commander Howard W. Gilmore as he lay wounded on the bridge of his embattled submarine, became legendary in the American Navy of World War II.

The scene was the South Pacific. The submarine USS *Growler* had just collided with a Japanese gunboat, and now machine-gun fire poured down onto the *Growler*'s deck. Two crewmen were already dead. The whole submarine was in peril each second that it remained on the surface. Gilmore was more concerned with the sub's fate than his own.

Lieutenant Arnold F. Schade, the *Growler*'s second in command, was standing under the hatch. He clearly heard the order: Take her down. But he hesitated. Bullets continued to rip through the hull. Schade climbed up the ladder and looked around, but couldn't see Gilmore. He dropped back down and pulled the hatch lid closed. An order was an order.

"OK, dive."

Gilmore's sacrifice, for which he was posthumously awarded the Medal of Honor, spared the *Growler* to fight another day. In fact, it fought for 19 more months. But it was still an ill-fated boat. Fifty years ago today, on November 8, 1944, the *Growler* was reported missing at sea—one of 52 U.S. submarines lost in World War II.

The Navy never discovered what happened to the *Growler*, or to many other lost submarines. One in every seven Americans who went to sea in a sub never came back—3,600 men, in all.

But the toll taken *by* U.S. submarines was awesome. Assigned mostly to the fight in the Pacific, they accounted for 55 percent of all Japanese ships destroyed in the war. They sank 201 enemy warships, including a battleship, eight aircraft carriers, 11 cruisers, 43 destroyers—and 23 Japanese submarines. Even more important, in a war against an island nation, was the toll of enemy merchant ships—1,113 vessels laden with foodstuffs, petroleum, and raw material for weapons, all things that Japan could not do without, all sent to the sea bottom.

This is the story of one of those submarines. This is the story of the USS *Growler*.

■

Then designated merely as SS-215, the 312-foot-long boat that became the *Growler* was launched November 2, 1941, at Electric Boat Co. in Groton, Connecticut, which a half-century later is still turning out submarines. Five weeks after the launching, when the Japanese attacked Pearl Harbor, the SS-215 was still in need of a crew.

Arnie Schade, now a retired three-star admiral living in Port Charlotte, Florida, was aboard an older-model sub in the Cape Cod Canal when the news came that the United States was at war. He remembers his first thought: "Get me on a submarine that's going to the Pacific!"

A 1933 graduate of the Naval Academy, he was assigned to the new boat at Groton as executive officer—XO.

In command was Gilmore, who had started in the Navy as an ordinary seaman, but then had qualified by competitive examination for Annapolis. Soon to be 40, he was advancing on middle age. Out of uniform, he might have been mistaken for a junior high school principal, except for the knife scars under his collar, left by thugs in Panama years earlier. His first wife had died of illness. His second wife was unconscious from a fall when he left for the Pacific.

Like all submarines then joining the fleet, the new boat was given the name of an aquatic creature—in this case a largemouth black bass. Almost no one aboard had ever heard of a growler.

Arriving at Pearl Harbor in the dead of night in June 1942, the *Growler* was quickly sent on the first of its 11 war patrols. Typically, a patrol would last two months. The sub would return for repairs; the men, for a two-week rest. Then they'd go back out again, rearmed with 24 torpedoes, each 18 feet long and weighing a ton.

From the git-go, Gilmore and the *Growler* had moxie. Sent out alone to attack a Japanese fleet invading the Aleutian Islands off Alaska, they managed to sink or damage three warships with a single barrage of torpedoes, an almost unheard-of feat.

Schade recalls: "It was the day before the 4th of July, and we went in about 5 o'clock in the morning, pitch dark. And there were these three Jap destroyers, right at the entrance to the Bay of Kiska. We went right in and picked them off—one, two, three."

Riding back into Pearl Harbor later, the *Growler* flew three small rising-sun flags from its periscope as symbols of its victories. Before its own death, the *Growler* would sink nine warships and 15 merchant ships in 2½ years at war.

"Believe me," said Schade, "when we were ordered back into Pearl Harbor, we were just about as cocky as any crew could be." As soon as their feet hit the ground, Schade remembered, the crew members set off "to raise hell."

"In the middle of the night sometime, I was dragged out of my bunk and told that my crew was getting a little disorderly and would I do something about it. I was still just the exec, but I was running the crew. So I went around and I rounded 'em all up, 'Get the hell back into your room and shut up and stop drinking!' "

Admiral Chester W. Nimitz, commander of the entire Pacific Fleet, sent word he wanted to see Schade at 8 that morning.

"He called me in promptly and said: 'I know you've got a good crew. They're well-trained. But they're a little obstreperous. You've got to do something about it.'

" 'By the way,' " Schade said Nimitz added, with only a hint of a grin, " 'what were they drinking? Sterno?' "

It was on the *Growler*'s fourth war patrol, starting New Year's Day 1943, that disaster first struck. Sailing from Brisbane, Australia, the boat set a course for dangerous hunting ground—the Japanese shipping lanes off Rabaul, New Guinea. On January 16, the crew spied a cargo ship and destroyed it with two torpedoes.

Then came the early morning of February 7, three weeks later. Off in the blackness an hour after midnight, the lookouts could see the outline of a Japanese ship, a gunboat of some kind. Gilmore commanded, "Battle stations—surface," and sounded the alarm: Bong! Bong! Bong!

They would attack from the surface. As captain, Gilmore's job was to remain above deck on the bridge. Schade, the No. 2 officer, would stand below in the conning tower at the controls. Two lookouts and three other crewmen were posted up top with Gilmore.

The *Growler* started to close in, maneuvering for a shooting position. But suddenly it was right on top of the gunboat. The Japanese ship must have turned in the dark and started for the *Growler.*

"Too close!" said Schade. The torpedoes, he recalls, needed at least 300 yards of running room.

"I said, 'We've got to back off somehow.' And that's when Gilmore made the decision to go in and ram it. He rang up full power and started charging on in."

The pointed bow of the submarine ripped into the side of the gunboat. From the deck of the Japanese ship, heavy machine guns opened fire at point-blank range.

The Medal of Honor citation reads: "Gilmore calmly gave the order, 'Clear the bridge!' and refusing safety for himself, remained on deck while his men preceded him below. Struck down by the fusillade of bullets and having done his utmost against the enemy in his final living moments, Commander Gilmore gave his last order: . . . 'Take her down.' "

Three of the men up top came spilling down through the hatch. All were wounded. "Blood and guts all over the place," Schade remembered.

One lookout and the officer of the deck never made it below. No one really knows exactly what happened to Gilmore. Schade saw no one at all when he looked out of the hatch in the dark.

After diving, the *Growler* lay low for a half-hour, at least. The Japanese gunboat could be heard groaning and collapsing in on itself as it gradually sank from the damage done in the collision.

The submarine wasn't in much better shape. Sea water gushed through dozens of bullet holes, each the size of a fist. The bow was twisted to port like a dislocated finger. Getting the *Growler* back to Brisbane was an exploit in itself.

Schade was now captain. While still at sea, he led a memorial service for Gilmore and the two other dead shipmates.

"We just assembled the crew and said some kind words—regretted that we lost him [Gilmore] and said we were going to carry on in his memory. What else can you say?"

■

On a submarine, for every moment of racing adrenalin and a pumping heart, there was a long stretch of boredom.

Bob Link of Absecon, New Jersey, says he was drawn to submarines by a movie of the '30s: *Hell Below*, a romanticized story of a sub in World War I that he saw at age 10 at the Royal Theater in Atlantic City.

The reality of life aboard a submarine was different from Hollywood's version, although Link says he would not have traded it for any other form of military service.

Men were "on watch" for four hours, then off for eight, in a cycle round the clock, day after day, week after week. A man might get a chance to stand lookout on deck. He might even gain permission, when the sea was calm, to go up top for a cigarette. Otherwise, he had to remain below in the dim lamplight.

The *Growler* would run all night on the surface, using diesel motors. During the day, it would lurk below, running on batteries. Living conditions were better than on the German U-boats that marauded against Allied shipping in the Atlantic. Unlike the Germans, the Americans had air-conditioning and flush toilets.

"We were all kids—18, 19, 20 years old," Link said. "The officers were only 10 years older than us, most of them."

The Submarine Service was an all-volunteer outfit; a man could quit anytime he wanted. Candidates were chosen for physical fitness, intelligence, and the ability to get along with others in cramped quarters for weeks at a time.

Link joined the *Growler* for its sixth, seventh, and eighth patrols. Two of the three submarines he served on during the war were sunk. "I lost a lot of friends," he said.

He was a "motor mac," a motor machinist third-class. His job was to help maintain the compressors, the blowers—the operating equipment. When the *Growler* was in combat while submerged, he reported to the control room to man headphones. When the boat was on top, he manned the deck gun.

Off watch, he was free to do what he wanted as long as he stayed out of the way. He loved to read. Very quickly, he had read all of the books in the *Growler*'s small library. He then began to bum books from the six officers aboard.

Link liked lookout duty, for the Pacific was often spectacularly beautiful. "There would be days," he said, "when the ocean was just like glass."

On those days, a lookout might spot a shark's fin cutting a wake through the water. "That could be scary as hell for a split-second, because you're looking for periscopes. You don't want another submarine firing at you."

Once, Link recalled, the *Growler* surfaced from underneath a school of fish. Sailors opened the hatch and saw their supper flashing and flopping on deck.

But the ocean could also be fierce. Link remembers running into a typhoon. "I think that was the most terrified I was at any time in the Navy—up on the bridge of a submarine during a typhoon. Your arms ache from hanging on."

Yet there was no experience like sitting helpless in a submarine while the enemy dropped depth charges on you. These were canisters of TNT rigged to go off at set depths. A sub would dive 300 feet or more and try to hide while a destroyer overhead zeroed in for a kill.

"There are guys who had far worse depth-chargings than I had, and there were some who probably had less," Link said. "All I know is, I heard them as loud and as close as I want to. It's like being in a 50-gallon drum with it closed—and somebody beating on it with a heavy hammer, if you can imagine that. It rings in your ears, the close ones."

■

Harry J. Messick watched the *Growler* hobble into port after its battle with the Japanese gunboat in February 1943. Word of Gilmore's dying command, "Take her down," spread rapidly, he recalls.

Australian repair crews had much work to do on the *Growler*, including giving it a new nose. They cut a steel plate in the shape of a kangaroo and welded it to the bow. From then on, the *Growler* had a nickname: the Kangaroo Express.

Schade, the new commander, asked Lieutenant Messick to come aboard. "He wanted me to replace the ensign who had been killed." Though 35 years old and a 17-year veteran of the Submarine Service, Messick had never been on a sub in combat. He would be with the *Growler* for six war patrols, including one of its most dramatic.

The time was September 1944. Early that year, American submarines had adopted a new tactic: They had begun to hunt in wolf packs as the German U-boats had always done. The *Growler* was the lead boat in a pack that included the USS *Sealion* and USS *Pampanito*.

Schade, by then, had moved on. The *Growler* was under command of T.B. "Ben" Oakley, and the pack was nicknamed "Ben's Busters." It was sent to search for convoys in the Formosa Straits. On September 12, at 1:10 in the morning, it found one.

Messick, now of Wynnewood, Pennsylvania, a onetime enlisted man who eventually rose to the rank of captain in the Navy, was the "plotting officer" for the *Growler*. "As soon as we picked up a convoy, I plotted its course. They would always have a 'zig' plan. I'd say, 'They're on course so-and-so; their speed is 12 knots.' "

At 1:50 a.m., Oakley was all set to fire from the surface at a large merchant ship. Suddenly, a Japanese destroyer appeared from nowhere, bearing down on the *Growler* at top speed.

Oakley ordered: "Clear the bridge." Remaining alone, he called for the *Growler* to swing around and fire torpedoes from all six of its bow tubes. This was the risky "down-the-throat" shot depicted later in many a Hollywood movie dealing with submarine action in World War II.

One of the torpedoes—maybe two, maybe more—hit home. The *Growler* turned away at full speed to avoid the concussion from the blast. But the sub and the destroyer continued on a collision course, carried by their momentum. Both turned, hard, and ended up side by side.

At that moment, Messick scrambled to the bridge. He looked over and saw the Japanese ship in flames.

"She's right alongside of us and she's going down. The Jap sailors are in white uniforms, clamoring over the gun turrets. . . . We found out the next day that the paint on our bridge had been seared from the intense heat" of the destroyer.

The same morning, the *Growler* had sunk another Japanese destroyer. The crew was exultant as it headed back to Pearl Harbor. But Messick, lying in his bunk, had a premonition of doom.

He dreamed he was drowning. He was under water, kicking, kicking to get to the surface, to get some air. He awoke pumping his legs. He had never before had such a dream. But he had it again a day or so later. He kept the dreams to himself. As it turned out, Messick was not on the next patrol. He was going to get a boat of his own; he was going to be a captain. He stood at the dock and waved with clenched hands over his head—Good luck!—as the *Growler* sailed for the last time.

He knew a man who tracked the subs. Periodically, he'd ask:

"How's the *Growler* doing?"

"He'd say, 'Well, she's doing fine.'

"Then, one day, he was evasive. I said, 'Hey, wait a minute. What's the score?' He said, 'Well, she's missing and feared lost. She got into a convoy, and they haven't heard from her since.' "

The *Growler* was gone.

27 • The Battle of the Bulge
December 16, 1944

It was a surprise German attack, and a big one. Winning cost the United States 80,000 casualties. But the Nazis were all but finished.

December 16, 1994

It was getting close to Christmas. In two days, snow would begin falling in the Ardennes forest. The war seemed to be settling down for a long winter's nap.

Six months had passed since the D-Day invasion of Normandy. The United States and its allies now had three million soldiers on the Continent. They had pushed the Germans out of France and all the way to their own border. Both sides lay back, exhausted.

Stanley Wojtusik, a 19-year-old private first class from South Philadelphia, had been on the front lines barely a week. His rookie 106th Infantry Division had just arrived from England, and had been sent to a quiet area to adjust to the war slowly.

"They told us, 'This is a recreational rest area. The only combat experience you'll have is going out on patrol and picking up Germans who want to surrender.'"

It wasn't yet dawn on December 16, 1944, 50 years ago today. With total surprise, the German army was about to launch its greatest offensive against the Western Allies in World War II. The battle would take its name from the huge indentation the Germans would make in the American lines before being propelled back in six weeks of desperate fighting. This was the Battle of the Bulge, the bloodiest conflict in American history, in which 19,000 GIs were killed, 20,000 captured, and 40,000 wounded.

When the Germans came, they came straight at Stan Wojtusik, standing guard duty in a long wool coat with his M-1 rifle near the

German border town of Auw.

The offensive opened with an artillery barrage. Thousands of heavy shells crashed through the fir branches of the thick forest. Then came a lull. Wojtusik peered into a foggy mist. From deep in the dark woods came a squeaking, clanking sound.

"The tanks were coming! I could see six or eight of them. Following the tanks were the German infantry. They were dressed in white. It was very frightening; they looked ghostly out there.

"We froze in that situation. There was no way in hell we were going to stop those tanks with M-1 rifles."

■

A surprise winter offensive was Hitler's idea. His generals had thought that it was too risky—that if it failed, it would speed Germany's ultimate defeat. In the end, the generals were right. But the Führer was a gambler, and he held the dice.

From all over Germany, Hitler had corralled old men and teenagers and put them in uniform. From practically nothing, he had scraped together 25 new infantry divisions.

From Russia, Hitler had recalled his best tank divisions. Together with SS troops, these *panzer* divisions led the assault along a 60-mile front in Belgium and Luxembourg, equipped with a terrifying new monster: the King Tiger tank. The initial thrust pitted about 200,000 Germans against only 83,000 Americans.

The objective was the Belgian coastal city of Antwerp. If Hitler could seize Antwerp, he would rob the Allies of a major port. He hoped to split the British forces in Holland from U.S. forces to the south and break the Anglo-American alliance. He might eat up the British army whole, as he very nearly had in 1940 at Dunkirk.

To get to Antwerp, he needed a *blitzkrieg*—a lightning war—to overpower the Americans who stood in the way. The avenue of attack was the same route that German armies had taken in World War I and again at the outset of World War II.

For some reason, American generals clung to the disproved notion that the Ardennes forest was impassable. They had placed just six divisions along the front: inexperienced ones such as the 106th, and tired, battered ones such as the 28th Infantry, which had suffered horrific casualties in the autumn fighting in the Hurtgen forest.

They weren't ready for the blow when it came.

■

A piece of shrapnel from an exploding artillery shell stung

Wojtusik in the face. He felt a burning sensation, but the deep cold helped numb the pain. He was in Company G of the 422nd Regiment. That morning, men fought in knots of four or five. There was no coordination, no direction. Every soldier battled for his own life.

"What we did was allow the tanks to go by us," said Wojtusik, now of Philadelphia's Holmesburg section. "We had no way of stopping them anyway. Then we tried to pick off their infantry."

He considered himself a decent shot, but he had never fired at a man. He now aimed at a German, 12 to 15 yards away. "I know I hit him in the side of the face," he said softly. "I saw him completely spin around in front of me."

Wojtusik, who eventually would become a prisoner, remembers that "everyone was shooting at the same time. . . . You didn't know if you hit [a German] or if it was the guy next to you."

The Germans were achieving a breakthrough. Panic reigned among the Americans. Telephone lines were down. The Germans had sent in 150 English-speaking commandos in American uniforms. The commandos turned directional signs on the roads, dynamited bridges—did anything they could to magnify confusion.

General Omar N. Bradley, commander of all U.S. troops, had no idea of the scope of the onslaught. Four hours into the battle, he felt enough at ease to leave the Luxembourg capital for a long drive to Paris, where he was to have dinner with Supreme Allied Commander Dwight D. Eisenhower.

That evening, General Eisenhower knew a little more. Bradley continued not to worry. But Eisenhower sensed the danger and decided to send the Seventh and 10th Armored Divisions as reinforcements. The next day, he ordered in two airborne divisions: the 82nd and 101st.

"Eisenhower was the first senior general to recognize what was happening for what it was—an attack on the largest scale possible, a scale larger than the Allies thought the Germans were capable of," said Temple University Professor Russell F. Weigley, a leading historian of the war in Europe.

Eisenhower's quick response may have saved the Americans in the long run. But it would take time for reinforcements to have an impact. It would be too late for the 106th Division. On December 19, two surrounded regiments—about 8,000 men—would surrender. It was the largest American capitulation in the war against Germany.

On the northern shoulder of the American lines, the Second and 99th Infantry Divisions were putting up a good fight on Elsenborn Ridge. On the south, the Fourth Infantry and Ninth Armored were hanging on. But in the middle, the bulge grew wider and wider.

In the 28th Division sector, the men in rear areas—clerks, cooks, members of the division band—were ordered to take up rifles. That division, too, was crumbling.

Norman Plumb of Erie, Pennsylvania, was a trombone player. He had marched with the band in Paris when the French capital was liberated. Now he was in the Belgian town of Wiltz. It was a couple of days into the battle. The 28th was pulling back, what was left of it. A soldier came around in a jeep, handing out hand grenades. "You better take these." Plumb climbed on a truck. There was panic in men's eyes. At a German roadblock, a machine gun opened up, but the truck broke through. There was no place to run. Down the road, an 88mm gun took aim at the truck.

"When that 88 hit that truck, it must have flown six or eight feet in the air—and me with it," Plumb said. The driver and others were killed. Plumb somehow survived, only to be taken prisoner a moment later. "Here stands a German lieutenant with a Luger. He shoves it in my ribs and says something in German. And that was it."

■

Three German armies were pushing across the front. On the north, the 12th SS Panzer Regiment broke through the Losheim Gap and raced for the town of Malmedy. The regiment had fought in the brutal winters of the Russian Front. Its leader was a fanatical Nazi, Lieutenant Colonel Joachim Peiper.

Hitler had handed down an edict: no mercy. The attack, he had said, should be preceded by "a wave of terror and fright." Soldiers should display "no human inhibitions." Peiper took the edict seriously. He left murdered civilians and POWs everywhere in his wake.

On December 17, Peiper's regiment was advancing on a crossroads two miles from Malmedy. Headed toward the same junction from the opposite direction was a truck convoy of Battery B of the U.S. 285th Field Artillery Observation Battalion.

Ted Paluch, a draftee from Philadelphia's Kensington section, was riding in the back of a canvas-covered truck, oblivious to the coming danger. "They fired and stopped the convoy along this road. We got out and went in the ditch. They were on the other side of the road. I never saw so many tracer bullets in my life going back and forth."

The Americans had no heavy weapons. A King Tiger rumbled up the road and slowly lowered its heavy barrel toward the ditch. The signal was pretty clear: Give up, or die. The Americans stood up and raised their hands. "They marched us up to the intersection, and they searched us," Paluch recalled. "They took my cigarettes, watch. I had an extra pair of socks in my pocket; they took that. Anything of value that you had."

What happened next was the worst atrocity committed against

American troops by the Germans in the Second World War. It became known as the Malmedy Massacre.

"They put us in a field; we were in a group," Paluch recalled. "They had a barbed-wire fence around us."

The German column began to move on down the road. As the German tanks and other vehicles passed the field, men opened fire on the GIs.

"Every tank and halftrack that passed was firing into us," Paluch said. "They were on the move, and they didn't have that many men. I guess they couldn't leave some men to guard us."

A few Germans came up close and shot the moaning wounded. Paluch had been hit in a hand, but made no sound. He lay still on the ground, playing dead among the heaps of Americans, probably 80 at least. A long time elapsed. Then someone got up and ran. Paluch and others followed. A half-dozen SS troops came out of a house and fired at the fleeing GIs. One chased Paluch down the road and shot at him. Paluch dived into a hedge and again played dead. The German looked at him—and went back to the crossroads.

After dark, Paluch escaped back to American lines.

■

As the Seventh Armored Division rolled forward to aid in the defense of St. Vith, a strategically important town in Belgium, it practically had to fight its way through a retreating tide of bedraggled, glassy-eyed, defeated American soldiers.

Philip Burnham of Villanova, Pennsylvania, remembered: "They'd come over the hill, some without any weapons, some with no overcoats, some with no helmets. They would go up to my men and say, 'You better get the hell out of here while you still can.' "

The Seventh Armored had been 60 miles north of St. Vith when it got orders to move at 5:30 p.m. on December 16. The first of its tanks reached the town the next day, in time to check the German advance. This was the fruit of Eisenhower's quick, decisive response.

Whoever controlled St. Vith controlled roads going in six directions. The Seventh Armored and remnants of other outfits formed a horseshoe around the town and dug in. The struggle for St. Vith raged for nearly a week. On December 18, at dusk, Captain Burnham was summoned to a strategy session next to a tank. The 48th Armored Infantry Battalion was going to try to drive the enemy out of Poteau, a village west of town. A major held a map. He pointed to a sunken railroad running through Poteau. Burnham and his 250 men of A Company were to seize the track bed and hold it.

Burnham went out to scout their objective. It was so dark he had to feel for the tracks. But no Germans were around. The company quietly took up position behind the steep bank.

"One of the non-coms came running over and said, 'There's a German machine gun over there.' I said, 'Don't tell me about it. Throw some grenades over there before they know we're here.' " With that, the fight was on. The Germans came crouching across an open field. Somewhere behind them, Burnham remembered, buildings were afire. The light silhouetted the Germans, making them easy targets. "They were in pretty close. We could hear the wounded out there who had got hit."

Toward midnight, Burnham was digging a foxhole. Suddenly, a mortar shell exploded. A shard of shrapnel hit an artery in his left leg. For him, the war was over. Medics took him to the rear, where a surgeon saved his life but had to cut off the shattered leg. A lieutenant took over A Company and continued the fight. Burnham found out later that his men had held out.

All around, similar small struggles were taking place. "The Battle of the Bulge," said Professor Weigley, "underlined the stubbornness of ordinary American soldiers."

On December 22, the Seventh Armored finally had to withdraw from St. Vith. U.S. forces wouldn't regain the town until mid-January. But the fight put up by ordinary GIs had slowed the German momentum and helped revive American morale.

■

Thirty miles south of St. Vith sits the Belgian town of Bastogne, the other vital road junction in the Ardennes. There, the 101st Airborne Division—sent in to fortify the American lines—found itself encircled and besieged by German forces.

The Germans offered the Americans a chance to surrender. Brigadier General Anthony C. McAuliffe sent a one-word reply—"Nuts!" The retort made him a hero to millions when it got into the papers back home.

The 101st was supposed to have been resting after months of combat. On D-Day, the Screaming Eagles had parachuted and flown gliders into Normandy. Later on, they had landed in Holland. At Thanksgiving, they had been granted a break.

"I had a pass to go to Reims and Paris," William Guarnere of South Philadelphia remembered. So when the order came to get into trucks and move out once more, "we were PO'd to no end," said Guarnere, a former staff sergeant who also lost a leg at the Bulge.

The division's 11,000 men began to reach Bastogne late on December 18, and they took up positions in the woods on the perimeter of town. Enemy forces were soon all around them. The Germans tried again and again to punch through but couldn't.

With roads cut off, the 101st and elements of other divisions inside Bastogne soon were short of food and ammunition. Snow began, and opaque skies prevented airdrops. The artillery shelling was constant.

"As soon as we got there, the Germans started probing," Guarnere said. "They were trying to find a weak spot. . . . It's like a fighter—jabbing and then backing off, jabbing. . . . There wasn't a tree standing. The shells just ripped them apart."

Guarnere had grown used to killing. "You step on a bug and you kill him, that's all. Not that you want to. It was survival, period. Survival of the fittest."

The job of airborne troops was to jump behind enemy lines, so they were used to being surrounded. But they had never experienced cold like this. They didn't have enough clothing, and they got what sleep they could in foxholes dug with folding shovels from their backpacks. Fingers, toes, and noses were prey to frostbite.

Relief had to come soon, or the defenders of Bastogne were doomed.

■

Enter George S. Patton Jr.

On December 19, Eisenhower had met with top British and American generals in Verdun, France. He had come to see the German offensive as not just a peril but also an opportunity. The German army had come out in the open. With luck, it could be crushed.

Lieutenant General Patton, in command of the Third Army, which was fighting in the Saar region, well south of the Ardennes, was at the meeting. Eisenhower asked him how soon he could counterattack.

"On December 22," Patton replied. "With three divisions."

Around the table, other generals scoffed. Patton was known to brag. He couldn't possibly disengage from the battle he was in, wheel 90 degrees to his left, travel 100 miles in deep snow—and go straight into combat. Not in three days.

Yet Patton did it.

At the head of his thrust was the Fourth Armored Division. Its goal: to rescue "the battling bastards of Bastogne," as men of the 101st had begun calling themselves.

John Gatusky Sr. of Ashley, Pennsylvania, was in the lead group, the 37th Tank Battalion. He rode in a tank with the battalion commander, Lieutenant Colonel Creighton W. Abrams, who a generation later would command U.S. forces in Vietnam.

With a cigar in his teeth, Abrams told his men: "This may provide us an opportunity to seriously defeat a major part of the German army and shorten the war." Abrams pushed the battalion round the clock. "We'd drive 50 minutes and then take a 10-minute break, 'cause it was a long haul," Gatusky recalled. He was the gunner in Abrams' tank, Thunderbolt. If anything got in the way, the battalion blasted it off the road. As the Third Army moved north, U.S. Army engineers worked to keep the bridges open. Leon Bass of Yardley was a sergeant in the 183rd Battalion of Combat Engineers, a segregated unit of African Americans. Under fire, the battalion rebuilt a bridge the Germans had destroyed at Martelange.

"We had to put up a structure that was strong enough to withstand all the trucks and armament that had to cross it so they could get up to Bastogne."

Eventually, he said, he saw Patton himself cross the bridge. "That was quite an experience to see this gentleman that had become a legend in his own time."

On December 23, the weather broke. Heavy B-17 bombers were suddenly in the sky, bombing the German forces. Cargo planes dropped supplies and weapons for the Bastogne defenders. On Christmas Eve, McAuliffe sent greetings to his men: "What's merry about all this, you ask? Just this: We have stopped cold everything that has been thrown at us from the north, east, south, and west."

Meantime, the Fourth Armored pressed on. On December 26, it broke into Bastogne. Gatusky doesn't remember a great deal of celebration, only relief all around.

The Battle of the Bulge was far from over, but now the Americans were the ones on the offensive.

■

It took until January 28 for the Americans, with British help, to erase the bulge. In all, 600,000 American soldiers and airmen fought in the Battle of the Bulge, far more than in any other battle ever. Though the United States had close to 80,000 casualties, the Germans had 100,000, or more. The Americans could replace their losses; the Germans could not. After the first 10 days or so, the drama was basically gone from the epic battle. It became a grinding, grueling war of attrition, one the numerically superior Allies were certain to win. The Battle of the Bulge wrung the last full measure of strength from the German army in Western Europe.

In the end, the battle did shorten the war. In the end, said Temple's Weigley, "the Germans did us a big favor."

28 • Iwo Jima
February 19, 1945

The words "Iwo Jima" recall the most memorable photograph of the war. They are also synonymous with a gruesome battle.

February 19, 1995

The Japanese could have no hope of holding Iwo Jima against the overwhelming might of U.S. forces in the late months of World War II. All they could do was make Marines pay in blood for every inch of that stinking, sulfurous sandpile.

And that they did.

The struggle for Iwo Jima, which began 50 years ago today, on February 19, 1945, became "the most savage and the most costly battle in the history of the Marine Corps," in the words of Lieutenant General Holland M. Smith, who led the Marines in the Pacific.

The 21,000 Japanese soldiers hidden in caves on the volcanic island sacrificed themselves almost to the last man to inflict maximum casualties on the invaders. In 36 days of ceaseless fighting, 6,821 Americans were killed and 20,000 wounded.

It was a supreme test of whether the United States was willing to pay the heavy price required to defeat a foe who preferred extinction to surrender. The affirmative answer is forever symbolized by a photograph of six Americans raising their flag in triumph atop Iwo Jima's Mount Suribachi.

To Joe Rosenthal, the civilian Associated Press photographer who took the famous picture, the Marines' determination and valor were "something that you almost couldn't believe. The island was amazingly well prepared for defense."

To William DiIenno Sr., a Marine who spent 27 days on Iwo Jima, it was an experience of hell on earth. He used a flamethrower to burn the Japanese out of their holes. Later, when he had to be evacuated with a bullet-shattered leg, it was almost a relief. "I didn't think I could ever get out of there."

To Thomas M. McPhatter, it was a rare chance for an African American Marine of that segregated era to prove himself in combat. But he wouldn't volunteer to go back. He remembers explosions everywhere, all the time. "It was just like a country fair," he says. "Only it was murder."

■

Army B-24 bombers had pounded the island for months. Navy ships had tried to soften it up with their big guns. But no amount of long-range fire was going to wrest Iwo Jima from the Japanese. That would take individual Marines.

Iwo Jima was the Japanese term for "sulfur island." The lumpy landscape was covered in black volcanic ash and wouldn't grow much of anything. Mount Suribachi, a 556-foot volcano, was its highest point. The location of Iwo Jima, 660 miles southeast of Tokyo, made it vital to Japanese air defenses. They had built three airfields on the small island, which measured $5\frac{1}{2}$ miles long by $2\frac{1}{2}$ miles wide.

The Americans, in turn, sought the island as an aerial fighter base to support bombing raids against Japanese cities. It also could serve as an emergency landing place for wounded B-29 bombers headed back to the distant Mariana Islands after raids on Japan.

The battle scenario seemed to promise a one-sided affair. The U.S. Navy by that stage of the war had all but wiped out the Japanese fleet, which otherwise might have aided the Japanese troops on land. And Japanese air power had been reduced almost to suicidal kamikaze attacks against U.S. ships. In ground forces, the 65,000 Marines outnumbered the Japanese by more than three to one.

But on Iwo Jima, the Japanese were led by a very capable general, Tadamichi Kuribayashi. He had learned hard lessons from the bitter Japanese defeats on Guadalcanal, Tarawa, Peleliu, and other Pacific islands.

This time, the Japanese would not waste themselves in frontal *banzai* charges. They would not even attempt to stop the Marines at the shore line. Instead, they would lie back in their caves and fortified bunkers until the Marines were on the beach. Then they would start blasting from their 800 artillery, mortar, and machine-gun positions. Almost never would they show themselves.

It was a kind of warfare that led to savagery on both sides.

The many miles of Japanese tunnels dug in the island seemed like gopher holes to the Marines. The enemy began to seem inhuman. Marines went into battle with "Rodent Exterminator" stenciled on their helmets.

The Japanese, in turn, dehumanized the Americans as "devils" and "beasts."

Colonel Joseph H. Alexander, a retired Marine officer and historian, said that by 1945 the fighting in the Pacific had become a war of revenge and annihilation—a get-even for Pearl Harbor, Bataan, Corregidor, and other U.S. humiliations early in the war.

"The Marines I talk to bear an almost frightening hatred still today for the Japanese," Alexander said in an interview.

■

To his chagrin, Tom McPhatter remembers that black Marines, themselves targets of racism, joined in degrading the Japanese as "monkey men."

"I kind of felt like they were monkey men, because that's what I was told—You've got to get rid of them!—until I saw one flushed out of the side of Suribachi with a flamethrower," McPhatter, now a retired Navy chaplain and Presbyterian minister, said from his home in San Diego. "Then I saw him being given blood plasma, and I recognized that this plasma was American blood. . . . I found out there was no difference in the blood of any of us."

McPhatter, then a sergeant, served in the Eighth Ammunition Company, which he recalls was manned by about 500 black Marines led by 10 to 12 white officers. Their contact with other white Marines was "almost nothing," he said. They were considered support troops, not assault troops. Their job was to carry ammo ashore and stack it.

The Marine Corps was the last of the U.S. armed services to enlist African Americans, in August 1942, and didn't integrate fighting units until after the war. But on a small place like Iwo Jima, with shells bursting all over, every Marine was in combat. The ammo companies were almost literally sitting on a powder keg.

"The enemy was firing all the time. Men were walking along and hitting mines. . . . There was no real sleep time for seven or eight days. . . . Nothing was still; everything was moving. A gun might be right behind you under a camouflage net. You'd feel the earth shaking and look back and see a ball of fire coming at you."

On their third or fourth day ashore, McPhatter said, the men of his platoon heard the pop-pop-pop of bullets exploding somewhere in the ammo dump. Japanese mortars must have started a fire in there. Someone had to extinguish the flames, or the whole ammo dump might blow.

McPhatter and others grabbed shovels and started throwing sand onto the fire.

"We wanted to put it out before it got to the hand grenades and other stuff that would set the whole dump off. The enemy must have sighted us, because as soon as we put the fire out, there was more fire coming in on us."

A bulldozer was brought in to cover the flames faster. But soon the fire was beyond control. A lieutenant hollered: "There's nothing we can do, men. Seek cover."

The platoon ran toward the beach, yelling out a password—"I think it was oak tree or something," McPhatter recalled—so that other Marines wouldn't shoot them by mistake.

And then, *Kaboom!* The ammo dump went up in a roiling, blackened mushroom cloud. "It was," said McPhatter, "the biggest explosion on the whole island during the invasion."

■

Bill DiIenno, now of Broomall, Delaware County, near Philadelphia, remembers that he didn't dare think about the danger. "You had to put it out of your mind or you'd go mad, you'd be so scared."

A private, he spent the first three days of the battle helping wounded Marines back aboard a transport ship. "That was a pretty awesome sight, pulling them up on ropes out of the boats. It was gruesome, especially knowing you were going in there yourself."

Once ashore, DiIenno was handed a flamethrower. This consisted of twin liquid-fuel tanks mounted on a backpack. A hose led from the tanks to a riflelike instrument with a trigger. A squeeze of the trigger would send a yellow tongue of flame 30 or 40 feet. The fuel burned at 2,000 degrees.

"My job was to get up close to those caves and fire the Japanese out. . . . The caves were pretty deep, and the heat of the flamethrower would penetrate. There's no escaping the heat. If the flame didn't actually get them, the heat would. They'd come running out—not necessarily on fire, but burned. Then they'd be shot."

Later on, he was given back his rifle. On March 17, St. Patrick's Day, he was with his squad attacking a Japanese position. "I think I was getting too brave or careless, because I was standing up too much instead of crouching."

Machine-gun bullets smashed his left leg above the knee. The femur was twisted at nearly a right angle. DiIenno flopped to the sand and writhed in agony. The medics couldn't reach him because he was in the line of fire. He lay there for hours, never losing consciousness despite the pain and loss of blood. Finally, the Marines laid down a smoke screen, and a medic and two stretcher bearers ran out to get him.

"When the corpsman arrived, he said, 'You're out of it now, Bill. You're going home.' I didn't believe him. I didn't think I could ever get out of there. . . . It was too much great news for me to comprehend it."

Fifty years later, DiIenno still lives with pain and a limp. He is retired from Yeadon Auto Body, a business he owned with his three sons. Of Iwo Jima, he says: "It was as much hell as you can imagine." For a decade, he had nightmares—not of flashing firefights in daylight but of the terrifying darkness at night, when the Japanese would sneak into foxholes with bayonets.

■

The raising of the Stars and Stripes atop Mount Suribachi lives as the most enduring image of the Second World War for Americans. Not the first flag-raising, actually. The second.

Joe Rosenthal has told the story repeatedly. No, he never told anyone that he had shot the first flag-raising, as people have suggested. No, his shot wasn't posed. Why some folks have insisted on knocking the photo, he doesn't know. Maybe it became just too famous.

Rosenthal, 83, lives in San Francisco, where in a five-decade career he worked for Wide World Photo, then the Associated Press, and finally the morning Chronicle. Too modestly, he calls himself a "journeyman news photographer" who one day at Iwo Jima "fell into a manure pile and came up with a rose."

Three times before, at Peleliu and other islands, he had gone with Marines into combat. At Iwo Jima, he landed on Day One with a boatload of 16 men and two carriages of mortar ammo. While the others toted weapons, he was loaded down with a big Speed Graphic press camera, the kind depicted in old Hollywood movies. As a backup, he carried a Roloflex camera in a watertight bag, along with a Hermes portable typewriter, film packs, two pairs of socks, and one K-ration.

His first picture showed the Marines lugging their carriages off the boat into the deep, black sand. "It was so soft that you plowed into it six or eight inches with every step," he remembered. "It was very tiring running even 15 or 20 feet."

"Once I was on shore, I could go anywhere I wanted. I was a civilian. I was not under anybody's orders, see. . . . My advance was from shell hole to shell hole."

He shot about 65 photos in 11 days on Iwo Jima. At day's end, he would often hitch a ride on a boat going back to the ships in order to send off his film. It would go on a plane to Guam and, from there, be sent via radio technology to the States. Each photo had to be approved by a censor.

On Day Four of the 36-day battle, the Marines captured Mount Suribachi and planted a flag. But the flag was too small to be seen from afar, and another group of Marines was sent up with a larger flag. Rosenthal come along when the second flag was on its way to the top.

A Marine photographer, Sergeant Bill Genaust, was there to capture the scene on movie film. Rosenthal, 5-foot-5, piled up stones and stood on them for a better angle.

"As I took my position, Bill Genaust came across. He said, 'I'm not in your way, am I, Joe?' I said, 'No, you're fine—heh, there it goes!' By being polite to each other, we both damned near missed it."

The flagpole was an old pipe left behind by the Japanese. Just as five Marines and a Navy medical corpsman hoisted it, the wind caught the flag and gave it a flutter. It was close to noon, and the overhead light gave the scene a sculpted quality.

Everything had come together—"serendipity," Rosenthal calls it—to create a great picture. But Rosenthal couldn't be sure of what his film had captured in a four-hundredth of a second. He made several more exposures of Marines grouped around the flag, raising their rifles in triumph. These, too, he sent back to Guam.

Within days, almost every newspaper in America had carried the shot of the flag going up. But Rosenthal hadn't yet seen it himself. He ran into another newsman who said: "It's a great picture. Did you pose it?" Rosenthal answered: "Sure."

"For some reason," he recalled a half-century later at home in San Francisco, "I thought he meant the group picture."

Thus began questions and doubts about the photo that linger to this day, even though there's no reason they should. The Marine Corps, for its part, has always loved the photo. It chose that image for its national memorial sculpture near Washington. Rosenthal recalled being seated at a banquet years later next to a four-star Marine general, who asked him: "Joe, what do you really think of the Marines?"

"I said: 'Well, general, in peacetime they can be an awful bore with their polish and strut. . . .' He kind of frowned. 'But if I find myself in a fight, I sure as hell want them on my side.'

"That was enough for the general to smile."

29 • Crossing the Rhine
March 7, 1945

The river was Germany's mightiest barrier—and its last line of defense against the Allied onslaught.

March 7, 1995

The mighty Rhine River had always been Germany's greatest defensive barrier. No invader had crossed the Rhine since Napoleon a century and a half earlier.

Then along came Sergeant Michael Chinchar and his GI buddies.

The place was the little town of Remagen, where a thousand-foot trestle bridge carried trains across the deep water. The time was 50 years ago today, March 7, 1945.

American and British armies were pressing toward the heart of Germany from the west. Plans called for a massive British thrust across the Rhine employing makeshift pontoon bridges and thousands of troops. Heavy casualties were expected, but a successful Rhine crossing could bring a swift end to the war in Europe.

All existing bridges had been wired with explosives. The Germans were holding them open until the last minute to permit their own fleeing troops to escape across the river to safety. One by one, they were blowing the bridges up.

"We never expected they'd let us capture a bridge," said Chinchar, of Saddle Brook, New Jersey.

Then, on the bright morning of March 7, a contingent of the Ninth Armored Division reached a summit above Remagen. The Americans looked down and, to their surprise, saw the Ludendorff Bridge still standing. Word came from higher up: "Grab that bridge." And so they did. This is that story, as remembered by Chinchar, who led the first platoon across the Rhine.

■

Once the resident of an orphanage in Nanticoke, Pennsylvania, Chinchar would receive the Distinguished Service Cross for "outstanding heroism and unflinching valor" on that day. But, really, he says, it was no big deal. It certainly wasn't something he expected would get his picture in Life magazine and his name in newspapers around the country.

And yet the capture of the bridge at Remagen was to become the stuff of Hollywood film, a famed event of World War II. General Omar N. Bradley, in command of all one million U.S. troops in northern Europe, wrote years later that hearing the "electrifying news" had given him "one of the most rewarding moments of my life."

That's how big a deal it was.

"We were a little surprised, I guess, at all the attention we got," Chinchar recalled at his home of 40 years in Saddle Brook, a blue-collar town in the shadow of Interstate 80 on the approach to New York City. He is 77 now, retired from a company that made printer's ink. He and his wife, Rose, married since 1949, were able to buy a little winter place in West Palm Beach. But their daughter is the one living there.

Chinchar spread out his memorabilia on the dining-room table—faded newspaper clippings, old photographs, Bronze Star, Purple Heart—and talked about a time that was.

He had been drafted into the Army in Wilkes-Barre, Pennsylvania, in 1941. His outfit, the 27th Armored Infantry Battalion of the Ninth Armored Division, had fought in the Battle of the Bulge. By March 1945, the men were hardened combat veterans.

Chinchar, though a sergeant, was acting leader of the First Platoon of A Company. The job normally belonged to a lieutenant, but casualties were making lieutenants scarce.

Riding in half-tracks—vehicles with rubber tires in front and tank treads in back—A Company was the spear-point of the whole Ninth Armored drive to the Rhine. The division was part of the U.S. First Army, led by General Courtney H. Hodges.

Not expecting to find a bridge intact, they planned to turn south at Remagen and ride along the western shoreline for 30 miles to link up with General George Patton's Third Army near Koblenz.

Then came the Ludendorff surprise.

World War II historian John Toland, in his book *The Last 100 Days*, wrote that when Brigadier General William Hoge, an assistant commander of the Ninth Armored Division, reached the summit and saw the bridge standing, he could hardly believe his eyes.

He immediately ordered tanks to descend the hill with infantry behind them. The tanks were to aim across the bridge and knock out any German guns protecting it. If the Germans hadn't blown it up at that point, the infantry was to try to cross.

Word was passed down the chain of command until it reached Second Lieutenant Karl Timmermann, acting commander of A Company. "We were supposed to go down into town on foot behind a couple of tanks, one platoon at a time," Chinchar recalled.

As the Americans crouched along the main street of Remagen, rifles at the ready, white flags appeared in second-story windows. The only people in town seemed to be civilians. Chinchar remembered that as his platoon neared the bridge, his buddy, Art Massie, suddenly fired off a rifle shot close to his ear.

"I said, 'What's the matter with you?'

"He said, 'I think I got him. I think I got him.'

"I said, 'Who?'

" 'A German. He was going to shoot you.' "

The two Americans ran behind a house. There lay a German soldier, clutching his groin and gasping in pain.

"I says, 'Let's put him out of his misery,' " Chinchar recalled.

"And Massie says, 'Mike, please don't. I'll get the medics.'

"I said, 'OK. All right.' I'm glad he did that. I'm glad he stopped me."

■

No German was in sight on the bridge. The men of A Company, whose lives were on the line, worried that the enemy was setting a trap. They feared that once they got halfway across, the Germans would set off explosives.

Timmermann went back for more orders. He told his three platoons to hunker down and wait for him. Hardly a moment had passed when another officer came up. He said to Chinchar: "I'm going to set up a machine gun to cover you while you cross the bridge."

Chinchar replied that he wanted to see where this gun was going to be located. So he followed the officer. Later, returning to his men, he found Timmermann standing there with his hands on his hips and an angry look on his face.

"Where the hell have you been?" Chinchar remembered him barking.

The lieutenant told the sergeant to get his men on their feet and start them across the bridge. Immediately! Chinchar was tired and worn out. He had just been chasing a German railway worker he had seen come out of one of two stone towers that stood as battlements on each side of the bridge. He also, frankly, was in a defiant mood.

"The way he talked to me, I got mad. . . . I said, 'The hell with you.

I'm gonna sit down here and get my breath.' "

Timmermann threatened to court-martial him. Chinchar answered: "Fine, here's my gun."

At that moment, a tremendous blast rocked the earth. Dirt, stones, and debris came down in a shower. The Germans had blown a hole 30 feet wide on the bridge-approach. His moment of disobedience, Chinchar realized, had saved his life. If he had jumped at Timmermann's command, he would have been right over the spot of the blast.

The enemy hadn't blown up the bridge, only the road leading up to it. The hole prevented any American tank or other vehicle from getting onto the span. The Germans, apparently, were doing anything they could to hold the bridge open even a moment longer, in case additional German troops might try to cross. Historians now know that Hitler had threatened to shoot any German soldier who detonated a bridge too soon.

But the situation was getting desperate for the Germans. The American Sherman tanks were firing from across the water. They could see more and more American helmets glinting in the sun. Time had come to reduce the bridge to a million sticks.

A second explosion ripped up the wooden planks and rails in the center of the span. American soldiers recalled seeing the bridge actually jump from its foundation. A heavy cloud of black smoke blanketed the whole valley. But as the smoke cleared, a cheer arose from the American side. The bridge showed a gaping hole. But, miraculously, it was still standing. A brave group of American combat engineers crawled out under the span to disconnect remaining dynamite charges.

Then came Chinchar's turn to go to work. Massie, he remembered, stepped out on the bridge and got in position to provide covering fire. He knelt beside a girder and put his rifle to his shoulder. Chinchar took off running, with others right behind him.

"To this day, I don't remember touching the boards. I thought I flew across there."

■

The citation for his Distinguished Service Cross—the Army's highest award for valor—says Chinchar charged "in the face of heavy machine gun, small arms, and direct 20mm gunfire."

The fact is, he remembers no enemy fire.

"They never talked to me before they wrote that. The real story wasn't exciting enough, I guess. . . . I can only tell you what happened to me. What happened to other people—if they got fired on or whatever have you—I don't know. Everybody was a hero, not me. Everybody.

I was just numb, that's all."

■

History records that Private Alex Drabik of Ohio was the first man to actually set foot on the ground on the opposite shore. Chinchar ducked into a tower and disarmed a German he found there. He pointed the man back across the bridge to the American side. Later, he said, he found that someone had shot him dead.

The many book and film accounts of the bridge crossing contradict one another again and again. Sergeant Carmine Sabia, also one of the first men across, remembers that, for sure, he was fired on.

The Germans, he remembered from his home in Boca Raton, Florida, "more or less surrendered" when the Americans showed up. There weren't many Germans to begin with.

Why the Germans didn't do a better job of defending the bridge—or at least blowing it up—remains something of a mystery. One thing is certain. The once-efficient Wehrmacht—the German war machine—was in tatters at this stage of the war. Most of its divisions had been sent to the Eastern Front to fight off the Russians. Surrender was only two months away.

"They were more or less retreating, and they were messed up," said Sabia, a retired telephone installer, originally from Brooklyn. "I understand they asked for some assistance [to defend the bridge], but they never did get it."

After the Germans let the bridge slip from their grasp, they tried like crazy to destroy it from the air. As U.S. Army engineers worked to shore it up, wave after wave of bombers were sent screaming down the Rhine to blast it apart.

After 10 days, the bridge simply collapsed, taking 30 American lives with it. By then, though, American engineers, working under fire, had been able to construct pontoon bridges nearby. The massive Allied thrust across a wide front was well underway.

The Americans never did get many troops or much equipment across the bridge at Remagen; it was the pontoons that carried the load. But the capture of the Ludendorff Bridge opened the door. The crossing of the Rhine was an important milestone of World War II, the breaching of Hitler's last barrier to defeat.

Chinchar was just glad to have had a role.

"But I have to tell you—I didn't do that much."

30 • The Battle of Okinawa
April 1, 1945

Kamikaze planes rained down on U.S. ships in a massive air-land-sea battle. The casualties—and bravery —were remarkable.

April 1, 1995

To reach the home of Desmond T. Doss near Rising Fawn, Georgia, you take the Desmond T. Doss Medal of Honor Highway. The folks around there are mighty proud of their neighbor up on Lookout Mountain.

As a 20-year-old in 1945, the shy, slim Seventh-Day Adventist became one of the most famous and unusual heroes of World War II. A strict believer in the Sixth Commandment—*Thou shalt not kill*—he refused to bear arms. But he was willing to serve as a medic, one of the most dangerous jobs the Army had to offer.

One day on the Pacific island of Okinawa, Private Doss rescued almost a whole company of men who had been cut down by Japanese fire while trying to capture an important hilltop. Crawling out among bullets and shell bursts, he dragged the wounded, one by one, to a sheltered spot behind a rock, tied a double-bowline knot around their chests and legs, and lowered them over a 35-foot cliff to safety.

"Dear God," he remembers praying over and over, "let me get just one more." It took all day, but he got them all. The Army estimated he had saved 75 lives.

It was an amazing story. But, then, Okinawa was a place full of amazing stories. The fight that began there 50 years ago today, on April 1, 1945, turned into the biggest combination land-sea-air battle of all time. Dragging on for almost three months, it was the last important American battle before the atom bomb ended the war.

Okinawa was the place where kamikaze planes inflicted massive damage on the U.S. fleet, sinking 36 ships and damaging 368 others—where Julian F. Becton of Wynnewood, Pennsylvania, led the destroyer USS *Laffey* in battling 22 suicide planes, five of which crashed into the deck, killing or injuring one-third of the crew. "You couldn't stop them, they came so fast," Becton, now a retired rear admiral, recalls.

It was the place where a single Marine Corps fighter squadron, later nicknamed the Death Rattlers, shot down 124 Japanese planes; where Charles W. Drake of Brookside, New Jersey, a member of that squadron, downed as many as five of those planes in a dizzying 20 minutes. "It was," he recalls, "a wild, wild scramble."

For more than 2½ years, U.S. forces had been fighting their way, from island to island, toward Japan; from Guadalcanal to Tarawa to Saipan to Guam to Peleliu to Iwo Jima.

In each place, the Japanese had refused to give up, even when they were clearly beaten. Their Bushido code of honor required them to die first. Great numbers of Americans died with them. The previous battle, at Iwo, had cost close to 7,000 U.S. lives.

No one was looking forward to Okinawa. It was to be the next-to-last hop in the U.S. island-hopping campaign. The final hop, according to plan, would be to Japan itself.

■

April 1 was Easter Sunday. As the soldiers and Marines of the U.S. 10th Army went ashore, a fleet of 1,200 ships established a protective ring around Okinawa. Stationed at the outer edge of the ring was a group of destroyers equipped with the latest radar gear. Their job was to warn the fleet—and the men on land—if planes were coming their way from Japan, only 350 miles to the north, or from major Japanese airfields on Formosa.

Becton, then a lieutenant commander, was captain of a destroyer on this "picket line." A 1931 graduate of the Naval Academy, he had been at sea in the Atlantic when the Japanese attacked Pearl Harbor. Later, he had been at the Naval Battle of Guadalcanal, one of the most intense sea fights ever. He had helped bombard Utah Beach when the Allies invaded Normandy. He had fought in the Battle of Leyte Gulf in the Philippines.

He already had experienced more combat than most sailors in history. But nothing in his experience prepared him for April 16, 1945.

As always, Becton's crew was at battle stations when the first glow of light warmed the sky. Dawn was the most dangerous moment of the day, when enemy planes could appear as if from nowhere. Becton was permitting a few men at a time to leave their stations to go to breakfast.

He knew kamikazes were coming his way, if not today, then tomorrow or the next day. The only chance the Japanese had to win the Battle of Okinawa was to sink the American fleet. The best weapons they had left were the brave kamikaze pilots who crashed planes loaded with TNT onto the decks of ships.

Kamikaze means "divine wind" in Japanese. The term referred to the miraculous salvation of Japan in the 13th century by a typhoon that blew away a Mongol invasion fleet. The Japanese longed for another miracle to blow away the Americans.

A few of the kamikazes were skilled pilots. Many more were just kids who knew little more than how to take off and steer their airplanes. Really, they were nothing more than guided missiles, or maybe smart-bombs. But they had a religious zeal to die for their emperor.

"They were all brainwashed, I guess," Becton said recently at his home. "You feared 'em, sure. They kept on coming. You could shoot 'em down, but more kept on coming after that."

At 8:20 a.m., a squall of kamikazes suddenly appeared as spots of white light on the *Laffey*'s radar screens. The planes were still eight miles away, to the north. The *Laffey* radioed the alarm to the fleet and got ready to defend itself.

Soon, lookouts with binoculars saw the first four planes: all Val dive-bombers, coming in from starboard. Becton's job as captain was to keep the ship turned sideways to the attackers, so all the deck guns could be brought to bear.

"But then the planes split," he said. "Two of them went for our fantail, and two of them were off to our left. We got the ones that were closest to us. . . . We shot them down and then swung around to the others. We got the third one and then . . . ."

And then a small vessel, a landing craft, got the fourth.

The guns suddenly fell silent. Men on deck began to cheer, but Becton barely had time to "exhale one deep breath of relief" before another dive-bomber appeared high in the sky. The ack-ack guns on the starboard side opened up. Some of them, double-barreled 20mm guns known to sailors as pom-poms, could spit out 450 rounds a minute. Others were 40mm guns that could do 160 a minute. The plane broke into pieces and splintered into the water.

Now the fight was beginning in earnest. Japanese planes were coming from what seemed like all points of the compass, from high and low. Wearing a steel helmet and a life vest, Becton had to stand out in the open so he could see what was going on.

"The first plane that hit us came right in over the stern," he said. The plane crashed into the big gun turret on the fantail. Then a second plane crashed into the ship. Then another. And another. And another. Each time one crashed, there was always a flood of gasoline from the plane—and one hell of a fire.

"Near the end of the action, one of my officers, Frank Manson, came to me and said, 'Captain, we're in pretty bad shape aft. Do you think you'll have to abandon ship?'

"It never entered my mind to abandon ship. The ship might sink under us. We might not be able to sail her. But I wasn't going to abandon her.

"So I said, 'No, Frank, I'll never abandon ship as long as a gun will fire.' "

That last statement, later conveyed by Manson to reporters, was to become a famous slogan in Navy history.

The *Laffey* remained in almost continuous combat for an hour and 20 minutes, an unheard-of length of time. Besides the five planes that crashed into it, there were two that dropped bombs on it. On its own, it managed to down nine of the 22 attackers. Thirty-two men aboard ship were dead and 71 were wounded. The ship couldn't be steered and had to be towed into port.

But it was still afloat. Fifty years later, it remains a famous ship of Okinawa, now a museum piece in dry dock at Charleston, South Carolina. For his role in saving it, Becton won the Navy Cross in recognition of "extraordinary heroism."

■

The planes that the *Laffey* didn't get, the CAP did. The acronym stood for combat air patrol. It was a job for Second Lieutenant Bill Drake and the three dozen other pilots of VMF 323, a.k.a. Death Rattlers.

Drake's friends knew him as "Duck." He had been a freshman at Dartmouth College when the war broke out. His father was a colonel in the Army Quartermaster Corps, "but I always wanted to fly." So he took naval cadet training, after which he had a choice: Navy or Marines. He chose Marines.

It wasn't until June 1944 that his squadron reached the Pacific. The battle for Saipan was wrapping up at that time, and Peleliu lay just ahead. But the squadron still hadn't seen combat months later when Okinawa came along. It was the pilots' first test in combat.

They passed; that's for sure. Twelve pilots, Drake included, would end up as "aces"—a recognition that they had shot down five or more enemy aircraft.

They flew the Corsair, the fastest plane in the Pacific. It could not twist and turn like its principal foe, the Japanese Zero, but it could outrun the "Zekes" by going 450 miles per hour. The ungainly looking Corsair had a gull wing and one giant propeller, stuck on a nose that resembled a basement water heater.

"A great airplane," Drake said.

The Marine pilots performed two jobs at Okinawa. One was to provide close air support for Marines fighting on the ground. The other was to help protect the fleet from kamikaze attack. Their base was at Kadena, an airfield on Okinawa captured from the Japanese.

A contingent of Marines, pinned down somewhere, would radio for an airstrike. Drake and his buddies would fly over and drop bombs or canisters of napalm on Japanese positions. Though napalm would be more closely associated with the Vietnam War a generation later, it was widely used late in World War II. Drake remembered it as "jellied gasoline—nasty stuff."

Close air support was important work. But aerial combat was much more glamorous.

Drake shot down his first plane on May 4. "That first one—I was almost more proud of that than the five I shot down later. . . . It was really a dogfight. Hundreds and hundreds of planes, and they were attacking the fleet."

The day he became an ace arrived a month later, June 3. That morning, he and three other pilots led by Lieutenant Cyril A. Dolezel had been in the air for about an hour, watching over the fleet. The destroyers on the picket line picked up radar blips indicating that a swarm of planes was headed their way from the direction of Japan. Drake and his buddies were alerted to intercept them.

They flew right to the spot where the destroyers had said they would find the Japanese planes, but none was in sight. Drake remembered hearing a panicky voice from the ships: "You're gonna pass 'em. You're gonna pass 'em."

He looked up, he said, and saw a thin layer of clouds. "As we broke through the clouds, there they were—24 of them, all Zekes, all very modern. We were in their blind spot, so we had time to get up and get behind them. We got behind them and started taking potshots at them. The first two I got were like shooting fish in a barrel."

The battle started at 18,000 feet and wound round and round, down and down. Besides flying skill, the Marines had two advantages to make up for the 24-to-4 odds. The first was speed—"If I got one on my trail, I'd dive away from him," Drake said—and the second was armorplating. The Americans had two inches of steel behind their seats; the Japanese had only a volatile fuel tank behind theirs.

Drake's Corsair had a bubble canopy. He constantly had to look up and around for the enemy planes. The Corsairs were painted navy blue; the Zeroes, brown.

His gun trigger was on the stick that controlled the direction the airplane was headed. A pull of his right index finger unleashed six .50-

caliber machine guns mounted three-and-three on the wings, a massive amount of firepower.

His left hand was on the throttle, which controlled speed, while his feet operated the tail rudder, right and left.

Pilots normally flew in pairs, one man protecting the other. But in a dogfight, Drake said, "it's every man for himself. . . . The reason I shot so many down is I picked on the poor pilots and ran away from the good pilots."

Each American plane had wing cameras, which followed the action. The officers who later studied the film credited Drake with four "kills" and one "probable" that day. He, too, won the Navy Cross for heroism. But the battle ended on a note of embarrassment. He found himself 200 feet over the water and totally lost.

"I picked up the radio and said, 'Mayday! I'm lost.' All of a sudden, I saw this plane behind me. I thought it was a Jap for a second, but it was a[n American] P-47. The poor bastard had to take me home."

■

Ashore, all this time, one of the most ferocious land battles of the Second World War was taking place.

The air-sea battle was awesome, with nearly 5,000 Americans killed. But the toll on land was even greater. About 7,000 soldiers and Marines were killed, including the 10th Army commander, Lieutenant General Simon Bolivar Buckner. At least 70,000 Japanese died, along with 80,000 native Okinawans.

"It was a very bloody affair," said historian Ronald Spector, author of *Eagle Against the Sun*, a well-regarded account of the Pacific War. In all, Okinawa cost the United States close to 32,000 casualties, including dead and wounded.

Yet Okinawa's fame has been eclipsed by Iwo Jima's. "I don't know why," Spector said in an interview. Iwo Jima, he said, was a smaller battle in most respects.

The island of Okinawa itself is many times bigger: 60 miles long and 18 miles wide. The Japanese knew they couldn't defend all of the shoreline there, so they withdrew to defensive positions and waited for the Americans to advance.

The job of blasting them out of their bunkers, trenches, and caves fell to units such as the Army's 77th Infantry Division, which included a young medic who already had proved his bravery on Guam and Leyte: Private Doss.

Doss had grown up in the Seventh-Day Adventist Church, whose members worshipped on Saturdays. At his home, then in Lynchburg, Virginia, his father had hung a framed scroll of the Ten

Commandments on the wall that depicted the biblical Cain murdering his brother, Abel.

"I looked at that picture hundreds of times. And I always wondered, 'How could his brother do such a horrible thing?' I reckon it put a horror in my heart for killing."

But he figured that being a medic meant he would be saving lives, not taking them. And that seemed OK.

"We were front-line doctors," he said from his sofa. "We had to go out ahead of our own lines to try to save life. And you exposed yourself to a lot of fire."

Hanging behind him, as he talked, was the same framed scroll of the Commandments he remembered from his youth. His house today sits on the piney crest of Lookout Mountain ridge, not far from the Tennessee line. At Okinawa, he said, his outfit was given orders to assault the Maeda Escarpment. That was a jagged hilltop, which dropped away in a sheer cliff. From there, the Japanese could direct artillery fire in all directions. His company decided to climb up behind the enemy: They would scale the cliff with ropes and ladders.

"We went up and pushed over against the Japanese position, got pinned down, and couldn't move," Doss recalled. Another company was supposed to take the opposite side of the escarpment, but word came that they had been "all shot up," he said.

"We had to take the whole thing by ourselves. How'd you like to be pinned down where you couldn't move and get an order like that? But Uncle Sam has to sacrifice lives. This was holding up the works."

The battle started on April 29. It was May 5 when Doss performed the principal deeds that resulted in his winning the Medal of Honor. President Truman himself would place the medal around his neck on the White House lawn in October 1945.

"We had orders to withdraw," Doss said, "but I couldn't leave my men. In combat, you get very closely attached to each other. When you see your buddy hit, you just can't leave him out there. It's like a mother with a house on fire. She don't think of herself; she's thinking about that child. And that's the way I felt about my men."

Exposing himself to mortars, grenades, and machine guns, he crawled out into the open and dragged the wounded back to cover. The Army at first said he had rescued a hundred. "I didn't see how it could be more than 50, and I still don't. So they settled on 75. I didn't think I'd get killed. But I felt it would be worth getting wounded if I could save just one more man. I kept praying for the Lord to help me, and He did."

Doss himself believes that what he did wasn't humanly possible.

"It's not what I did, but what the Lord did. To me, it was as much a miracle as what I read about in the Bible."

31 • The Liberation of the Death Camps
April 12, 1945

America learns why it had been fighting. Eisenhower was so shaken that he made sure the world could never forget what he saw.

April 9, 1995

We are looking through the eye of an old 35mm movie camera. The scene is a Nazi concentration camp. It is April 12, 1945, a bright, white day—and a cold one, judging from the bulky coats that many of the GIs are wearing. General Dwight D. Eisenhower, supreme Allied commander in Europe, has come to witness for himself the horrors that U.S. Army troops have begun discovering in recent days in camps all over Germany.

A pentagon-shaped cluster of five stars glimmers from each of the commander's shoulders. He is wearing his familiar "Eisenhower jacket," waist-length and expertly tailored. The stiff cap on his head bears the emblem of an eagle with arrows clutched in its talons. At age 54, Ike looks fit, trim, and very much a man in charge.

We follow him as he walks briskly into the main compound at Ohrdruf, the first of numerous Nazi camps liberated in the four-week period before Germany's surrender on May 7, 1945. Ike is trailed by an entourage ranging from privates and sergeants to three-star General George S. Patton Jr. and four-star General Omar N. Bradley. Their boots kick up only a little dust; the ground is hard. Bradley has a holstered pistol under his left arm. Patton is decked out in riding breeches.

Cut to a ragpile of human bodies—scraggly, skeletal bodies with white, tight skin—tossed every which way in the dirt. All of them appear to be men. There must be scores of them, dressed in cotton, pajama-like uniforms with prison stripes. Many still have blankets around shoulders as thin as coat hangers.

They lie in twisted, obscene poses, arms and legs bent at angles no gymnast could achieve, as if they'd been slammed to the ground by the machine gun bullets that killed them. The pants of some have slipped down, an indignity even in death.

We focus on Eisenhower's face and then Patton's. The Army Signal Corps photographer who has shot this silent footage seems to want the same thing we want a half-century later—to see how these generals, who know the carnage of battle, will react to what they are seeing now.

Patton looks ill; Ike, angry. Hands on his hips, Eisenhower listens impatiently to something that Bradley is saying, drops his head in a motion of exasperation, and spits out an epithet.

Next, the generals are led to a woodshed. The double doors are open; it's dark inside. The camera takes us in. We see bodies, bodies, bodies—naked, shriveled bodies, stacked like fire logs, six or seven rows high. These men appear to have been starved, then shot. Their cheeks are as bony as knees and elbows. Their skin is white marble, riddled with sores and smeared with dried feces. One man dangles head-down with his eyes open, his lips caked with a white powder. This makes him appear to be foaming at the mouth, but the powder is probably lime, thrown over the cadavers to hold down the stench.

An even grislier sight awaits. We now follow the supreme commander and his party as they approach the cold remains of a funeral pyre set at the edge of a woods. Here, scores of bodies have been laid on a grill of railroad tracks, then burned with gasoline. The fire must have been intense; the steel rails are curled like spaghetti.

The bodies can scarcely be distinguished as human anymore—blackened skulls encrusted with flesh; hints of feet and foreheads among the ocean of ashes. One ghoulish head rests its cheek gently against a rail, as if napping.

Patton stops. Wearing a helmet with white stars on it, he very slowly swivels his head, left, right. Eisenhower continues on, hands clasped behind his back.

The camera again focuses on Ike. The humanity has gone out of his face. Under the visor of his cap, we see one eye, close up. It is the fierce, cold eye of a hawk.

■

This is how America learned of the Holocaust. It was only when U.S. troops began stumbling onto concentration camps as they overran the heart of Germany in April 1945 that America came to realize the absolute evil of the Nazi regime.

Eisenhower was so taken aback by what he saw in Ohrdruf that he ordered the Army film turned over to newsreel companies, which distributed it to movie houses across the United States. Theater managers everywhere reported shocked silence among their audiences.

The historic film is preserved today in the storehouses of the National Archives at College Park, Maryland. Reference number: 111-ADC-8568. Source: War Crimes Commission. It remains a silent, irrefutable witness to the atrocities of Adolf Hitler's Germany.

"This is why we fight," the newsreel narrators intoned. Indeed, the growing realization of just what the Nazis had been doing out of the world's sight seemed to give greater meaning to the sacrifice of Americans killed or maimed in battle.

War means killing; every soldier knows that. But this was something different. This was mass murder.

There had been reports for years that the Germans were murdering Jews and others—dissidents, priests, Poles, Gypsies, Jehovah's Witnesses, the physically handicapped, the mentally retarded. Terrifying stories, smuggled out of Germany, had appeared in newspapers, including sketchy reports that the Nazi regime actually intended to exterminate all of the Jews of Europe. Yet the world had not expected Ohrdruf. No one could yet calculate that the Nazis had murdered between five million and six million Jews, two-thirds of Europe's pre-war Jewish population. Several million other people also disappeared in Nazi hands.

"Eisenhower did not know the extent of the horrors of those camps, and he was completely shocked by it," says historian Philip Rosen, director of the Holocaust Awareness Museum at Philadelphia's Gratz College. "He knew they were not nice places, but he had no idea of the horror. There's knowing and then there is *knowing.*"

The Soviet Red Army, advancing on Germany from the East, had come upon extermination camps in Poland as early as July 1944. But the Nazi SS had had time to prepare for the Soviets' arrival, and they had cleaned up and covered over much of the horror. Many of the inmates, in fact, had been moved to the camps in Germany. The Soviets invited Western newsmen to see what remained of the Majdanek camp, but their reports somehow never had much impact back in the States.

In January 1945, the Red Army had liberated Auschwitz, where 1.5 million people—90 percent of them Jewish—had been gassed. The Auschwitz slaughter dwarfed the killing at Ohrdruf and all other camps in Germany combined. But American leaders had not seen Auschwitz themselves, and they were reluctant to believe the Soviet reports.

Within Germany, the SS operated slave-labor camps, not extermination camps as at Auschwitz. There were no gas chambers. But these camps were maybe even more horrible places. Instead of dying quickly, inmates worked until they succumbed to disease or starvation or abuse. Then, as in death camps, bodies were mostly burned in ovens.

Ohrdruf, which supplied labor to a nearby munitions plant, was not even the biggest camp in Germany, nor the worst. Others— Buchenwald, Nordhausen, Dachau—would attain greater reputations in succeeding years for the scope of atrocities committed there.

But Ohrdruf was first to be uncovered, on April 4, eight days before Ike's historic visit. The SS troopers who had been stationed there, fleeing in advance of the U.S. Fourth Armored Division and 89th Infantry Division, had hurriedly tried to cover up their crimes by opening up with machine guns on the last of what had once been 10,000 prisoners. At least the dead would not talk. But some inmates remained alive to greet the American soldiers as they arrived.

Eight days later, the high-ranking generals went to inspect Ohrdruf. Each later wrote of the experience.

Bradley: "The smell of death overwhelmed us even before we passed through the stockade. More than 3,200 naked, emaciated bodies had been flung into shallow graves. Others lay in the streets where they had fallen. Lice crawled over the yellowed skin of their sharp, bony frames. A guard showed us how the blood had congealed in coarse black scabs where the starving prisoners had torn out the entrails of the dead for food. . . . I was too revolted to speak."

Patton: "This was one of the most appalling sights I have ever seen. One of the former inmates acted as impresario and showed us first a gallows where men were hanged for attempting to escape. The hanging was done with a piece of piano wire, and the man hanged was not dropped far enough to break his neck, but simply strangled by the piano wire. . . . Two prisoners next to be hanged are required to kick the plank from under him."

Eisenhower: "I have never felt able to describe my emotional reactions when I first came face to face with indisputable evidence of Nazi brutality and ruthless disregard of every shred of decency. Up to that time I had known about it only generally or through secondary sources. I am certain, however, that I never at any other time experienced an equal sense of shock."

"Indisputable evidence" of Nazi war crimes was a necessity. In the First World War, says Eisenhower biographer Stephen Ambrose, the "Huns," as Germans were often then called by their enemies, had been falsely accused of committing atrocities in Belgium and the parts of France they had occupied.

"There were crude propaganda posters showing Germans with babies on the end of bayonets," said Ambrose, a leading historian of the

Second World War. "After the war, it became clear that what our propaganda had said had happened had *not* happened."

It was like the case of the boy who cried wolf. When the wolf finally came, no one wanted to believe.

"It was very hard for the World War II leaders . . . to believe the stories about the concentration camps," Ambrose said, "because that generation had been fooled in World War I."

Ike's grasp of the need to overcome this reluctance to believe the truth remains one of his great contributions as supreme commander. Holocaust survivors, who today gnash their teeth at every suggestion by some neo-fascist nut-case that the camps never existed, remain grateful to Eisenhower for preserving the record—and not just on film.

He issued orders that any GI who could possibly be spared from the fighting for even an hour or two should visit a camp. These American boys became witnesses, too. He gave instructions that German townspeople near the camps be required to go through them, so they could never say they hadn't known what went on. Townspeople were also made to dig graves and clean up filth in the camps.

On April 18, he cabled General George C. Marshall, the Army chief of staff back in Washington, asking that a dozen congressmen and a dozen newspaper editors be put on a plane right away and sent to Germany to take a look at the camps. Two representatives from Marshall's office drove over to the Capitol at noon on April 20, and two days later a delegation was en route.

Joseph Pulitzer, publisher of the St. Louis Post-Dispatch, led the group of newspapermen who went at Ike's invitation. In a dispatch from Germany, he told readers: "I came here in a suspicious frame of mind, feeling that I would find that many of the terrible reports that have been printed in the United States before I left were exaggerations, and largely propaganda."

But after seeing the camps, he had changed his mind. The reports, he said, "have been understatements."

■

The day after his Ohrdruf shock, Ike had a surprise visitor at First Army headquarters in Marburg, Germany. It was his son, John S.D. Eisenhower, 10 months out of West Point and newly promoted to first lieutenant.

Overnight, the Allied command had received word of the death of President Franklin D. Roosevelt. Altogether, it was a disturbing time. That evening, Lieutenant Eisenhower joined his dad, General Courtney H. Hodges, and several of their aides for dinner. They sat for a long time smoking and talking at a big table after the dishes were cleared.

Inevitably, the concentration camps came up. On April 6, two days after discovering Ohrdruf, U.S. troops had liberated Nordhausen. On April 11, they had found Buchenwald.

"Dad was still pretty shaken," John Eisenhower recalled in a recent interview. A military historian, he lives on Maryland's Eastern Shore, where he is writing a book about the War of 1812.

"You come into these camps and it hits you right in the face—this awful stench, bodies falling apart," he said. "Of course he was jarred by it. The difference between him and other people is, he was in a position to do something about it."

During the after-dinner conversation in Marburg, Ike mentioned that Patton—legendary old "blood and guts," as the newspapers called him—had become sickened while at Ohrdruf, walking away to throw up. Ike himself seemed to be pondering the nature of his enemy—these Germans he had been fighting since 1942, starting at Morocco in French North Africa.

"He knew the Nazis could be beasts," John Eisenhower said. "But [the camp] took it out of the realm of the theoretical. . . . He was angry; he was *angry!*"

Years later, Hobart R. Gay, a general who had been with Ike at Ohrdruf, wrote that as the military leaders had been waiting for a ride out, an enlisted man had bumped into a German camp guard and had giggled nervously.

"General Eisenhower fixed him with a cold eye," Gay wrote, "and when he spoke, each word was like the drop of an icicle.

" 'Still having trouble hating them?' "

One thing that gave Ike some hope for the Germans as a people, he told his dinner companions, was the story of the mayor of Gotha, the town nearest Ohrdruf, and his wife. After being made to view the camp, they had gone home and hanged themselves out of shame.

John Eisenhower's visit with his father was short. A day or so later, he recalled, he had an opportunity to visit Buchenwald himself—and seized it. "I might not have paid much attention," he conceded, "if I hadn't talked to Dad."

The young lieutenant and his driver entered alone in a jeep. He had his camera. Army medics were feeding and caring for the former inmates who still remained. Many of them, he recalled, continued to die from the effects of prolonged malnutrition.

Eisenhower met a Belgian, a political prisoner still wearing his baggy prison suit, who volunteered to be his guide. They spoke in French. The guide showed him the barracks, the crematorium, the piles of bodies with tattoos on the legs, the chamber where inmates had been hanged on hooks.

The bodies of three Germans lay in a separate heap. "They were

SS guards," Eisenhower recalled, "and they were pretty freshly killed. I don't know what the circumstances were. One was lying on his back, a handsome devil. He had a rope burn around his neck."

Camp survivors were clustered around the bodies, sluggishly, almost gently, kicking them. The guide said aloud, "*Amerikanisch Offizier!*" and the group parted to give the officer a better look.

"I felt like an intruder," Eisenhower recalled. "I'm barging in on people's grief and people's tragedy. Here comes this scrubbed lieutenant with a camera. But they didn't treat me as an intruder. They treated me as an honored guest."

Lieutenant Eisenhower snapped a couple of pictures and turned to leave with a mumbled word of thanks. The survivors closed back in, and resumed kicking the corpses.

■

Shouldn't America —and the world—have known what was going on? Couldn't we somehow have intervened in what might be the worst crime in history? These questions still haunt us today.

Throughout the '30s, the Nazis had singled out Jews for abuse, especially after *Kristallnacht*—the "night of broken glass" in 1938, when synagogues were desecrated and store windows smashed in Jewish communities all over Germany.

After Hitler's rise to power, many European Jews had tried to escape to the Americas. More tried to get out after the war began in Poland in 1939. But instead of opening the door to refugees, the United States and other nations threw up barriers to immigration, Jewish or otherwise. These nations feared being flooded by refugees from battle zones. But there was also a strong element of anti-Semitism in their actions, as historian David S. Wyman writes in his book *The Abandonment of the Jews*, the authoritative account of American response to the Holocaust.

We know, now, that the Nazis' decision to commit genocide—to attempt to wipe out Jews entirely—was reached in 1941 after German troops had gained control of Poland, Ukraine, the Baltics, and other areas where most of Europe's Jews lived. On July 22, 1942, the Nazis began to deport Jews from the Warsaw Ghetto on trains bound for the new Treblinka extermination camp. Other death camps were also springing up in Poland.

Reports got out that Jews were being taken from occupied countries. But to where? And for what purpose? In August 1942, a German industrialist passed word of mass exterminations to a Swiss friend, Gerhart Riegner, in the Geneva office of the World Jewish Congress. Riegner passed the word to the U.S. consulate, which passed it to

Washington, with a note that it had the "earmarks of war rumor inspired by fear."

The State Department paid little heed. The whole notion of genocide was too fantastic to be believed.

Riegner waited for action, for a response—for *something!*—from Washington. None was forthcoming. Rabbi Stephen Wise, head of the World Jewish Congress, based in New York, then tried to get a rise out of the State Department. Wise was able to reach high up the department ladder to Sumner Welles, the undersecretary. But Welles continued to sit on the report, and it took Wise until December 8 to get a meeting with Roosevelt.

Roosevelt, whom Jewish leaders had always considered a friend, seemed distracted. But he ended the meeting with a promise: "We shall do all in our power to be of service to your people in this tragic moment."

Evidence of mass murder continued to mount. Occasional stories appeared in newspapers. "But who reads the small items on Page 15?" Wyman, a retired professor at the University of Massachusetts, said in a recent interview. "It got buried deep in the paper. This was the case most of the time."

In July 1943, Jan Karski, a Pole who had been inside the Belzec camp and escaped, arrived in Washington as a courier from the Polish underground and gave the president a firsthand account. "I am convinced there is no exaggeration in the accounts of the plight of the Jews," he said. "Our underground authorities are absolutely sure that the Germans are out to exterminate the entire Jewish population of Europe."

Roosevelt was genuinely shocked and sympathetic. But his response, then and later, was that the best way to save Jews—and all oppressed peoples of Europe—was to defeat Hitler as quickly as possible. It wasn't until late November 1944 that he was persuaded to establish a Jewish Refugee Board to aid in rescue. Between then and the end of the war, about 200,000 Jews who otherwise might have died made it to the United States, many through neutral countries.

Wyman said that if rescue efforts had happened sooner, more Jews might have been saved from Hungary, Romania, and Bulgaria—the German-allied nations that were last to deport Jews.

How many more?

"You can't tell," he said. "Half to two-thirds [of the Jews killed in Europe] were already dead by the time we really knew what was happening. I would say another 200,000—and possibly 400,000."

The people at their desks in Washington knew far more than military leaders actually fighting the Nazis. Wyman said he doesn't fault Ike or other generals for any lack of action; they were going all out to win the war.

In fact, he said, "it would not surprise me if they were unaware. . . . I have no way to prove it, but I would have reason to expect they did not know. The sources of information did not give it to them in any amount."

■

If Eisenhower was surprised, ordinary soldiers were dumbstruck. Arthur C. Dietrich, of Canfield, Ohio, remembers well. He appears in a well-known Army Signal Corps photograph of GIs staring at the Ohrdruf funeral pyre. A blowup of the photo hangs prominently in the new United States Holocaust Memorial Museum in Washington.

One day, his outfit, the 537th Ordnance Heavy Maintenance Co., was loaded onto trucks and driven to the camp. "They took us in there more or less to show us what was going on—the atrocities that had been committed. They said they were taking us to show us what had been done . . . what we were fighting for, you might say. A lot of the German soldiers we went up against, they were just kids like us. You didn't really feel that hostile toward them. I think that's one of the reasons they wanted to show us this.

"There were some of the survivors there. They looked like they hadn't been fed for weeks. But what got us most was, they had buildings with dead bodies stacked up in them. They were nothing more than skeletons with skin on them."

Dietrich, now 71, a retired machinist, is of German descent. "I saw my name on mailboxes all over Germany." He remembered it was hard for him to believe that people like himself could have committed such crimes. But here was proof.

The photo of Dietrich at Ohrdruf shows a dozen and a half men looking at the blackened mass of bodies. Their vehicles wait behind them. No one is talking. Dietrich stands right in front with his left hand in his pocket and his right hand hanging at his side.

He had encountered death before, but never this "sweet, sickening smell," he recalled. A buddy had a camera and took some pictures. He has seven or eight of them himself. "You couldn't hardly call them souvenirs. But I've shown them to people."

When he got home after the war, he didn't say much about what he had seen. "Not really. We didn't speak about much of anything in the war. You got home and thanked your lucky stars that you made it in one piece. And then you went on with your life. You thought about it a lot, but didn't talk about it much."

Some time ago, a neighbor in Canfield told him he didn't believe the camps had ever existed. Dietrich asked him why not. "Well, he'd heard that." So Dietrich got out his photos. "After seeing my pictures, he said, 'Well, I guess it did happen.' "

Throughout April and May 1945, thousands of American troops visited one concentration camp in Germany or another. The British army, which had liberated Bergen-Belsen, sent its soldiers through that chamber of horrors.

Richard Crane, who visited the camp at Landsberg soon after it was liberated, remembered that inmates had tried to kiss his hand. "I admit that I drew back a little bit. I was afraid they might be diseased. I remember that with some shame and regret."

He felt doubly guilty, he said, because "as a Jew, I should have been particularly sensitive." Part of his family had been in America a long time; his mother's grandfather had fought for the Union in the Civil War. But on the other side, his family was relatively new to America. His father's parents had emigrated from Eastern Europe, and he may well have had distant cousins in some of those camps.

Now a retired sales rep living in Ardmore, Pennsylvania, Crane was a captain in the Army. Because he had traveled in Europe before the war and spoke a little German, he had been assigned to a military government unit. He followed the fighting troops into towns seized by force and helped re-establish civil order.

He remembered that German civilians invariably denied that they had known anything of camp atrocities. The Army went to great lengths to show the horrors to them, often by displaying gruesome photos.

"While I was there, big posters appeared on walls and so on—scenes of dead bodies piled like cord wood, some of them naked and some in striped uniforms. . . . They asked the question in German, *Who is guilty?*"

■

A half-century later, hundreds—no, thousands—of Americans of retirement age remain witnesses to the Holocaust. It is just what Eisenhower had in mind when he ordered all available units to be taken out of combat long enough to tour a concentration camp.

Eisenhower seems to have thought of himself primarily as a witness. There was little else he could do with respect to the Holocaust in the spring of 1945. His armies provided food and medical care for camp survivors. But the idea of taking rescue measures was moot at that point. The last camp to be discovered, Mauthausen, in Austria, was liberated on May 5, two days before the Nazi surrender.

With the collapse of the German government, the Allies found themselves with responsibility for the care and housing of seven million to nine million displaced persons all over Europe, many whose homes had been destroyed by fighting and some who had been camp inmates. By the end of 1945, around six million had been repatriated. About 400,000 "DPs" were eventually permitted to emigrate to the United States.

Today, historians give Eisenhower a great deal of credit for his role as supreme witness to the Holocaust. Words of his are inscribed on the exterior wall of the Holocaust museum in Washington. They are taken from a letter he wrote to General Marshall days after his visit to Ohrdruf:

"The things I saw beggar description. . . . The visual evidence and the verbal testimony of starvation, cruelty and bestiality were so over-whelming. . . . I made the visit deliberately, in order to be in a position to give firsthand evidence of these things if ever, in the future, there develops a tendency to charge these allegations to propaganda."

■

February 8, 1995. It is a bitter night on the campus of West Chester University in the Philadelphia suburbs. A foot of snow lies like hardened concrete. Leon Bass, a veteran of World War II, stands before an audience of about 200 students in the Schmucker Science Center auditorium. He is telling them about Buchenwald.

"I saw the walking dead—people who had been denied all the basic things. . . . They were skin and bone. They were walking skeletons. They had deep-set eyes and heads clean-shaved. They were struggling so hard to stay on their feet, holding onto one other."

Bass, an African American serving in a segregated outfit, the all-black 183rd Combat Engineering Battalion, had arrived in Europe as "an angry young man," he said—angry at the flagrant racism he had encountered both in and out of the Army.

Bass, who came from Philadelphia, had had no experience of Jim Crow laws in the South. When he had tried to drink from a water foun-tain while in training in Georgia, a white voice had barked, "Hold on, boy, you don't drink here!" This was the "white" fountain. Over there was the "colored" fountain.

By April 1945, when he entered Buchenwald, he was a combat vet-eran. He had served under fire in the Battle of the Bulge. Yet he could-n't escape feeling the Army didn't want him. "What in the heck was I doing here?" he remembered asking himself. "I felt my country was using me, abusing me—putting me out there to fight and die," while at the same time denying him the ordinary freedoms of an American.

Oh, yes, he had known racism. But he had not seen genocide, and he was not prepared for what he experienced with his own eyes at Buchenwald. "It was the shock of my life. . . . I was upset. My stomach was queasy. I was going to be sick. I needed a breath of fresh air."

He walked to the gate to wait for the others. He began to understand, he said, that what Buchenwald represented was racism carried to the ultimate degree. He came to understand "that all of us can suffer . . . that we shouldn't compare pain—just understand it. . . . I saw a link and a connection between my experience in life as an African American and what had happened to the people in Europe."

The experience, he said, forever changed his view of life.

Many years later, as principal of Benjamin Franklin High School in North Philadelphia, he walked by a classroom where a Holocaust survivor was describing her experience to a group of black students. "She had come to the school to share her pain. They had their own pain. The young men were rude; they wouldn't listen."

Dr. Bass intervened. *What she is telling you happened! I know!* The students quieted down and listened. They looked at the tattoo on the survivor's arm. They asked questions. They shook her hand. And they left the room in silence.

Afterward, Bass remembered, "she told me *I* had something to share; I should share *my* experience." That was in 1970. Ever since, he has been standing up as a witness to the Holocaust. In the past year alone, he said, he has given more than a hundred speeches on the subject of racism and anti-Semitism. "I have traveled from the East Coast to the West Coast; from the North to the South."

A good teacher, he had a lesson this night for the students at West Chester, his college alma mater. One day years down the road, he told them, Holocaust survivors will all be dead. So will the GIs whom Ike sent into the camps to be witnesses.

Then, it will be *their* responsibility to testify to the truth, he told them. It will be the responsibility of those who have heard him speak to stand and say, "Don't tell *me* it never happened—because *I* heard it from Dr. Leon Bass. And *he* was there."

32 • The Death of FDR
April 12, 1945

The grief was universal. So was the sense of sadness that he died before he could see the victory he had helped bring about.

April 12, 1995

L ike Lincoln's, his funeral train would pass through Philadelphia. And again, a mournful people would stand by the thousands along the track to weep at a great man's passing.

Fifty years ago today, on April 12, 1945, Franklin Delano Roosevelt—for 12 years the president of the United States, the man who had led the nation through the Great Depression and very nearly to final victory in World War II, whose radio voice seemed as familiar to most Americans as that of a family member—was struck by a cerebral hemorrhage at his vacation cottage in Warm Springs, Georgia. He muttered, "I have a terrific pain in the back of my head" and slumped over.

Two days later, after funeral services at the White House, a train carrying Roosevelt's body departed from Washington's Union Station at 11:03 p.m., pulled by two Pennsylvania Railroad locomotives. In the last car were the Roosevelt family and Harry S. Truman, the new President. Truman, an unknown quantity to most of his countrymen, had told a gathering of reporters: "Boys, if you ever pray, pray for me now."

The train was bound for the Roosevelt home along the Hudson River in Hyde Park, New York. Its route took it through Baltimore, Wilmington, and on toward 30th Street Station in Philadelphia.

At every depot and roadway overpass, in every open field and on every hilltop that afforded a view of the tracks, citizens stood in silence, heads bowed, hats in hand, as the train passed in the blackness.

Only once in the nation's past had there been such an outpouring of grief. That was at the death of President Abraham Lincoln, mortally wounded by an assassin 80 years before that very night, April 14, 1865. Lincoln's body, too, had taken a long railroad journey home, to Springfield, Illinois. Thousands of people had walked past Lincoln's coffin when it lay in state for a day at Independence Hall in Philadelphia.

Roosevelt, too, seemed a martyr—his life cut short at age 63, not by a bullet but by the stress of his long, crisis-filled tenure in office: three terms plus three months. Four times, voters had elected him to lead them.

"He was the only president we ever knew," remembers Clarence Harris, 67, a faculty member at Cheyney University. "Our first thought was, 'What are we going to do now?' "

There would be less opportunity for Philadelphia to say goodbye to Roosevelt than to Lincoln. The train bearing Roosevelt's body was only passing through—and at 2 in the morning.

At 30th Street, 5,000 people had crowded into the main waiting area more than an hour before the 12-car train pulled into the station. Police had to close the stairway to the tracks, for fear that people would be pushed to their deaths.

"But still they came," The Inquirer reported, "tumbling off trolley cars which halted in front of the Market Street entrance, alighting from automobile after automobile in the driveway to the west, and converging upon the terminal on foot."

Police estimated the crowd at 50,000. Farther up the track, at North Philadelphia Station, 10,000 had gathered. All the way to Hyde Park in Upstate New York, the scene was much the same.

"People felt such a terrific loss," says Betty Berg, 89, of Huntingdon Valley, Pennsylvania, who had headed the first Women's Auxiliary Army Corps detachment in Philadelphia. "It was a devastating thing that happened."

■

In the half-century since Roosevelt's death, perhaps only one event has so united Americans in heartache: the 1963 slaying of President John F. Kennedy.

FDR, as headline writers called him, had been in power so long and had presided over such momentous times that he had come to seem permanently the president, said University of Pennsylvania professor Bruce Kuklick. He was "kind of Clinton, Bush, and Reagan, all rolled into one."

Of course, anyone who got a close look could see that his physical condition had deteriorated. In photos taken at the Yalta Conference that February, his head hung down and his shoulders drooped. He had a look of deep fatigue. That familiar, jaunty pose—the crescent-moon grin, the proud chin, the upturned cigarette holder—was long gone.

Republicans in the previous election, in 1944, had questioned FDR's health. But not to worry, his personal physician had said. All he needed was "some sunshine and more exercise." In fact, doctors had diagnosed Roosevelt with a serious case of congestive heart failure, but the diagnosis was hidden from voters.

Since 1924, after developing leg-crippling polio, he had traveled regularly to Warm Springs to soak his limbs in a natural pool of water that maintained a temperature of 86 degrees, winter and summer. He had acquired a small piece of property there: his "Little White House," as the press called it, with four white pillars in front.

On April 12, a muggy Thursday in the western Georgia hills, FDR was at the cottage, taking a breather from Washington, where that day a group of Army leaders was advising Congress that the Germans were close to surrender. In the Pacific, a battle raged on Okinawa, the last steppingstone before the planned invasion of Japan.

FDR's wife, Eleanor, wasn't at Warm Springs. Instead, Roosevelt was accompanied by Lucy Mercer Rutherford, whose presence was known to the President's daughter, Anna, but kept secret from Eleanor. Franklin's affair with Lucy years earlier had nearly broken his marriage. He had promised never to see her again. Eleanor later felt that she had been betrayed by both her husband and her daughter.

The President was going through his mail before lunch while portrait-artist Elizabeth Shoumatoff painted him in oil. In the room was FDR's cousin, Daisy Suckley.

Harvard historian Doris Kearns Goodwin, in her war-era biography of the Roosevelts, *No Ordinary Time*, recounts the President's last moment:

"At one o'clock, the butler came in to set the table. . . . Roosevelt glanced at his watch and said, 'We've got just fifteen minutes more.' Then, suddenly, Shoumatoff recalled, 'he raised his right hand and passed it over his forehead several times in a strange jerky way.' Then his head went forward.

"Thinking he was looking for something, Suckley went over to him and asked if he had dropped his cigarette. 'He looked at me,' Suckley recalled, 'his forehead furrowed with pain, and tried to smile. He put his left hand up to the back of his head and said, 'I have a terrific pain in the back of my head.' And then he collapsed."

Goodwin, in an interview, said it can almost bring a tear to her eye to think that Roosevelt didn't live to see the victory in World War II that he had worked so hard to bring about.

"There is a sense people have that he gave all of his energy to the country, and that if he had not decided to run for the presidency that fourth time, he might have lived much longer."

Though hated by big business for his Depression-era programs—an alphabet soup of bureaucracies, many of which still thrive today: the FTC, the FDA, the ICC, the FDIC—Roosevelt was loved by the people his programs benefited.

Americans today place their money in federally insured bank accounts, a Roosevelt creation. Retirees draw Social Security, a Roosevelt creation. Many who served in the war owe their educations to the GI Bill, a Roosevelt creation.

During the war, Roosevelt's warm, reassuring voice on the radio helped inspire utmost effort from Americans, not only on distant battlefields but on farms and in defense plants at home. It was Roosevelt who, at the Casablanca Conference in 1943, committed the Allies to the goal of achieving unconditional surrender from both Germany and Japan.

To mark the 50th anniversary of his death, a monument to Roosevelt is going up near the Capitol in Washington. The government is putting up 80 percent of the $52 million cost, with donors contributing the rest. The work started in October.

Soon, Roosevelt's monument will take its place where most Americans think it belongs: with George Washington's and Thomas Jefferson's. And with Lincoln's.

■

As they do with Pearl Harbor, people still remember where they were and what they were doing when they heard that Roosevelt was dead.

Brooks E. Gray of Philadelphia's Wynnefield section, then a private first class in the Marine Corps, remembers: "I was on Guam, on mess duty—a bright, sunny day. I'm scrubbing pots and pans when the announcement comes over that the President had died."

Roosevelt, he said, "was sort of idolized, especially by black people," who credited him with advances in civil rights. It was Roosevelt who had pushed for creation of the Fair Employment Practices Commission, which sought with limited success to break down race barriers in defense hiring during the war.

Gray recalls that a Marine sergeant, a fellow African American, came to him and said, "Well, Brooks, we don't know what we're in for now with that man from Independence."

By that he meant Truman, who was from Independence in Missouri, once a slave state. As things turned out, Gray noted, Truman would be the man who in 1948 would abolish segregation in the armed forces.

On the home front, reports of Roosevelt's death that Thursday broke on the wire services in late afternoon, Eastern War Time. Newspapers and radio stations were flooded with calls asking whether it was true. At 6 p.m., White House secretary Stephen T. Early made the formal announcement.

Mary Jane Freedley of Haddonfield, New Jersey, then a college student whose parents were Republicans and not admirers of Roosevelt, recalls a universal sense of shock and sadness.

"We didn't see the pictures of it like you would today on the television," she said. People sat close to their radios and bought "extras" published hurriedly by the newspapers.

James N. Reaves, later a Philadelphia police inspector but then a young officer, remembers: "Everybody was almost crying. Even myself. I mean everybody. There was no one that said a bad word, a harsh word, about the guy. You know, the war was still on, and we were concerned what was going to happen now that our leader was gone."

The funeral was scheduled for 4 p.m. Saturday. The papers carried the schedule for the special train that was to take the President's body home late that night. Reaves was supposed to be off that day, but he was called in to help check the safety of the Pennsy tracks in the area between the zoo and 30th Street.

"They just wanted us to walk the tracks to make sure everything was all right. We searched the tracks for anything that might cause a problem."

There was no school that day, of course, since it was the weekend. Most businesses closed their doors, at least during the hour of the funeral. Philadelphia's two hometown baseball teams, the Phillies and Athletics, were supposed to play a "City Series" game, but it was called off. All flags were at half-staff. Pennsylvania Governor Edward Martin ordered liquor stores closed.

That weekend, department stores used their newspaper advertising space for epitaphs. "Together with the sorrowing peoples of the world," said Strawbridge & Clothier, "we mourn the loss of Franklin Delano Roosevelt, President of the United States, Molder of History, Heroic Champion of Freedom."

Come late evening Saturday, the throngs began to gather along the tracks and at stations.

Harris, a telecommunications professor at Cheyney University, was then a teenage worker on the evening shift at the Scott Paper plant in Chester, just outside Philadelphia. On his way home, he remembers, he saw people converging on 30th Street from every point of the compass.

He said of Roosevelt: "He was loved very much."

33 • V-E Day
May 7, 1945

Germany's surrender was a big deal, but the pent-up joy was muted by Washington, which knew the warfare that still lay ahead.

May 7, 1995

The Associated Press flashed the first report from London at 3:26 p.m., English time. In Philadelphia, it was 9:26 on a warm Monday morning. As radio stations blurted out the short message, the city began to blow off long pent-up emotions.

At last, after days of false rumors, Germany had surrendered. World War II in Europe was over.

It was May 7, 1945—50 years ago today.

Lucy Cipriano Gentile, then a billing clerk at the Esso oil company office in Center City, remembers a "snowstorm" of paper instantly beginning to fall onto 12th Street, six floors below her window.

"We used to have something that resembled the shredders they use now," she said. "There was all kinds of wastepaper. We just went to the window and threw it all out. . . . Everybody above us and below us and across the way was doing the same thing."

Her brother, Lawrence, was a soldier in the European Theater, and her boyfriend, Dominic, was a Marine in the Pacific. "I was happy for my brother, and I figured that the fighting with the Japanese would be over sooner if the Germans gave up."

Workers poured out onto the pavement, waiting for the party to start. Cars blared their horns. Phone lines became jammed as people started calling one another to ask, Did you hear?

The news flash was followed by a further report from Edward Kennedy, the Associated Press bureau chief in Paris. The surrender, he wrote, occurred at 2:41 a.m. in Reims, the Champagne capital of France. The Germans, represented at the table by Field Marshal Alfred Jodl, had agreed to lay down their weapons unconditionally. Lieutenant General Walter Bedell Smith, chief of staff to five-star General Dwight D. Eisenhower, had signed for the United States. Representatives of Britain, France, and the Soviet Union also had penned their names.

Strangely, there was nothing about this momentous event hours earlier on any other wire service. Not one word from United Press. Nary a peep from International News Service. In Washington, reporters raced to the White House to be there when President Harry S. Truman formally announced victory in Europe. A term had already been coined for the historic moment: V-E Day. But Truman was said to be in a meeting.

The crowds on Center City streets continued to expand throughout the morning. At the lunch hour, they became throngs. Everyone was milling around, waiting for word from Truman. Mayor Bernard Samuel ordered that all air-raid sirens be sounded the instant of the announcement.

Subsequently, a statement from the president was handed to reporters: "There is nothing I can or will say to you."

With that, the cork got stuck in the bottle. The expected explosion of celebration was reduced to a fizzle. All over Washington, even from within the White House, officials were saying in stage whispers, Yes, it's true. Why, then, wasn't Truman saying it?

"The letdown became noticeable shortly after 1 p.m., and pronounced after 2 p.m.," The Philadelphia Inquirer said.

The office workers eventually wandered back to their desks. There was little else to do.

■

Germany, indeed, had surrendered. A week after Hitler's suicide in a Berlin bunker, with Allied troops swarming over the country, his military successors had called it quits. The fighting that had begun September 1, 1939, with Germany's *blitzkrieg* against Poland had ended after 5 years, 8 months, and 6 days.

Unlike World War I, this war really had developed into a global matter. The fighting against Japan, the last of the original Axis powers, would persist through the summer of 1945. In Europe, North Africa, and elsewhere within the reach of Hitler's forces, tens of millions of people were dead. Among them were as many as 6 million Jews, victims of the Holocaust.

Truman's delay in making the surrender announcement was the result of a pledge he had made to withhold the news until 9 a.m.

Eastern War Time the following day, so that the news could be released simultaneously in Washington, London, Paris, and Moscow. May 8 was formally declared V-E Day in the Western Allied countries. The surrender was ratified at Soviet Red Army headquarters in Berlin on May 9, which is still recognized by Russians as Victory Day.

The partying resumed in Philadelphia with Truman's announcement, but some of the effervescence had been irretrievably lost.

Sixteen of the 17 reporters invited to witness the surrender ceremony at Reims had also withheld the news. They had done so under censorship orders from Eisenhower's headquarters, officially designated as Supreme Headquarters Allied Expeditionary Forces.

Only Kennedy broke the embargo. After racing back to the AP's office in Paris after the surrender, he had begun typing up the story. He said later he had felt that there was no military-security reason for the censorship—that it was "purely political." He had decided to break the news, he said, after hearing it made public by the Germans on German radio.

"I thought we were there as reporters—that the end of the war was news," he later explained.

While he typed, he told an assistant to get the AP office in London on the phone and give it the "flash." The man he spoke to in London, Lewis Hawkins, didn't recognize the assistant's voice and wasn't sure how to react. Kennedy grabbed the phone: "This is Ed Kennedy, Lew. Germany has surrendered unconditionally. That's official. Make the date Reims, France, and get it out."

Hawkins went to do that, while a typist got on the line to take dictation of Kennedy's story. He slowly read aloud about 300 words from a 1,500-word story, and then the line went dead—reason unknown. Contact could not be re-established.

Soon thereafter, Kennedy found himself in a storm of controversy. His press credentials were suspended by Eisenhower's headquarters. For six hours, the entire Associated Press was suspended. Reporters from news outlets that had heeded the censorship signed a letter condemning Kennedy and demanding his punishment. On May 9, after other reporters had been allowed to file their stories, Kennedy's full dispatch at last appeared in newspapers. A blunder or not, it was vivid reporting:

After he had signed the four instruments of surrender, and after the representatives of the Four Powers had signed them, Jodl asked for permission to speak. He was told that he might.

He held himself stiffly erect. His voice was low and soft. "With this signature, the German people and armed forces are, for better or worse, delivered into the victors' hands." Jodl finished speaking and sat down. A moment passed in dead silence.

As supreme commander, Eisenhower had refused to meet any German officer until the surrender had been signed. Jodl and a German naval officer, Grand Admiral Hans Georg von Friedeburg, were led up a flight of stairs to another office. The door opened:

Eisenhower and his deputy, [British] Air Chief Marshal Sir Arthur Tedder, were waiting. They stood behind Eisenhower's small desk.

Jodl entered first, followed by [Friedeburg]. . . . Friedeburg looked out the windows. Only Jodl, his bald head gleaming beneath naked electric light bulbs, looked the American and British commanders in the face.

Again, there was a moment of heavy silence. Then Eisenhower spoke. He was brief and terse as always. His dark blue eyes were hard . . .

In clipped sentences, Kennedy wrote, Eisenhower told Jodl that he would be held personally responsible for any German disobedience from that point onward. The supreme commander stopped speaking. The meeting clearly was over. Jodl bowed stiffly and turned to go out. When the Germans were gone, in a scene that Kennedy apparently was unable to witness, Eisenhower finally let go of his emotions. He was a very controlled man, so they didn't go far.

A wide grin crossed his face.

■

The people happiest to hear that the Germans had quit were, of course, the ones the Germans had been fighting.

Lewis J. Truhan, a merchant seaman who throughout the war had faced the German submarine threat in the Atlantic, was aboard a ship at anchor in the Netherlands.

"We had known it was only a matter of days," he remembered from his home in Bellmawr, Camden County, New Jersey. "We knew things were happening, and we were camped on the radio, trying to get the Armed Forces Radio service. . . . Elation was the word. We heaved a great sigh of relief. But we wondered what was going on in the Pacific. We couldn't foresee that the war was going to be over as far as we were concerned. We were just going to have to turn around and go over there."

Paul Fussell, an infantry lieutenant then recovering from a wound at a military hospital in France, felt the same dread.

"The end of the war [in Europe] left me with no other feeling than depression, because that meant I had to go to Japan and fight there," said Fussell, a University of Pennsylvania professor. "It did not mean the end of the war at all. It meant the transfer of a battlefield from one side of the world to another."

On May 9, Joseph P. Barrett, a soldier in the 474th Anti-Aircraft Battalion, wrote a jaunty letter to his sister Catherine back home on

North Croskey Street in Philadelphia. She saved it and wrote "souvenir page" on the envelope, which had been stamped: "Passed by Army examiner."

"Hello, Kate,

"How's the girl? Well, your worrying for now is over. V-E Day is here and gone. It is now V-E plus sixteen hours, three minutes and thirty seconds. . . . Now all that we need is . . . RHD Day—Return Home Day."

Barrett could joke then. Having gone ashore at Normandy on D-Day and having fought his way all across Europe to the heart of Germany, he had been one of the lucky men.

He had lived to see the victory.

34 • Hiroshima
August 6, 1945

This was the day the United States dropped an atomic bomb on Japan. Eight days later, World War II was over.

August 6, 1995

From 31,000 feet, Hiroshima was unmistakable. The seven branches of the Ota River delta glinted like mirrors. Squirrel tails of factory smoke drifted in the August haze.

Captain Theodore Van Kirk, navigator of the Enola Gay, leaned over the shoulder of the bombardier, who was lining up his target: the T-shaped Aioi Bridge in the middle of the city.

"I could point out the various landmarks," Van Kirk remembers a half-century later. "We just wanted to make sure that everything was right." He noted in his log that seven ships were docked in Hiroshima's harbor.

For three years, the United States had been secretly working to develop the world's first atomic weapon. Now came the deliverymen. It was fifty years ago today, August 6, 1945.

Sitting in the pilot's seat of a B-29 Superfortress, Colonel Paul W. Tibbets got ready for the plane to lurch upward the moment it dropped its load: a 9,700-pound bomb, 10½ feet long and 29 inches wide, ironically nicknamed Little Boy.

Tibbets and crew would have about 45 seconds while the bomb fell to get away. Little Boy would then detonate with a force equivalent to thousands of ordinary bombs. Tibbets hoped it would speed the end of World War II, forcing the Japanese to finally face defeat.

"I've never said that we won the war," Tibbets says today. "But we were the convincers. We showed them the futility of continuing—that they'd be annihilated if they did."

At 8:15 a.m. Hiroshima time, the bomb dropped from the belly of the bomber. Tibbets rolled the plane into a dive to gain speed and veered away from the city in nearly a U-turn.

The roar of the engines attracted the attention of Tadataka Sasaki, a Japanese soldier. He was outdoors, pushing a cart of breakfast dishes. He had paused to look into the shallow moat surrounding the pagoda-shaped Hiroshima Castle, which loomed large over the city. "I'd hoped to see some carp."

"I heard somebody say, 'That's a B-29!' " he remembers. "I looked up."

At that instant, the A-bomb exploded. The only thing Sasaki saw was a flash. It was like looking into the sun—a burst of pulsating colors. He was knocked unconscious. He came to in the moat. The back of his uniform shirt and pants were burned away, and his skin bubbled with blisters. But most horrifying was this: The mammoth castle was gone! Just like that, it had vanished.

■

The atomic bombing of Hiroshima was the deadliest and most destructive event ever caused by man. The date of August 6, 1945, marks the beginning of a frightening age in which humankind, after countless eons on Earth, has attained the power to destroy itself.

Not only was the Hiroshima Castle gone, so was almost everything in the city center. The bomb exploded 1,700 feet above the ground, as planned, to spread the damage a maximum distance. For a split-second, heat in the uranium core of the bomb reached millions of degrees.

At street level, the temperature topped 3,000 degrees. Buildings, trees, and people ignited as easily as tissue paper. One person sitting on the stone steps of the Sumitomo Bank left only a heat-ray shadow—still visible 50 years later in a glass case at the Hiroshima Peace Memorial Museum.

The death toll reached 140,000 by the end of 1945, according to the official estimate in Japan, and climbed for years afterward because of delayed radiation effects such as leukemia and other cancers. Ninety-two percent of the 76,000 buildings in the city were destroyed or damaged.

The atomic bomb was so powerful that it created its own weather. So much dust was hurled into the atmosphere that storm clouds formed. An hour after the blast, dirt-blackened rain, laden with radioactivity, began falling north and west of the downtown area.

Together with the atomic attack on Nagasaki three days later, the bomb did, indeed, convince Japan to quit. Even after Nagasaki, where 70,000 people were killed, Japanese militarists had wanted to fight on.

It took the emperor to say that enough was enough.

On August 14, 1945, Japan agreed to Allied demands for unconditional surrender.

The United States had been preparing 650,000 men to invade Kyushu, Japan's westernmost island. Based on their experience in Okinawa, the generals expected 268,000 to be killed or wounded. The following spring, a second army was to invade Honshu, where Hiroshima is located.

Historians still wrangle over how many lives—American and Japanese—would have been lost. Japan had been preparing for a suicidal fight; women and children were trained to resist invaders with sharpened sticks, and Army leaders had called for "100 million deaths with honor."

But Harold M. Agnew, a young atomic scientist who flew in an escort plane on the Hiroshima attack, has no doubt that saving American lives alone was reason enough for the bomb. Frankly, he says, American life seemed more important at the time than Japanese life.

"I have no qualms," he said at his home in Solana Beach, California. "I think we really made a contribution. . . . It brought a very rapid end to a very terrible war."

Agnew, who in later years headed the U.S. atomic-weapons laboratory at Los Alamos, New Mexico, said he met young Americans who believe, as most Japanese do, that dropping the bomb was morally wrong because it was so terrible a weapon. But he once met an old Japanese soldier who told him, "You saved my life. I would have given my life for the emperor."

■

Colonel Tibbets was the best the Army Air Forces had. When the United States had made its first air raid against the Germans, Tibbets piloted the lead plane. When General Dwight D. Eisenhower had gone to war in North Africa, Tibbets flew him there. His photo had appeared in Life magazine. He had flight-tested the B-29 bomber.

A man of 30 in 1945, he was round-faced and had heavy black eyebrows. He was married and the father of two small boys.

Tibbets was blunt and demanding but didn't insist on petty rules. He'd had enough of those, starting with military school in Illinois as a kid. "If you did your job," he said in an interview, "that was good enough for me."

In September 1944, he had been summoned to Colorado Springs, Colorado, to appear before General Uzal Ent, commander of the Second Air Force. He wasn't told why. Outside Ent's office, he was met by a lieutenant colonel who probed him with personal questions, including one about the time when at age 19 he had been arrested for making out with a girl on a Florida beach. After an hour of this, the officer finally said, "OK, we'll go in."

Ent sat behind his desk. Sitting with the general were a scientist from Los Alamos and a Navy officer. The man who had asked all the questions was introduced as a security officer for the top-secret Manhattan Project, the multibillion-dollar effort to build the atomic bomb.

Tibbets, who later became a brigadier general and today is retired from commercial aviation in Columbus, Ohio, remembered: "I had had three courses in physics in college. I understood the word "atomic"; I understood the word "energy." I won't say that I understood Einstein's theory, but I knew what they were talking about."

He was told his job: He was to develop a strike force to carry the powerful new weapon to a target in either Germany or Japan. He would be given an armada of 15 B-29s and 1,800 men, including ground crews and security forces of his own. His first task was to pick subordinates. He chose Thomas W. Ferebee, his bombardier on past missions, to train bombardiers in the new outfit, the 509th Composite Group. Van Kirk, his longtime navigator, would train the navigators.

Van Kirk remembered Tibbets saying, "We'll be doing a special job. We'll be going overseas again. If it works, we can either end—or materially shorten—the war." He sensed not to ask questions: "I knew he wouldn't tell me any more. You could sense by his tone of voice, that was it."

The son of a truck driver from Northumberland, Pennsylvania, Van Kirk was known as "Dutch." He had completed a year at Susquehanna College and had flown 58 bombing missions, many with Tibbets.

"If Paul had a weakness, it was as an administrator," Van Kirk said at his home in Marin County in California. "He was not a paperwork guy. . . . He doesn't brook fools easily. But, on the other hand, he was extremely loyal to people."

The 509th trained at a remote airfield in the desert at Wendover, Utah. "I had more authority than the chief of Air Force has today," Tibbets said. "I didn't have to report to anybody."

To practice dropping an enormous bomb, the air crews dropped dummies they called "pumpkins." At high altitude, anti-aircraft fire would not be a concern. The biggest danger would be getting away from the blast shock wave. They'd have to be at least eight miles away for safety. Of course, they would already be six miles up.

As training went on, Tibbets visited Los Alamos, where he met J. Robert Oppenheimer, scientific director of the project. Tibbets recalled an incident that showed Oppenheimer's astonishing mental prowess.

He and the physicist were walking down a hall. Oppenheimer suddenly turned and went back to a door they had passed. In a room, a man
was seated at a desk, staring, with head in hands, at a blackboard covered with "all kinds of hieroglyphics."

Oppenheimer, Tibbets said, "walks up, takes an eraser, reaches
down to the left-hand corner. He rubs something out and puts some
other numbers in there. "And this guy, he stands up and he says, 'I've
been looking for that mistake for three days!' "

The "guy" was Italian physicist Enrico Fermi, perhaps one of the
most brilliant scientists in history.

On July 16, 1945, two months after Germany's surrender, a test
bomb was exploded in the New Mexico desert. By then, Tibbets had
moved his group to Tinian, a small Pacific island 1,700 miles south of
Japan. When the bomb was ready, so was the 509th.

Van Kirk remembers the date he left the States. It was June 25,
1945, the day his son, Tom, was born back in Northumberland.

■

Tinian—captured from the Japanese in June 1944—had the
world's biggest airport, with six runways, each nearly two miles long and
the width of a 10-lane highway. The island was shaped a little like
Manhattan, though larger, and the streets were laid out like
Manhattan's. The 509th was housed in the Columbia University area on
the "Upper West Side" of the island.

Tinian was 6½ hours from Japan. Each evening, Van Kirk would
watch as hundreds of B-29s from the 20th Air Force took off to fire-
bomb Japan. These planes already had reduced most of the enemy's
principal cities to ashes.

Van Kirk, who today is retired from the DuPont company, agrees
with Tibbets that the atomic bomb itself didn't win the war. "The war
was won. But it *did* stop the killing."

On July 26, the Navy ship *Indianapolis* reached Tinian with Little
Boy after a 10-day voyage from San Francisco. That day, half a world
away in Potsdam, Germany, leaders of the United States, Britain, and
the Soviet Union issued an ultimatum to Japan: Surrender or face
"prompt and utter destruction."

Japan had passed word to the Soviets that it might consider peace
talks, but not on terms of unconditional surrender. American leaders,
after four years of struggle, were in no mood to bargain. They believed,
besides, that Japan would never quit. They had just seen Japan sacrifice
70,000 men on Okinawa in a suicidal cause. About 32,000 Americans
had been killed or wounded.

The go-ahead to use the bomb came directly from Washington.

After the war, Tibbets recalled, he was invited to meet President Harry S. Truman at the White House. Truman asked if anyone had given him a "hard time" about the bomb.

"Oh, once in a while," Tibbets recalled replying.

"I'll tell you what," Truman said. "If they do it again, you refer 'em to me. I'm the guy that sent you out there to do it."

The next decision was a target. Tokyo and many other cities were out, since they already had been devastated. The military wanted a "virgin" target, Tibbets said, so it could more easily calculate bomb impact. "It would have a certain effect on steel; it would have a certain effect on wood. . . . They wanted to see what the damage was. It was strictly a scientific research project from that point of view."

Hiroshima, Nagasaki, and Niigata headed the list. At the last minute, Niigata was scratched, and Kokura was added.

At 11 a.m. August 5, men assigned to the mission gathered in a Quonset hut for a briefing. Agnew, the young scientist from Los Alamos, was present. He recalled that the steel hut was air-conditioned; he had never experienced air-conditioning before. The men sat on wooden benches in summer khakis.

"We were told we were going to bomb tomorrow," Agnew said. "They told us the primary target is going to be Hiroshima, and then they showed us where there were going to be submarines in case we crashed.

"I wanted a gun. They wouldn't let me have a gun because I was a civilian. Some guy gave me his rosary, which really wasn't what I had in mind at all. But I took it."

Seven of Tibbets's 15 air crews would participate. Three would fly ahead to check weather. Two would accompany the bomb plane with scientific instruments to measure the blast. Agnew would fly in one of these. The final plane would be stationed on Iwo Jima, halfway to Japan, in case the bomb plane broke down.

The crews of the three planes that would fly all the way to Hiroshima were at the briefing. Captain William S. "Deke" Parsons, a Navy weapons expert, explained what the powerful new weapon was expected to accomplish. But even then, "the word 'atomic' was not used," Van Kirk said. "It wasn't used until we were on the airplane."

Parsons intended to show film of the test explosion in New Mexico. But the projector wouldn't work, and he had to show still pictures. The sight of the mushroom-shaped cloud that had towered up from the test site was still pretty impressive. Parsons explained that the bomb would have the force of 20,000 tons of TNT.

Tibbets had decided to pilot the bomb plane himself. He took over a plane normally piloted by Captain Robert A. Lewis, who would move over to the copilot's seat. Ferebee would be the bombardier; Van

Kirk, the navigator. Parsons would arm the bomb in flight. The rest of the 12 men aboard would be from Lewis's crew.

The plane had not had a name; Tibbets now gave it one. He ordered the nose painted with the words "Enola Gay." It was his mother's name.

His father had wanted him to be a doctor, but his mother had supported his ambition to fly. "The old man had said, 'If you want to fly airplanes, go kill yourself.' "

After the briefing, the airmen had time to themselves before a final briefing at midnight. Agnew remembered that he scrawled a message on Little Boy.

"I wrote my name on it, my wife's name, and my daughter's name—and some nasty words for the Japanese . . . something like 'a present' or 'the hell with you.' "

At 2 a.m. on August 6, the crews arrived on the flight line in trucks after a breakfast of eggs, ham, and pineapple fritters. The Army knew this was a historic moment, and the Enola Gay was emblazoned with lights for military photographers. "We had a big ceremony, I remember that," said Agnew. "It was sort of like the opening of a drugstore."

At 2:45, the Enola Gay took off. Slow, bomb-laden B-29s sometimes rose a few feet and crashed. With his special load, Tibbets was determined to gain safe takeoff speed. Lewis, he recalled, became frightened he'd run out of runway.

"On average . . . we took off at 140 miles an hour. . . . We're going down the runway and we pass 140. Bob gets nervous and tells me to 'lift off, it's 140.' . . . He grabbed hold of the yoke and started to pull on it. I told him, 'Get your goddamned hands off the yoke. I'm flyin' this airplane.' "

The Enola Gay rose up "as nice as could be," Tibbets said with a smile. "From there on out, it was so routine a flight that it was dull."

■

It was a drowsy tropical night with a sliver of crescent moon. Van Kirk navigated by the stars.

The Enola Gay climbed to 4,700 feet and headed north-northwest over Saipan, an island that U.S. forces had bought with 14,000 casualties a year earlier. On Saipan, Japanese soldiers died almost to the man in suicide charges. Japanese women and children jumped off cliffs rather than fall into American hands.

Tibbets had stocked up for the 13-hour flight with a large supply of pipes, cigars, and cigarettes. "I was drinking coffee and puffing on my pipe most of the time."

Over Iwo Jima, site of another bloody battle, the Enola Gay got into loose formation with its escort planes, the Great Artiste and an unnamed B-29 bearing the number 91.

Dawn was coming up. The planes now rose to bombing altitude. The big, cigar-nosed B-29 was the world's first pressurized aircraft, and it enabled fliers to ride in shirtsleeve comfort. Three more hours passed.

"You could see the coast of Japan from a hundred miles away," Van Kirk remembered.

As the plane drew close, the bomb-bay doors flopped open. Once Ferebee had the Aioi Bridge in the cross-hairs of a Norden bombsight, the bombsight itself controlled the timing of the drop. Agnew, in the Great Artiste, was waiting for a radio signal that the drop was imminent. The Great Artiste opened its bomb doors, too—to permit the scientists to drop their instruments.

"If you read the early newspaper accounts from Japan, they say the bomb came down on a parachute. . . . But it wasn't the bomb; it was our gauges that came down on the parachute."

By Tibbets's watch, it was 17 seconds after 9:15 a.m. when Little Boy began its plunge. His watch was on Tinian time, an hour ahead of Hiroshima time.

The Enola Gay lurched, as expected. Tibbets rolled the aircraft into a 155-degree turn—as much strain as it could withstand before the tail ripped off.

Van Kirk counted the seconds before the blast. "We saw the bright flash in the airplane, that's all," he said. "It was like turning on a light bulb in a closet."

"When the shock wave hit," Van Kirk remembered, "somebody yelled, 'Flak!' Then the tail gunner said, 'No, it wasn't; it was a shock wave—and here comes another.' " Bob Caron, who operated the only guns on the plane, actually had seen the shock wave coming. "We didn't understand why it kicked us twice," said Agnew. "Well, one was the blast. The other was the reflection off the ground."

Tibbets tasted lead in his mouth. He learned later that radioactivity from the atomic explosion had caused electrolysis in the lead fillings of his teeth.

From a safe distance, he finally looked back. Hiroshima was covered in boiling black dust. It reminded him of a bubbling tar pot.

A funnel cloud was shooting up like a poisonous mushroom. It rose to the height of the plane and kept rising. Van Kirk remembered it as mostly white. Agnew recalled "a dirty, gray-brown mess." Tibbets thought it had purple in it. "You could see the turmoil going," said Tibbets. "There was fire and there was dark smoke and there was light smoke. It was rolling and tumbling as it went up."

A half-century later, seated at a restaurant table in Alexandria,

Virginia, he was asked: "Did you think about the people in the city?"

"No," he said. "I knew that I'd be ineffective if I started to worry about that. So I schooled myself in Europe—I was going to drop the bombs; I wasn't going to worry about what happened."

■

Tadataka Sasaki had been enjoying the morning sun as he pushed the cart of breakfast dishes alongside the moat. The temperature was 81 degrees; the humidity, 80 percent. At 7:09 a.m., air-raid sirens had wailed after one of the weather planes from Tinian was sighted. But the alert had been called off at 7:31 when the plane turned away, and now people were starting to relax.

For some reason, there was no alarm this time.

Sasaki never felt the blow that knocked him into the castle moat. As he came to in the water, he looked around and saw "nothing but stone walls. All the trees were completely blown away. It made me feel like I was in a different spot." The earth-colored shirt of his enlisted man's uniform was in tatters, and his white pants flapped like kite tails. His arms, back, and legs were white with blister sacs.

"It was like I had another skin all over me. . . . I was just trying to figure out what had happened. I was stunned. I didn't really know what to do."

Now 75, Sasaki spoke in an interview at his 15th-floor apartment in the port city of Kure, a 40-minute train ride from Hiroshima. Of 60 men in his ordnance unit, he was one of two who survived. Today, he is a skillful amateur photographer. He bears the scars of his burns. He believes that the water of the moat quenched his skin and saved his life.

For years, he said, he hid his story. In Japan after the war, A-bomb survivors were ostracized. People feared that radiation poisoning might be catching. Children of survivors often had trouble finding mates because potential spouses feared they might pass on bomb-related genetic defects, though no such case has ever been documented.

"So I closed my mouth," Sasaki said, "and I never told anyone." His son and four daughters are healthy, and today he has four grandchildren. In recent years, he has begun to speak up.

He recalled that when he came to, one of two men he had been walking with at the instant of the blast was bleating, "I'm hit, I'm hit." The other had disappeared. Sasaki wandered back to his post, but could find no one in charge. Hiroshima, with an estimated 43,000 military personnel within its borders on that day, was the largest military center in western Japan. But the A-bomb had instantly destroyed the command structure.

The only army that Sasaki could see was "an army of walking

ghosts"—people like himself whose blistered, peeled skin dangled from their arms and fingers. They shuffled along with hands held high in front of them. Sasaki remembered that his own pain was lessened if he lifted his hands higher than his fast-pumping heart.

A diorama in the Hiroshima Peace Memorial Museum recreates the look of these people. For the American visitor who recalls the drive-in horror movies of the 1960s, one word instantly comes to mind: "zombie."

Human corpses lay in dense, black clumps. For some reason, the dead horses loom largest in Sasaki's memory. Their haunches were so enormous. In the distance, he could now see mountains. Before, they had been hidden by the buildings of the city. A locomotive lay derailed along its tracks. Even the wooden ties were afire. Sasaki walked toward the Kanda Bridge to escape the heart of the city, but the span was also in flames. He decided to cool his flesh in one of the river branches.

Others, naked or half-naked, were doing the same. No one seemed to try to cover himself or herself. In their suffering, the people of Hiroshima were beyond modesty. Sasaki waded in, but the water made the pain worse. The tide was low, revealing a sandbar in the river. He climbed onto the sandbar, but soon had to return to the water. "It was a very sunny day, and the air was so hot—I couldn't take it."

Back and forth, he went. In-out, in-out. He began to notice that many people in the water and on the sand had stopped moving. Death was starting to extend its claim.

Gradually, the bridge burned itself out, and Sasaki got across. He made it to an army facility in the northeastern part of the city. There, he began to vomit, the first sign of radiation sickness. Then he passed out. He would remain hospitalized for three months.

"It is a miracle," he said, "that I made it through."

■

Just a moment before the bomb struck, Suzuko Numata, then 22, had been standing at a window in the Hiroshima Communications Bureau, watching shirtless men do calisthenics on the roof. "The sky," she recalled through a translator, "was a brilliant blue—not a cloud in sight."

In her hand, she held a wet rag, which she had been using to wipe off the desks in the office where she worked. Abruptly, she turned away and went downstairs to rinse out the rag and dump her water bucket. She was shielded in the hallway when the bomb went off.

The flash illuminated the hallway with "a beautiful light," Numata recalled in an interview at the Peace Memorial Museum. "It was red, yellow, green, and orange, combined." Knocked out by the concussion, she awoke in the dark. She had been blown out of the hallway and was under a pile of wreckage. The weight was crushing. She called out for help, but got no response.

Then, luck intervened again. A man suddenly pushed away the ceiling plaster, desks, and other debris on top of her. Numata looked down at herself and saw that her left leg was cut to the bone below the knee. Funny thing, it didn't hurt.

The man threw her over his shoulder and started downstairs. "We were enveloped in smoke," she recalled. Had her rescuer been delayed even moments, she would have died in the fire.

Outside, the man deposited her on the ground. Burned people lay all around, some appearing scarcely human. Numata looked back toward the building and saw flames darting from windows. The flames, she thought, looked just like red curtains flapping in a wind.

Numata found herself in a playground in front of the communications bureau. She wondered what had happened to her father and sister, both of whom had also been in the building. Her father, she would learn, somehow had escaped injury. But her sister, Fusako, 20, was badly hurt.

With a start, Numata suddenly heard Fusako call out her name. She whirled around and spotted her sister lying a few yards away on the concrete. "Glass fragments were sticking out of her body," Numata remembered. As the sisters huddled together, storm clouds began to accumulate overhead. The day grew dark, and heavy rain began to fall. It was a kind of rain that no one had ever experienced. The initial drops left black splotches wherever they hit.

"I didn't have any idea that it was the black rain, as people call it," Numata said. "Later on, people said it contained radiation. But I had no idea at the time. What I do remember is how beautiful the flashing light was."

All that day, and the next, and the next after that, the Numata sisters lay on the playground. Suzuko's leg might have been saved had she been given proper treatment. Instead, she received only a tourniquet. Eventually, the leg had to be amputated below the knee.

To this day, the sisters have had medical problems. They live together in the city of their birth. Neither ever married.

Like others, Suzuko Numata went decades without speaking about the bomb. Now she speaks up. "I am beginning to feel I have a mission—to tell this to the rest of the world."

■

Most people in Hiroshima never saw the mushroom cloud rising directly above them. Their view was blocked by a roiling cloud of dust that hung low over the city. This was the bubbling tar pot that Tibbets had witnessed from high altitude.

Nine miles from Hiroshima on Eta Jima, an island military base in the Inland Sea, the mushroom cloud was clearly visible—awesome, frightening, and puzzling.

Isao Wada, who was being trained in piloting a suicide-boat to fend off possible attacks on Hiroshima by sea, was indoors when the sky lit up like a magnesium flare. After a moment came the roar.

Wada ran outside and looked toward the city, where the cloud was already climbing toward the stratosphere. It seemed almost alive as it twisted and heaved and churned. "It was white," he said in an interview, "but it became gray, and it got darker and darker."

A barber today, Wada lives above his shop on Senda Dori, a busy avenue in the rebuilt city. Sitting on a tatami mat in his apartment, he struggled to describe the look of an atomic cloud. Japanese filmmaker Akira Kurosawa has imagined it as a great eye, opening wide. Wada thought perhaps that a gas tank had blown up, but the cloud was far too big, and it kept rising, rising, rising.

By midday, Wada and other troops of the Atatsuki Corps were ordered to cross over to Hiroshima on boats to help restore order. Landing at Ujina port, he and his unit reported to an army command post at the Hiroshima Tram Car Company. They were then sent into the city.

Wada remembers it as a journey into the heart of darkness. Burned, maimed, naked stragglers were coming the other way. Their flesh was the tint and texture of a skinned tomato. Bodily fluids dripped from the tips of their fingers.

"They did not know where to go. They were just wandering around. I saw many people like that."

Reaching the Miyuki Bridge, Wada was ordered to gather wounded and carry them to a relief station there. Little could be done for them. A study years later would conclude that 90 percent of the 270 doctors in Hiroshima died in the atomic bombing, along with 93 percent of the 1,650 nurses.

Wada recalled the smell of burned flesh. He remembered thinking, "Meat is burning."

Before he left Eta Jima, he had been issued bread rations for three days. "But I could not eat anything for two days," he said, "because of the smell." All day, he worked. That night, he slept out in the open with the injured. The night chill would take its toll on thousands of the people with serious burns. Wada wouldn't realize how much of a toll until he awoke the next morning.

"When night came, it was very dark," he said. "There was no electricity in the center of Hiroshima. I could not see my surroundings. In the morning, I realized I was surrounded by dead bodies."

His job now changed. The work was mostly gathering the dead.

"I was not used to seeing a dead body," he said through a transla-tor. "So I would touch it with a stick, trying to see if it was alive or dead. But after a time I got used to seeing the dead bodies, and I could touch them by hand."

Most of the dead would never be identified, nor even counted.

Among the estimated 350,000 people in Hiroshima on August 6, 1945, were 3,200 native-born Americans of Japanese descent whose par-ents had sent them, before war broke out, to study in Japan. Among the unidentified dead were thousands of Korean slave laborers who had been taken from their homeland to work at the Mitsubishi Heavy Industries shipyard.

Wada had to go into the river branches to pull out corpses that the tide was carrying toward the sea. He and other men would place the corpses on the bank, dig a pit, and put the bodies in the pit. They would scavenge for wood and put the wood atop the bodies. Then they would throw gasoline on the pit and set it afire.

After seven days in the city, Wada went back to Eta Jima, where he began to have diarrhea. "This was a symptom," he said, "of exposure to a high dose of radiation."

His hair fell out; his mouth bled. He, too, had become an atomic-bomb casualty, merely by working amid radioactive dust.

■

Sixteen hours after the world's first atomic weapon had been loosed on Hiroshima, President Truman announced the news in a radio broadcast to the American people. He told them that a single air-plane, dropping a single bomb, had damaged much of a city. He knew it would be a hard fact for them to comprehend.

"It is an atomic bomb," he said. "It is a harnessing of the basic power of the universe. . . . We are now prepared to obliterate, more rapidly and completely, every productive enterprise the Japanese have above ground in any city. We shall destroy their docks, their factories, and their communications. Let there be no mistake—we shall com-pletely destroy Japan's power to make war. . . . If they do not now accept our terms, they may expect a rain of ruin from the air, the like of which has never been seen on this Earth."

Truman's words may seem harsh today, a half-century later, in a time of peace. But Americans were tired, so tired of war.

Today, many historians on both sides of the Pacific argue that the atomic bomb wasn't necessary to end the war, that Japan was at the end of its rope and could not have continued fighting much longer. In all probability, these historians say, the American invasion would not have been necessary.

But if the war had continued even a month longer—a week longer, a day longer—additional Americans would have died in battle and in Japanese prison camps. And that was not a tradeoff, after four years of war, that Americans were willing to make.

Three days after the Hiroshima attack, a B-29 nicknamed Bock's Car appeared over Nagasaki. At 11 a.m. on August 9, 1945, that city, too, was destroyed.

The military leaders of Japan still could not agree on surrender, but Emperor Hirohito intervened. Japan sent word to the United States through neutral Switzerland that it accepted the Potsdam Declaration, the terms for surrender laid out by leaders of the Big Three nations at their Potsdam meeting in July.

Today, 50 years later, Tibbets, the commander of the 509th Composite Group, the pilot of the Enola Gay, likes to think he helped bring the most awful war in history to a more rapid conclusion than it otherwise would have had.

If the Japanese had had the bomb, he reflected, they would have used it, too.

"There is no way to fight a war without killing people," he said. ". . . You don't think if they went after the General Motors plant in Detroit that women and children would be spared, do you? That's my point. You can't distinguish. Everybody contributes to the war effort—to the ability of that nation to defend itself. So what you're out to do is to destroy their ability to wage war, and, unfortunately, that means killing.

"I don't think I've ever done anything to indicate that I'm a savage person," he said. "I don't feel that way. I don't like to see bloodshed any more than anybody else does."

35 • V-J Day
August 14, 1945

Two atomic bombs had convinced Japan—the emperor, actually—that it was time to accept the Allies' demands for surrender.

August 14, 1995

The United States had been at war for three years, eight months, and seven days. Somehow, it seemed even longer. When peace came, it was as if a deep, chronic pain had suddenly stopped hurting. It took a moment to accept that, at last, it was gone.

And then America exploded with joy.

Fifty years ago today, August 14, 1945, the Empire of Japan notified the Four Powers—the United States, Britain, China, and the Soviet Union—that it would accept terms of complete surrender. The worst catastrophe in human history—the Second World War, in which tens of millions of people from 51 warring nations had died of battle wounds, deprivation, and murder—was over.

"It was such a great relief, a feeling of thankfulness that our men won't be killed anymore," recalled Beverly Blackway, now of the Johnsville section of Warminster, Bucks County, whose husband-to-be was off in the Navy.

Blackway, 18 at the time, was working behind the soda fountain at Powell Drug Store in nearby Abington at 7 p.m. when, after a long day of rumor and expectation, President Harry S. Truman announced that the Japanese really had given up. Within a minute, the word had flashed across the news wires and was being broadcast on radio. Blackway ran out to the sidewalk, where a Greyhound bus was passing by on Old York Road. The people on the bus were letting out a cheer.

"That gave me goose bumps," she remembered. Suddenly, she

craved to party. "Mr. Powell gave us each $5 after we closed, which was a lot of money in those days." She persuaded her brother, a veteran of Omaha Beach, to chaperone her and some friends on a bus trip to Center City Philadelphia, where *real* partying was going on.

"At one time between 9 and 10 o'clock," The Evening Bulletin reported, "Market Street throngs were packed so tightly shoulder to shoulder that only a tank could have driven through them. A slow drift with the logjam was the only way to escape it."

The Bulletin's electric "flashcast" above the intersection of Broad and Chestnut Streets spelled out the words, "Your doughboy will be home soon. Yell—Yell—Yell."

The authorities had ordered bars closed the moment that peace was announced, but homemade wine and beer appeared from cellars all over the city. Mayor Bernard Samuel personally sounded the air-raid siren in the City Hall tower—12 blasts of 30 seconds each.

More than 200 people were treated at hospitals for injuries in the mayhem. One man, at 24th and Montrose Streets in South Philadelphia, fired six shots from a .38-caliber pistol into the pavement. The fragments wounded a woman and five children.

Former Philadelphia Police Inspector James N. Reaves, then a young patrolman, remembered: "The fire engines were running up and down the streets, sounding their alarms. This kept up for several hours. In fact, the police vehicles were doing the same thing."

The celebration was far wilder than when Italy had surrendered in September 1943; wilder than when the Germans surrendered in May 1945. It was wilder even than when World War I came to an end in 1918. It was perhaps the wildest party in city history, rivaled only by the celebration in April 1865 that began with the news that General Robert E. Lee had called it quits at Appomattox.

Of 16,112,566 Americans who served in the war, 294,597 had died in battle. An additional 113,842 had failed to return home because of accident or disease, and 670,846 had been wounded. In addition, thousands of civilian merchant seamen had lost their lives during the Atlantic U-boat war, in which 3,843 Allied merchant ships were sunk.

Alone among major belligerents, Americans had not had their homeland invaded or their cities bombarded. But there was hardly a family that had not lost a son or a brother, a cousin or a nephew.

Mayor Samuel told his people, "The City of Philadelphia has paid a heavy price for victory. More than 5,000 of our servicemen and women have given their all in defense of American ideals. Nearly 30,000 have suffered wounds on the battlefield. Homes have been broken up and family life disrupted. Great financial sacrifices have been made."

And now the war was over!

Ended! Finished! Kaput!

■

The atomic bomb had done it.

General Douglas MacArthur, who on September 2, 1945, would formally accept the surrender on the deck of a battleship anchored in Tokyo Bay, believed that, in the absence of the A-bomb, the Japanese might have preferred national suicide to surrender.

Only this "new and most cruel bomb," as Emperor Hirohito called it, could ever have overcome the shame that Japanese felt at giving up, especially while two million of their soldiers remained at arms, MacArthur thought. It provided them a way to quit and "save face," he told aides.

On August 6, an atomic bomb had been dropped on Hiroshima, destroying the city. Three days later, a second bomb fell on Nagasaki. That evening, Japan began to seek a means of surrender.

It had taken two atomic bombs, not one, to convince Japan that its position was hopeless, said Stanley Weintraub, a Pennsylvania State University professor and author of a new book on the final months of the war, *The Last Great Victory*. "The wake-up call was the Nagasaki bomb," Weintraub said in an interview. "The first bomb didn't do it. The military lived in hope that it was our only bomb and an experiment." The fact that the Soviet Union, Japan's powerful neighbor on the Asian mainland, had declared war against the empire on August 8 also fed the sense of doom.

About 11 on the night of the Nagasaki strike, Hirohito entered an underground bunker in Tokyo to meet with his Supreme War Council. The six members were split, 3-3, on whether to fight on. General Koreakira Anami, the war minister, insisted that Japan could still repel an Allied invasion. The navy commander thought so, too. All of the council members agreed that Japan could never surrender if it meant that the emperor had to abdicate the throne.

"In August of 1945, the emperor of Japan was a demigod; he literally was worshipped," Weintraub said.

In prior decades, the emperor's political power had been restrained somewhat; the country was now dominated by generals and admirals. But no one dared dispute Hirohito when he spoke. And now he did so. He rebuked the hardliners, saying that continuing the war could only mean Japan's destruction. Hirohito said he feared for the Japanese people and their culture. It was unbearable, he said, to think that his soldiers would have to be disarmed, unbearable to think that some leaders might face punishment as war criminals.

"It cannot be helped," he said.

There was no longer a need for a council vote. It only remained for the government to contact the victors and see what could be done to preserve the throne. The Allies, in their Potsdam Declaration, had left the door open for Hirohito to remain. They had demanded the unconditional surrender of Japan's military forces, but pointedly had said nothing about the emperor.

It would take a few days to sort out details, during which the world public became aware of the peace overture from Japan. Each day, the papers in Philadelphia were full of speculation on when peace would come. Japanese generals, Weintraub said, still hoped to prevent a military occupation of their homeland, still hoped that they themselves might be able to disarm the troops. The United States, in the person of Truman, was unmoving. Yes, Hirohito could stay—as a figurehead only. No other deals.

On the day of surrender, Hirohito himself delivered the news to his people in a radio broadcast.

"He had never spoken in public," said Weintraub, "and his voice did not seem imperial. It was thin and weak. But those who heard it realized that this was the emperor and the war was over."

"We, the emperor," Hirohito began, "have ordered the imperial government to notify the four countries, the United States, Great Britain, China, and the Soviet Union, that we accept their joint declaration. . . . To continue the war under these conditions would not only lead to annihilation of our nation, but the destruction of human civilization as well."

Japan had never surrendered in any war. Now, enemy forces would be coming to occupy the homeland. Other things would change, too. The emperor no longer would be considered divine. And the Japanese people, Hirohito said, were no longer to consider themselves "superior to other races, fated to rule the world."

With that, said Weintraub, 2,600 years of Japanese history came to an end.

■

The United States that emerged from World War II was also vastly changed, a nation far mightier than the one attacked by Japanese aircraft at Pearl Harbor on December 7, 1941. In less than four years, one America—economically depressed, inward-looking—had disappeared. Another America—an economic colossus and world superpower—had emerged.

Journalist I.F. Stone wrote: "We emerge from the war the Midas of nations. While other countries rise from the ruins appalled by their poverty, we are baffled by our wealth."

The enormity of the American accomplishment in winning the war could hardly be overstated. The United States had fought two wars simultaneously on opposite sides of the globe. Holding off the Japanese with one hand early in the war, Uncle Sam had combined with his allies to smash Nazi Germany. Then he had turned his full attention on Japan. All the while, he had helped arm and feed his main allies, the British and the Soviets.

It was a victory not only of American courage but also of American industry. Admiral Isoruku Yamamoto, commander of the Japanese Combined Fleet, had feared that if Japan failed to knock out the U.S. Pacific Fleet in one blow at Pearl Harbor, it would succeed only in awakening a sleeping American giant.

U.S. industries, which had virtually shut down during the worst of the Depression, had begun to revive in 1940 when America started to re-arm for war. After Pearl Harbor, unemployment virtually disappeared, and cities had to import thousands of workers to meet the production needs of factories and shipyards.

"The war rescued the country from the Great Depression," said Russell F. Weigley, a Temple University history professor. "It put money in people's pockets, and the prosperity was linked to a sense of national purpose." Much of people's money went straight into war bonds, which paid for the ships and tanks and airplanes. Besides enduring hard work and worry, Americans on the home front put up with shortages and rationing, loss and loneliness.

Looking back 50 years later, it is possible to see that while the end of the war heralded a period of great prosperity for America, it marked the start of a prolonged and continuing decline for the old cities of the Northeast and Midwest. Wartime spending had helped make Philadelphia one of the greatest industrial centers on the planet. The city proper had about 350,000 wartime manufacturing jobs, according to Philip Scranton, a professor at Rutgers University.

"The city number goes straight down, with a few up-bumps, from 1945 to the present," Scranton said. Today, Philadelphia has fewer than 100,000 manufacturing jobs. Tens of thousands of other jobs have disappeared from the cities of Camden and Chester and other factory centers. Many of those jobs were replaced—in the suburbs—by the growth of electronics, pharmaceuticals, and other new industries. Many workers followed these jobs to the suburbs.

But all of that was in a dimly lit future when Beverly Blackway and other celebrators raced to Center City to party on the wonderful night of V-J Day—Victory over Japan Day.

On August 17, 1945, she wrote to Richard, her intended:

"Darling, the war is over. I'm so happy. Now I know that you will be back. I am so full of things to say that I just can't express them. Gosh, now you can probably come home soon. You're coming back, you're coming back!"